M000311956

Dec. 4, 2013

ADVANCE PRAISE

"Proactively engaging customers is the answer to creating and leveraging loyal customers. VK describes how to do just that with clear, authoritative logic. A must read for executives facing dynamic marketplaces, fast-moving competitors, and the realities of a digital communications and communities. The five metrics will become classic tools of future executives and students of management."

—Dave Aaker, **Vice-Chairman of Prophet Brand Strategy, Professor Emeritus of Marketing Strategy at the Haas School of Business, UC Berkeley and an advisor to Dentsu Inc.**

"Engaging the customer is the holy grail in today's paradigm shifting, big datafied, socially networked, exponential rate of change environment. With *Profitable Customer Engagement*, VK has presented an invaluable construct to the increasingly complicated, but never more important role of CRM to organizations of all stripes. He has done a remarkable job of explicating the distinct components of customer engagement, while presenting a set of analytical tools that bring each into clear focus for actionable, marketing programs that will optimize customer lifetime value. It's a must read!"

—Alan Beychok, **CEO, Benchmark Brands/FootSmart, USA**

"As customer touchpoints proliferate it is imperative that marketers know the depth of engagement of their best customers. In this landmark book, VK raises our understanding to the next level, with a rigorous approach to managing each facet of engagement."

—George Day, **Geoffrey T. Boisi Professor; Professor of Marketing, Co-Director, Mack Center for Technological Innovation, Director, Emerging Technologies Management Research Program**

"To be successful a firm must engage and satisfy its customer profitably. VK provides the frameworks and metrics for firms to be successful in customer engagement. He provides compelling examples to illustrate substantial gains in profits from successful implementation. Whether you are building a brand, maintaining your brand, or managing for profitability, this book provides you with the tools that you need."

—John R. Hauser, **Kirin Professor of Marketing,**
MIT Sloan School of Management

"This book is destined to be a classic from a real Legend in Marketing!!! It is a MUST READ for managers in ALL for-profit industries!!! Why? Based on years of research, Dr V. Kumar (VK) details the processes a firm can follow to become profitable using an innovative and impressive set of metrics. Furthermore, VK demonstrates the value of implementing these metrics. This is the ONLY book in the market that can provide valuable information for every firm regardless of industry. As such, this book is unparalleled. Most business pundits propose a 'silver bullet' that is demonstrated via case studies to work in a small number of firms. Unfortunately, most managers discover that these 'silver bullets' miss the mark for their businesses. Instead, VK shows that there is more than one way for a firm to profitably engage with its customers. Each way is carefully defined, measured, managed, and shown as a blueprint that managers can follow to achieve sustainable profits. Moreover, this book is loaded with case studies and implementation stories. As a result, VK offers convincing evidence that this is no magic bullet—it is a tried and true guide to long-term business success."

—Timothy Keiningham, **Global Chief Strategy Officer &**
Executive Vice-President of Ipsos Loyalty

"Companies that want to be winners have to go beyond just making and selling more products. They need to deepen their engagement with their customers and have ways to measure the engagement level of their individual customers. VK has done the best theoretical and empirical work that I know in this field. This book will be an 'eye opener' for most companies."

—Philip Kotler, **S.C. Johnson Distinguished Professor of**
International Marketing, Kellogg School of Management,
Northwestern University

"Dr V. Kumar has once again identified a timely and critical way to maintain a competitive advantage and drive continued profitability at a time when many companies are focusing on cost-cutting strategies rather than their customer base. This book shows in a clear and straightforward manner multiple ways a company can identify profitable customers and more important, keep those customers loyal and profitable to your brand by engaging them in a manner that in some ways makes them co-producers of what they are purchasing. Driven by metrics developed through rigorous research involving both large and small companies, Dr Kumar suggests a number of new engagement strategies that are certain to lead to guaranteed profits. These strategies are described in a clear manner and illustrated by various real-world case studies. This book is a must read for both C-level executives and customer-facing employees."

—*Robert P. Leone*, **J. Vaughn and Evelyne H. Wilson Chair and Professor of Marketing, M.J. Neeley School of Business, Texas Christian University**

"While firms generally recognize that their customers are the source of their growth and profitability, most fall far short of optimizing their customer engagement process. As V. Kumar shows in this important new book, customer engagement optimization goes far beyond the direct, economic profitability of individual customers. Customers provide positive (or negative) profit contributions through their social networks, their referrals, and their knowledge or knowhow. Drawing on decades of research, VK provides the conceptual framework, the measurement processes and the marketing strategies firms need to optimize the customer engagement process. This book provides a blueprint for increased profitability through improved customer engagement and is destined to become a classic."

—*Gary L. Lilien*, **Distinguished Research Professor of Management Science, Penn State and Research Director, Institute for the Study of Business Markets**

"This is the best book on measuring customer engagement value, period! It is very comprehensive, highly readable, and simply engrossing. It is also conceptually rich, scientifically rigorous, and managerially relevant."

—*Jagdish N. Sheth*, **Charles H. Kellstadt Professor of Marketing, Goizueta Business School, Emory University**

"In today's globally competitive environment, differential advantage is shifting from product-related advantages which can be easily copied to the ways that companies engage with their customers. In this book, internationally renowned Professor V. Kumar develops a highly useful and innovative 5-component model for how companies can design and implement such engagement strategies profitably. Backed by sound and rigorous academic research as well as numerous illustrations, Professor Kumar's recipe for competitive advantage should be studied and utilized by any company that wishes to survive and be profitable in the marketplace today."

—*Russ Winer*, **William H. Joyce Professor of Marketing Chair and Marketing Department Academic Director of Stern Center for Measurable Marketing, New York University**

Profitable
Customer Engagement

Profitable
Customer Engagement

Concepts, Metrics, and Strategies

V. Kumar

www.sagepublications.com

Los Angeles • London • New Delhi • Singapore • Washington DC

First published in 2013 by

SAGE Response
B1/I-1 Mohan Cooperative Industrial Area
Mathura Road, New Delhi 110 044, India

SAGE Publications Inc
2455 Teller Road
Thousand Oaks, California 91320, USA

SAGE Publications Ltd
1 Oliver's Yard, 55 City Road
London EC1Y 1SP, United Kingdom

SAGE Publications Asia-Pacific Pte Ltd
33 Pekin Street
#02-01 Far East Square
Singapore 048763

Published by Vivek Mehra for SAGE Publications India Pvt Ltd, typeset in 11/14 pt Adobe Garamond Pro by Diligent Typesetter and printed at Saurabh Printers Pvt Ltd.

Library of Congress Cataloging-in-Publication Data

Kumar, V.
    Profitable customer engagement : concept, metrics, and strategies / V. Kumar.
    pages cm
    Includes bibliographical references and index.
    1. Customer relations—Management. 2. Branding (Marketing). 3. Profit.   I. Title.
    HF5415.5.K8636   658.8'12—dc23   2013   2013034437

ISBN: 978-81-321-1340-9 (HB)

The SAGE Team: Sachin Sharma, Alekha Chandra Jena, Nand Kumar Jha, and Rajinder Kaur

"A book is a powerful tool for change but the inspiration behind it is what makes you take the first step. This change is not always the easiest but some people show their undying support and relentless motivation to make you believe that you can create this change."

—With that, I dedicate this book to

Dean H. Fenwick Huss

For providing unconditional support of our efforts at the
J. Mack Robinson College of Business, Georgia State University

Thank you for choosing a SAGE product! If you have any comment, observation or feedback, I would like to personally hear from you. Please write to me at contactceo@sagepub.in

—Vivek Mehra, Managing Director and CEO,
SAGE Publications India Pvt Ltd, New Delhi

Bulk Sales

SAGE India offers special discounts for purchase of books in bulk. We also make available special imprints and excerpts from our books on demand.

For orders and enquiries, write to us at

Marketing Department
SAGE Publications India Pvt Ltd
B1/I-1, Mohan Cooperative Industrial Area
Mathura Road, Post Bag 7
New Delhi 110044, India
E-mail us at marketing@sagepub.in

Get to know more about SAGE, be invited to SAGE events, get on our mailing list. Write today to marketing@sagepub.in

This book is also available as an e-book.

CONTENTS

List of Illustrations   xi

List of Abbreviations   xv

Foreword: From a Thought Leader by David J. Reibstein   xvii

Foreword: From a Business Leader by J. Patrick Bewley   xix

Preface   xxi

Acknowledgments   xxiii

1. Introduction to Customer Engagement   1

     Engaging with Your Customers: Marketplace Evidence   4

     Understanding Profitable Customer Engagement   7

     Why Value Customer Engagement?   9

2. Metrics for Engaging Customers   17

     A Firm's Approach to Customer Engagement   17

     Conceptualizing CEV: An Integrated Framework   20

     Customer Brand Value (CBV)   25

     Customer Lifetime Value (CLV)   28

     Customer Referral Value (CRV)   31

     Business Reference Value (BRV)   35

     Customer Influence Value (CIV)   35

     Customer Knowledge Value (CKV)   38

     How Does It Help Organizations?   42

     Conclusion   43

3. Brand: "Is That What You Think of Me?"   46

     Connecting Brands with Customers   48

     Need to Measure Brand Value   51

     Aggregate versus Individual Brand Value   54

The CBV Framework   54
Measuring CBV   62
Maximizing CBV   63
Conclusion   63

4. Valuing Customer Contributions: The Future Looks Green!   **66**
Introduction: Why Measure Customer Value?   66
Traditional Measures of Customer Value: Backward-looking
    Metrics   67
Defining CLV: The Forward-looking Metric   70
Measuring CLV   72
Drivers of CLV   77
Maximizing CLV to Ensure Profitable Customer Engagement   78
Future of CLV   109
Looking Beyond CLV   110

5. Linking Brand Value to Customer Value   **113**
How to Link the Brand Value to Customer Value   113
The Role of Brand Communication in Linking Brand and
    Customer Value   115
Strategic Implementation of Managing Brands and Customers   116
Conclusion   130

6. Customer Referrals   **132**
Introduction: Valuing the Word That Goes Around   132
Conceptual Background   135
Defining CRV   147
Measuring CRV   147
Maximizing CRV   152
Linking CRV and CLV   154
Linking CBV and CRV   168
The Value of References in the B2B Setting   171
Measuring BRV   172
Drivers of BRV   177
Maximizing BRV   182
Linking BRV and CBV   186
From Referrals to Influence   189

7. Customer Influence Value: Really! Where Did You Hear That?   **191**

Introduction: Social Media   191
Social Media Landscape   192
Why Social Media Can Be Powerful   193
Successes and Failures in Marketing through Social Media   196
Defining Customer Influence Effect (CIE) and Customer
    Influence Value (CIV)   199
A Seven-step Framework for Creating Successful Social Media
    Marketing Campaigns   199
Implementation of the Seven-step Framework   203
Implementation of the Seven-step Process in HokeyPokey   206
Measuring CIV: Calculating the Effect and Value of Social
    Media Influence   212
The Campaign Results and Implications   216
Computation of CIV   218
Implications of CIV for Social Media Marketers   218
Encouraging and Maximizing CIV   221
Avoiding the Pitfalls in Social Coupon Launches   227
Interrelationships   234
Social Media Marketing (SMM): Version 2.0   240
A Sample Framework for Implementation   241

8. Please Help Us Help You...   **246**

Introduction: The Value of Customer Knowledge   246
Defining Customer Knowledge Value (CKV)   251
Measuring CKV   251
CKV Measurement Strategy   255
Impact of Social Media in CKV   264
Encouraging and Maximizing CKV   265
Applying CKV in Business   267
Interrelationships   269
Conclusion   275

9. Managing Customers in a Multi-dimensional World   **278**

Managing the CEV Framework   279
Organizational Challenges   288
Database Management   291

The Future of Customer Engagement 294
Conclusion 297

Glossary 299
Index 304
About the Author 312

LIST OF ILLUSTRATIONS

EXHIBITS

3.1	Role of Branding	46
4.1	Optimal Allocation of Resources at IBM	85
7.1	Calculating the Effect and Value of Social Media Influence	219
9.1	Management in Motion—Building Brand Value	282
9.2	Management in Motion—CIV	285
9.3	Management in Motion—CKV	287

BOXES

6.1	Optimal Referral Seeding Strategy—A Research Study	142
6.2	The Campaign Targeting the Affluents	161
6.3	The Campaign Targeting the Advocates	161
6.4	The Campaign Targeting the Misers	162
6.5	Microsoft Customer Reference Program	172
6.6	SAS Reference Program	173

FIGURES

1.1	Product-centric Approach to Profitability	11
1.2	Customer Engagement Approach to Profitability	13
2.1	The CEV Framework	21
2.2	Five Core Dimensions of CEV Framework	22
3.1	2012 Hyundai Veracruz	47
3.2	Mercedes-Benz E-Class	49
3.3	Hyundai Genesis	49

3.4 Sales Data for Brands A and B 52
3.5 The Change in Brand Value and Net Income for Samsung (2001–2005) 53
3.6 The Change in Brand Value and Net Income for Nokia (2001–2005) 53
3.7 CBV Framework 56
4.1 CLV Measurement Approach—A Conceptual Framework 73
4.2 A Sample List of Strategies to Ensure Profitable Customer Engagement 79
4.3 Wheel of Fortune: Strategies Used for Maximizing CLV 81
4.4 Managing Loyalty and Profitability Simultaneously 83
5.1 A Strategic Implementation of Managing Brands and Customers 116
5.2 Jessica's Measured Brand Value 118
5.3 Jessica's Estimated and Optimized Brand Value 119
5.4 Jessica's CLV Curve Measured at Different Times 120
5.5 Customer Life Cycle Brand Management: An Integrated Framework 121
5.6 Segmentation Strategies to Manage CLV and CBV 122
5.7 Migration from Acquaintances toward True Loyalists 125
6.1 Sample Referral Program by Sprint 134
6.2 Sample Referral Program by Scottrade 134
6.3 The Customer Referral Process 137
6.4 Sample Referral Program by Ashworth College 138
6.5 Position of Hubs, Fringes, and Bridges in a Social Network 143
6.6 Sample Referral Program by Roku 154
6.7 The Relationship between CLV and CRV 156
6.8 Customer Segments (by CLV and CRV) for the Telecommunications Firm 159
6.9 Campaign Results for Affluents Segment 163
6.10 Campaign Results for Advocates Segment 164
6.11 Campaign Results for Misers Segment 165
6.12 The Relationship between CBV and CRV 169
6.13 The Relationship between BRV and CBV 187
7.1 Social Media Landscape 193
7.2 Facebook and Twitter—Social Media Giants—A Quick View 194
7.3 Power of Social Media 195
7.4 Kenneth Cole Tweet 197

7.5   Seven-step Framework for a Successful Social Media
       Marketing Campaign   201
7.6   Drivers of Influencers   202
7.7   HokeyPokey   204
7.8   HokeyPokey's Goals for Social Media Marketing   205
7.9   HokeyPokey Social Media Marketing Project Timeline   205
7.10 First Step   206
7.11 Second Step   206
7.12 Third Step   207
7.13 Fourth Step   208
7.14 Fifth Step   209
7.15 Sixth Step   211
7.16 Happy Family Enjoying HokeyPokey Ice Creams   212
7.17 Distribution of Number of Conversations versus Ice Cream
       Creations   213
7.18 Seventh and Final Step   214
7.19 Conceptual Approach for Measuring CIV   215
7.20 ROI—Results of the Campaign   217
7.21 Daily Deals—Indifferent to Unpopular   223
7.22 Social Media Failure   224
7.23 Tracing the Dollars   225
7.24 The Relationship between CIV and CBV   237
7.25 Activity Diagram   242
8.1   The Quirky Process   250
8.2   Conceptual Approach to Measure CKV   252
8.3   CKV Measurement Strategy   255
8.4   Feedback Response Strategy   261
8.5   The Relationship between CKV and CBV   271
8.6   The Relationship between CKV and BRV   274
9.1   Implementing the CEV Framework   280
9.2   Customer Feedback Flow within an Organization   290
9.3   Types of Data   295

TABLES

1.1   Examples of Customer Engagement Initiated by Companies   5
2.1   Comparison between CRV and CKV   37

3.1	Experiment Results	47
3.2	Summary of Key Metrics across Top Luxury Brands	48
4.1	Transaction Details of Amy	76
4.2	Drivers of CLV in B2B and B2C Settings	78
4.3	Effect of the Drivers of Cross-buy	90
4.4	Sales Campaign Comparison in Telecommunications Industry	94
4.5	Average Customer-based Metrics of Single-channel and Multichannel Shoppers	100
5.1	ROI of the Campaign—Telecommunications	125
5.2	ROI of the Campaign—Financial Services	125
5.3	Expected Gains in CLV—Financial Services	125
5.4	Brand Awareness of Brand X Retailer	127
5.5	Brand Image of Brand X Retailer	127
5.6	Brand Trust of Brand X Retailer	128
5.7	Brand Affect of Brand X Retailer	128
5.8	Brand Purchase Intention of Brand X Retailer	128
5.9	Brand Loyalty of Brand X Retailer	129
5.10	Premium Price Behavior	129
5.11	Brand Advocacy	130
6.1	Intentions versus Actual Referral Behavior	142
6.2	Degree Centrality and Referral Rates	146
6.3	Tom's Referral Behavior in a Financial Services Company (Semi-annual Data)	150
6.4	Customer Rankings by CLV and CRV for a Telecommunications Firm	155
6.5	Campaign ROI for the Telecommunications Firm	166
6.6	Profit Projection for the Telecommunications Firm's Campaign	167
6.7	Reference Impact of Classic University	176
6.8	Influence of the Drivers of BRV	179
6.9	Client Firm Analysis for BRV and CLV	184
6.10	Segment Description for High- and Low-BRV Clients	185
7.1	Study Findings	230
7.2	Merits of Regulated Social Marketing—A Comparative Look	243

LIST OF ABBREVIATIONS

A&F	Abercrombie & Fitch
ARPRO	Allocating Resources for Profit
B2B	business-to-business
B2C	business-to-consumer
BRV	business reference value
CBV	customer brand value
CCV	customer collaborator value
CEV	customer engagement value
CIE	customer influence effect
CIV	customer influence value
CKV	customer knowledge value
CLV	customer lifetime value
CMO	Chief Marketing Officer
CRV	customer referral value
CPG	consumer packaged goods
CRM	customer relationship management
CSS	customer spending score
GM	General Motors
HP	Hewlett Packard
NPV	net present value
OM	opinion mining
PCV	past customer value
P&G	Procter & Gamble
ROI	return on investment
RFM	recency-frequency-monetary value
SI	stickiness index
SMM	social media marketing

SOW	share of wallet
SoLoMo	Social/Local/Mobile
SUR	seemingly unrelated regression
UML	Unified Modeling Language
VOC	voice of customer
WACC	weighted average cost of capital
WOM	word of mouth

FOREWORD
From a Thought Leader

Many companies spend millions of dollars in an effort to attract customers, as no business can survive without customers. But, to attract customers and not keep them is an absolute road to failure. The key to any successful business is customer retention. BASES, a marketing research firm that has a long history of new product testing, discovered years ago that repeat purchase was the number one metric indicative of success. Yet, the majority of marketing spending remains focused on customer acquisition.

Dr V. Kumar (VK) has spent a rich career focused on understanding profitable customer engagement. He has led a stream of research all around understanding the mechanisms that drives customer engagement that leads to having a profitable customer base. He shares his years of research and working with companies with us in this powerful book, *Profitable Customer Engagement*. It starts with carefully selecting the "right" customers—those that are profitable. This requires not simply looking at who has been profitable for the firm, but those, if handled correctly, have the potential to become profitable customers. It then is followed by an understanding of what engages the customer so they are happy with the product/service and are very likely to become repeat customers. But, his latest insights are in understanding the greater value of customers beyond their purchases—how they influence others to engage with our products and services as well. This book clearly extends into today's world of social media with plenty of depth to allow us to quantify what few others have been able to do, the impact of social media. He also shows us to realize some customers bring additional value by the feedback they provide allowing us to improve our offerings, not just for that customer, but for numerous others.

The four basic tenants of Profitable Customer Engagement centers on (1) customer lifetime value, (2) customer referral value, (3) customer influence value, and (4) customer knowledge value. Customer lifetime value is directly linked to the firm's profits, while the other three are linked, but indirectly. These principal components of customer engagement are not merely concepts, but can be measured and tracked. The book has separate chapters on each of these pillars and details how to measure and use these concepts to enhance overall profitability. This is very well illustrated with a rich set of examples. Dr V. Kumar then illuminates for us how each of these measures directly contributes to profitability and return on investment (ROI).

One of the key components of the book is how each of these measures is on an individual level. Each customer has his/her own customer lifetime value, customer influence value, etc. With the emergence of BIG DATA we now have the opportunity to start tracking which of our customers are offering what value and how this can be enhanced by focusing on the key component of customer engagement. Some customers may not be profitable today, but with the right stimulus directed to the critical component, their value can be increased. The roadmap to doing this is extremely clear throughout the book.

Dr V. Kumar has based his work on rigorous research, but the book is not only based on these findings, but riddled with scores of engaging examples that we can all identify. You cannot read this book without coming away with a deep understanding of how to engage your customers.

—David J. Reibstein
Chairman of the American Marketing Association and
The William S. Woodside Professor and Professor of Marketing
at The Wharton School, University of Pennsylvania

FOREWORD

From a Business Leader

In my work over the last two decades as a CEO and a business leader of some of the world's most sophisticated data and analytics companies, I have gotten to watch something very special happen. I have seen the transformation of the marketing discipline within organizations. Simply put, marketing organizations have become scientific. This paradigm shift of marketing from art form to a science has many parallels to the changes that the manufacturing disciplines within businesses went through in the 1990s.

For a group of business professionals (marketers) who like to quote John Wannamaker's famous retort, "Half my advertising is wasted, I just don't know which half," this transformation is greatly overdue. In 2012 alone, that number of "wasted advertising" was in the hundreds of billions of dollars.

Marketing's available technology, data, and methods have undergone a consonant proliferation. From the early days of e-commerce, marketers witnessed an emergence of anonymous click-stream data about user behaviors which gave them insights in minutes that historically took months to generate. We marketers were greatly unprepared to assemble or understand these data streams about customers.

Anytime humans have experienced this type of renaissance of information, it takes the work of pioneering individuals to show us the way forward. In the same way that physicists gave us explanations to gravitational, electromagnetic, and nuclear forces, Dr Kumar has given us fundamental explanations of the marketing discipline.

In typical fashion, VK has returned tour de force to provide us marketing practitioners our equivalent of Grand Unified Theory. In this latest work *Profitable Customer Engagement*, he links a customer's individual value with their referrals, influence, and knowledge and ties that to the effects on brand

and shareholder value. This provides a holistic framework that can be applied at the center of your marketing strategy.

The foundations established by his work in 2008 *Managing Customers for Profits* gave us practitioners the tools required to put Customer Lifetime Value at the center of our marketing strategy. With these tools, I have been able to help leadership of many of the world's greatest brands around the globe explain to their CEOs, CFOs, and Board of Directors why investing in a customer-centered strategy was important.

One of the most significant successes based on Dr Kumar's pioneering work was being able to demonstrate to European mobile handset manufacturer that minute improvements in consumer engagement were worth nearing a half of a billion euro of additional sales in just a three-year time frame.

In this book, Dr Kumar takes his work in *Customer Lifetime Value* to the next level, giving us even greater accuracy and predictive power. VK then expanded on this substratum with his more recent scientific works, allowing us to understand and accurately measure the new phenomenon of influencers and referrals in a way that links to the bottom line. The addition of customer influence value and the significant evolution of customer referral value provide us with the mechanics to accurately quantify our social media efforts.

With customer knowledge value being added to the framework, we can now understand how to link voice of the customer initiatives to the critical research phase of product development. As consumer demands of products and services rapidly increase, the expectation for turn times and new releases rapidly decreases. The ability to link investments in this area to a more holistic customer engagement strategy has been tremendously important in my work implementing marketing strategies.

I'm looking forward to leveraging this ground breaking work to set the vision and strategy of many of the world's best brands in the years to come.

Congratulations and keep up the je ne sais quoi VK!

—J. Patrick Bewley
Big Data and Analytics Entrepreneur
jpbewley@post.harvard.edu

PREFACE

The business world, as we know, is constantly evolving from making just great products/services to now creating profitable, loyal customers. If the changing scenarios are any indication, it can well be said that if you don't find ways to make your customers stay, they have every reason to walk away with your competitors. There is a constant pressure to make the bottom line grow. While you may have great products/services, if you don't have the right customers, you might as well be packing your bags. How to make the profits from your loyal customer base sustainable? A recent phenomenon that has caught the attention of many business executives and thought leaders is along the lines of how to engage the customer base more proactively. This proactive customer engagement has become imperative and crucial for sustaining profitable businesses. The power of the customers' word of mouth has not been capitalized yet by the businesses. Social media channels are proliferating and customers participate in these channels voluntarily. Further, customers have become more informed about their needs and wants and are willing to articulate their exact needs to the firms. Thus, with so many ways to get the customer base engaged with the firm, the question that needs to be answered is: How can a company make all forms of customer engagement profitable? Targeted at top/mid-level management of small, medium and large business-to-consumer (B2C) and business-to-business (B2B) enterprises, this book provides in-depth knowledge about the various customer engagement strategies that a firm can undertake to gain maximum profitability from each of its customers while ensuring their continued loyalty. Is there a way to monetize customer engagement? Indeed there is. This book proposes several *concepts* and methodologies to measure customer engagement by developing a framework that includes the multi-dimensional aspects of customer engagement. Methodologies to monetize these components are proposed, tested, and validated in the real-world scenarios in order to maximize the profitability of the customers.

This book identifies four dollar *metrics* and one attitudinal metric that can help manage customer engagement. The four dollar metrics include—customer lifetime value (CLV), customer referral value (CRV), customer influence value (CIV), and customer knowledge value (CKV). Customer brand value (CBV) is the attitudinal metric. The book starts with the basic understanding of customer engagement and then delves deeper into each of the components in the subsequent chapters. We approach each chapter by first defining the concept, describing the way to measure it, and then provide several *strategies* to maximize it. It is extremely important to understand that each of these concepts can be interrelated and together they help manage customer engagement as a whole. The book concludes with strategies to identify the relevance of the different metrics and the need to maximize them, based on the company objectives. The uniqueness of the book lies in the fact that each of these concepts has been implemented by many companies that have reported success. These concepts have passed the test of rigor and relevance and these studies have been published in several top scientific journals. The book illustrates the concepts through many global examples for comprehension of readers from all around the world. This book is a synthesis of a decade-long effort in the area of customer engagement and has been made possible by working with my past and current doctoral students.

ACKNOWLEDGMENTS

I wish to express my sincere thanks for the support and encouragement offered by our university President Mark P. Becker and Provost Risa Palm for keeping us engaged productively.

I want to thank Angeliki Christodoulopoulou, Anita Iyer, Amber McCain, Nandini Bala, Narayani Sharma, and Rachelle Jackson for their assistance in the preparation of this manuscript. I would like to also thank Bharath Rajan, and Sarang Sunder for their suggestions at various stages of the manuscript. I would also like to thank Riddhi Shah for helping me manage the writing process. I would like to particularly thank Renu for copyediting the manuscript. I want to thank my co-authors in each of the studies referenced in this book for their contribution. I am deeply indebted to the editorial team at SAGE for their patience and consistent encouragement, and for accepting this manuscript for publication.

Chapter 1

Introduction to Customer Engagement

Find answers for...

- What is customer engagement?
- How does customer engagement help businesses?
- Why should firms value customer engagement?

Companies are constantly looking to improve their customer relationship management (CRM) strategies and practices. While doing so, one question that all successful companies seem to be asking is—*Is CRM activity adding value to our company?* The strategic process of CRM pertains to selecting customers that a firm can profitably serve, and shaping interactions between a firm and its customers. The goal of CRM is to optimize the current and future value of the customers for the firm. This pursuit toward higher profits has often led companies through the path of introspection regarding customer practices by analyzing all the avenues of customer profitability. These empirical investigations have provided directions for critical questions such as:

- Who are our most profitable customers?
- How can we manage and reward customers based on their profitability?
- How do we identify the "right" products/services to sell to the "right" customers and at what time?
- How do we optimally allocate marketing resources to maximize profitability?
- How do we hold on to our profitable customers?

These questions continue to dominate the agendas of marketing managers and the C-level executives in the boardroom.

An important outcome of measuring and maximizing customer profitability is clearly evident from the constantly evolving landscape of customer management. Companies are consciously moving away from a product- and sales-centric philosophy to a customer engagement philosophy. The underlying principle of a product-centric philosophy is to sell products to whoever is willing to buy. In such organizations, the aim of all business functions will be on solving the needs and problems of customers by developing appropriate product solutions. Typically, managers of companies with this type of orientation would focus on: (*a*) How many customers can we sell this product to? (*b*) How can we strengthen our product development and increase market share? (*c*) What type of new product features should we introduce and how do we highlight their advantages? (*d*) How can we improve product profitability and market share so that the firm performance is enhanced? While such an approach may be worthwhile in some situations, the pitfall of such a focus is that companies tend to ignore customer-specific needs that are crucial in determining their relationship with the firm. When companies do not factor in customer relationship needs, customers are likely to defect to competition.

On the contrary, the customer engagement philosophy advocates developing a portfolio of customers (a specific set of valuable customers) and nurturing relationships with these customers. Under such an approach, companies typically focus on: (*a*) How many products can we sell to this customer? (*b*) How can we highlight the product benefits that align with customer needs? (*c*) Which customers segments can we focus on and how should we develop relationships with these customers? (*d*) What customer metrics should we use to measure the firm performance? Several firms that have moved away from a product-centric to a customer engagement philosophy have reported huge gains in profits. For example, while casinos such as MGM Grand and Caesar's Palace focus on attracting as many customers as possible for profit, Harrah's success results from its ability to identify and pursue serious gamers.[1]

An important element of the customer engagement philosophy is the management of profitable and unprofitable customers. When companies compute customer profitability and identify the unprofitable customer segments, they are immediately inclined toward "firing" such customers. Though this instinctive decision of firing unprofitable customers at times helps businesses in staying profitable, it has been proven wrong many times too.

Consider the following instances:

- In July 2007, Sprint "fired" around 1,000 of their customers who were calling the company's call center too often and using more of their resources. The customers who were fired were not customers who couldn't pay their bills, but they were customers who frequently called in and complained. This resulted in financial losses for Sprint.[2]
- When FedEx discovered that some of their customers, who had negotiated discounted rates in return for consistent shipping orders, were not bringing in sufficient revenue (and expecting expensive residential deliveries), they demanded that these customers pay higher rates. While some customers accommodated these higher rates, customers who refused to pay more were told to take their shipping business elsewhere. In effect, FedEx selectively fired their high cost, unprofitable customers by charging higher prices while offering discounts to their valuable customers.[3]
- Peeled Snacks, makers of dried fruit-and-nut snack packs, found that the high slotting fees, and the demand by the grocery store to have periodic sampling events and discounts were eating into their already slender profit margins. Unable to cope with these demands, Peeled Snacks decided to not supply to such grocery chains, and instead started focusing on convenience stores and other "grab and go" locations such as gift shops, gyms, and movie theatres. This move proved to be profitable for Peeled Snacks, as some convenience stores provided profits nearing 50 percent on a bag of snacks that retailed at $2.49, compared to the few pennies that the grocery chains were offering.[4]

The above examples are just a sample of corporate actions in dealing with unprofitable customers. However, they do raise some important issues on profitable customer management techniques. Did these companies have a clear idea about the "future" profitability of the customers, as against how profitable the customers were at the time of firing? In this regard, it is important to use a metric that computes the "future" profitability of a customer, and not rely only on historical profit contribution. That is, had these companies computed the future profitability of customers, it is possible that some of these unprofitable customers would have indicated future profit potential. In such a case, some of those customers could have been "saved" from being fired, thereby not only bringing in profits but also lessening the consumer whiplash effect. Further, if these companies had determined the future profit potential of these customers; is it still acceptable to fire the unprofitable customers? It is possible that the loss-making customers were using a product category that was not suitable for them, therefore causing losses. In such a scenario, promoting appropriate products/services to up-sell and/or cross-sell to such customers could make them profitable in the future. Another way would be to revisit the choice of communication channels used. If these customers had been migrated to low-cost communication channels with varying communication intensities, it is possible that their loss-making potential would have been decreased, maybe even making some of them profitable. The alternate scenarios provided here, apart from helping companies manage unprofitable customers, contribute toward the larger purpose of CRM—to *engage* with your customers.

ENGAGING WITH YOUR CUSTOMERS: MARKETPLACE EVIDENCE

The concept of customer engagement, as popularly understood by companies today, relates largely to the customer experiences as manifested by customer or company-initiated communication efforts. Examples of these customer experiences include interactions with the brand offerings, responses to advertising efforts, level of participation in the marketing communications efforts, and engaging in word-of-mouth (WOM) advertising on social media channels, giving valuable feedback, among others. Table 1.1 provides popular instances of companies engaging with their customers.

Despite the growing appreciation and inclination toward customer engagement, companies have so far not been able to assess the benefits that engaging would bring in to the company accurately. The answer, therefore, lies in quantifying customer experiences and deriving value out of it through customer management strategies. In other words, the introduction and usage of credible metrics in customer engagement efforts will go a long way for companies to identify, nurture, grow, and maximize customer engagement.

This leads to the next issue—what aspect of customer engagement is to be maximized? Focusing only on the efforts and outcomes that maximize direct and indirect customer engagement is not sufficient. The key to engaging

Table 1.1	Examples of Customer Engagement Initiated by Companies

How do they engage?	Who does this?
Offer more products and related accessories.	Apple sells cases and new gadgets for its main line of products (computers and phones at http://store.apple.com). New developments and upgrades are released every year to continue the customer buying experience.
Track purchase history, observe what customers are buying, and determine how to adjust marketing and product mix to spur continued purchases.	Cellairis is an international producer of cell phone accessories. When they realized a large percentage of their customers were young girls, they launched a Justin Bieber line of cell phone accessories (https://www.cellairis.com/justin-bieber-iphone-case) that largely expanded their business.
Understand customer behaviors and their specific purchase triggers that will help optimize the marketing mix.	Blendtec's "Will It Blend" videos on YouTube grabbed consumer attention. The program has far surpassed 100 million hits altogether, and sales have skyrocketed.[5]
Create discussion areas and topics via social media sites.	Domino's offered a limited number of free artisan pizzas to people who "liked" the Domino's Facebook page, and gained referrals through the "likes." They also created a Facebook widget that customers can post on their Facebook walls.[6]
Be more personalized. Track and keep records of customer interactions that can be retrieved by any agent whenever the customer calls/visits next.	Great clips, the hair salon, tracks the hair styles and the stylist of a customer and these can be retrieved during the customer's subsequent visit to ensure the customer has the same satisfying experience with them.
Letting customers be the brand ambassadors.	The bourbon maker, Maker's Mark uses its grassroots ambassador program to market the product. They offer freebies and business cards to customers who sign up and spread the word to people and local bars about the brand.[7]
Be available at all times. A 24/7 communication channel ensures that customers can engage with the company at any time.	Customer Call Centers or Care Services are examples of such platforms.

(Table 1.1 Continued)

(Table 1.1 Continued)

How do they engage?	Who does this?
Provide incentives in exchange for feedback.	Skiddle.com, the event promotion website, held a contest with a grand prize of tickets to any festival of the winner's choice in exchange for feedback about their website.[8]
Make the customer feedback process easy and effective.	LinkedIn.com allows users to give feedback or mention problems through a sidebar while still on the original site page.
Strong presence in the social media portals makes feedback easier.	Zappos and Delta Airlines' twitter interactions with customers ensured fast responses, and quick solutions.[9]
Gain WOM and referrals when customers genuinely like it.	Pinterest keeps its customers engaged by ensuring that its core demographic like the service, and earn positive referrals in the process.
Offer rewards for successful referrals.	Several banks and telecom service providers offer rewards for successful referrals. For instance, First Tennessee Bank offers a $50 referral reward (https://www.referlive.com/firsttennessee).
Create an experience that can be enjoyed by a group of people.	"Donate a Friend" blood drives ask participants to bring a friend along to donate blood.[10] March of Dimes Foundation volunteers create teams and are required to invite/recruit other people for their team.[11]

with customers profitably is in recognizing the sources of profit contribution. Companies should strive to engage with their customers while ensuring overall firm profitability. This corresponds to directing all efforts to maximize *profitable* customer engagement, as opposed to just customer engagement. Customers in general, engage with firms in four different ways (*a*) by buying the firm's product, (*b*) by referring the firm to other prospects using the firm's referral program, (*c*) by influencing other customers/prospects through online social media channels, and (*d*) by providing feedback to the firm. When companies can quantify and measure the customer's engagement (each of the above-mentioned four types), customer engagement becomes more meaningful and actionable. Such an approach would not only cultivate customer engagement, but also lead to growing the bottom line of the companies.

Conceptually, customer engagement value (CEV) is the total value provided by customers who value the brand such that they engage with the firms (*a*) through their purchase transactions, (*b*) through their ability to refer other customers to the firm using the firm's referral program, (*c*) through their power to positively influence other customers about the firm's offerings in the social media, and (*d*) by providing a feedback to the firm for product and service ideas.[12]

This book identifies different metrics that would aid firms to capture/measure CEV. This chapter elaborates the need to value customer engagement and customer engagement approach to enhance profitability.

UNDERSTANDING PROFITABLE CUSTOMER ENGAGEMENT

Business wisdom suggests that customer purchases indicate the level of engagement with the company, apart from determining customer profitability. Research has shown that profitable customers exhibit important characteristics such as (*a*) buying intensively over time, (*b*) buying multiple product categories, (*c*) returning a moderate amount of purchases, (*d*) responding to the marketing efforts, and (*e*) membership in the company's loyalty program, among others.[13] All these indicators suggest the level of customer engagement with the company. What about customers who are unprofitable? When companies identify customers with poor profit potential, they are often tempted to "fire" such customers. The question we need to ask here is—is firing unprofitable customers the only option? Or, do we have other options that will help the companies to deal better with these customers?

When customers do not contribute profits through their purchases, companies should revisit their product portfolios to ensure that the product offerings fit in with the needs and expectations of the customers. In case of a mismatch of product ownership, identifying and promoting the right product options will go a long way in increasing customer profitability. While promoting related and relevant products to improve profitability does make good business sense, it is only helpful up to a certain level. In other words, what happens if no more changes are possible to the product portfolios of the customers to make them more profitable? This situation is possible when customers are constrained by personal income levels (determined by their size of wallet) and lifestyle choices that are likely to prevent them from buying some product categories, even though they may yield high margins. When encountered with such situations, it is imperative for companies to revisit their intensity of marketing communication and refrain from making any major marketing investment in them. When they do come knocking, however, companies should extract the maximum profit from every transaction since these customers may not come again.

Apart from their direct contributions, customers can also contribute indirectly through several ways. One such popular option is by promoting customer referrals.[14] Incentivizing existing customers to bring in new customers through customer referrals works well in determining the engagement and profitability of a customer. Referrals are crucial as they have the potential to reduce acquisition costs for the firm and bring in future revenue. Because referral programs reward existing customers, firms encourage customers to make recommendations to others. In many ways, these referring customers can be thought of as non-employee salespeople earning a commission from the sale and can be an effective way of bringing in new customers. For instance, companies such as AT&T and DIRECTV have introduced a value-oriented referral incentive program that rewards both the referral and the referring customer. AT&T rewards both the referral and the referring customer $25 whenever a referral activates a new, qualifying AT&T wireless service. These incentives seem to be in proportion to the relative value of each customer segment. This concept that is popular in a business-to-customer (B2C) setting has also been extended to accommodate a business-to-business (B2B) setting, wherein firms are influenced to purchase based on references (or testimonials) from other firms who are already clients of the selling firm.[15] This allows the managers of the selling firm to identify the best references to use, in order to influence potential client firms to purchase products and services in the future. Regardless of the business setting, it is important to incentivize the right customers to provide referrals or references. This is because incentivizing an unprofitable customer is likely to bring in customers of similar profit potential who would severely undermine the company's bottom line.

A second option to promote indirect profit contributions by customers is through their online presence. In many product categories, information sharing, WOM, and online interaction can significantly affect others' behavior through (*a*) increased persuasion and conversion of others to customers, (*b*) the recipient customer's continued usage of a product, and (*c*) changes in their share of wallet.[16] Past research has found that consumers who had communicated with an early adopter of a telecommunications product were 3–4 times more likely to respond to an offer for the product.[17] Evidence from the marketplace also suggests that WOM can play a significant role in a firm's sales and marketing efforts (see Table 1.1). In an online setting where customers belonging to various geo-demographic segments actively communicate with each other, WOM can significantly affect the desirability of continued (or even increased) product/service usage by other customers. In this regard, harnessing the power of WOM in the online medium is an important way to shape and positively impact the product usage and engagement of the customers.

Finally, companies can also embellish customers' indirect profit contributions by actively seeking their review/feedback on the products/services. Customer input can be a valuable resource. This can be done in a variety of ways, but most notably through customers' involvement in the product development process. For instance, the ice cream retailer Ben and Jerry's encourages customers to participate in the new product development process by sponsoring a contest where customers can suggest the "best new flavor." In this regard, several companies are using the Internet and social media to involve customers in several aspects of the new product development process and across product categories ranging from customized laptops to fashion accessories. Aside of aiding in new product/service creation and innovation, customer feedback is also vital to quality/service improvement efforts, complaint management, and service recovery that forms an important part of customer satisfaction. In short, customers can add value to the company by helping understand customer preferences and participating in the knowledge development process.[18] Since this is essential to the creation of successful new products that create value, contribution of customers to this value creation needs to be captured and included as part of profitable customer engagement.

WHY VALUE CUSTOMER ENGAGEMENT?

The concept of profitable customer engagement is a relevant topic in the current landscape of customer management, and is receiving increasing attention from the academic and business communities. With the vibrant social media climate, engaging with customers has become a key objective of companies.

The importance and immediacy of this concept stems from its applicability to a wide range of business types and functions. It applies to firms of various sizes (small, medium, and large), the B2B and B2C industries, the customers in the contractual and noncontractual business settings, companies selling products or services, and firms with transactions that are onetime or continuous in nature. Given this wide spectrum of usage, understanding customer engagement and cultivating it in a manner that would also ensure profits is of vital importance.

Customer engagement has been in practice for quite some time, but only by quantifying the value derived from customer engagement can companies justify their efforts. In order to ascertain the value added by the engagement efforts, companies should identify, understand, and manage not only individual customers' purchase behavior, but also attitudes. In other words, companies must not stop with encouraging customers to buy more intensively over time. They should also encourage their customers to refer more customers to buy products/services from the firm, talk to (and in the process, influence) other customers and prospects to transact with the firm, and exchange information (in the form of customer feedback) with the firm. Companies should bear in mind that the customer perceptions drive each of these above-mentioned activities and hence companies should take necessary actions to create a positive brand image of themselves in the customers' mind. When this heightened state of customer engagement is effectively tracked and managed, firms will increase their profits. To understand the concept of profitable customer engagement, it is important to review the prevailing business wisdom to earn profits. Figure 1.1 illustrates the conventional product-centric approach to profitability adopted by businesses.

As is evident from Figure 1.1, companies begin on their path to profitability by providing innovative product/service offerings. Several organizations have ingrained innovation as a top priority and believe that if they investigate customers' needs and innovate, they will acquire new customers easily. Such a focus will inevitably lead to higher levels of satisfaction for all customers. Consequently, higher levels of satisfaction lead to higher levels of loyalty, which, in turn, lead to higher profitability. In other words, when firms create value for their customers through superior and innovative product offerings it will, in turn, lead customers to create value for the firms. While this path to profitability sounds reasonable, it does suffer from three key weaknesses.

Figure 1.1 Product-centric Approach to Profitability

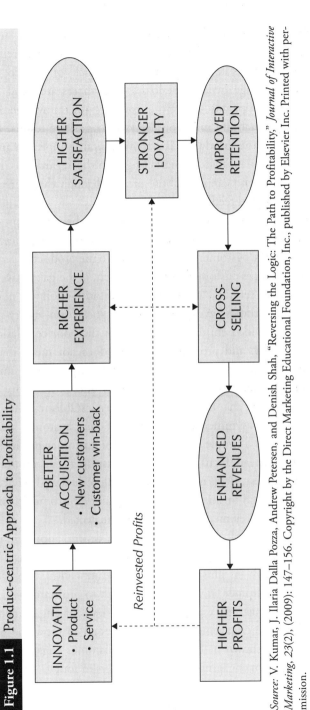

Source: V. Kumar, J. Ilaria Dalla Pozza, Andrew Petersen, and Denish Shah, "Reversing the Logic: The Path to Profitability," *Journal of Interactive Marketing*, 23(2), (2009): 147–156. Copyright by the Direct Marketing Educational Foundation, Inc., published by Elsevier Inc. Printed with permission.

First, there are several risks attached to the development of new products that include high initial investment outlay and product failure. As a result, a failed new product is not just a marketing setback for the firm but is often accompanied by huge investment losses in both research and design, and in promotional campaigns. Therefore, focusing on innovation as a starting point toward profitability may not always bear positive results. Instead, engaging customers as coproducers is a more desirable approach and is part of the emerging dominant logic of marketing.[19] In this regard, it is important to engage customers who can contribute profits through their direct purchases and their referrals and feedback.

Second, the level of satisfaction that a customer has with a product or service is dependent on (a) the richness of the customer experience and (b) the expectation that the customer has with regard to the product or service.[20] Even when the experiences customers receive are rich, if the gap between expectation and perceived service is small, the level of satisfaction will not be high.

Finally, several studies have questioned the satisfaction-loyalty-profitability link and have provided empirical evidence for the poor correlation between satisfaction, loyalty, and profitability.[21] This does not mean that customer satisfaction or customer loyalty is not important any more. It simply implies that the linkages between satisfaction, loyalty and profitability have to be assessed in a correct manner. It has now been established that these links are non-linear and asymmetric.[22] Therefore, taking customer satisfaction or customer loyalty as a simple proxy measure for customer profits is not sufficient anymore. Instead, focus on measuring customer-level profitability holds the key. Nevertheless, firms almost always use product and service quality to influence profits, and in this regard, the impact of customer satisfaction and customer loyalty as key mediators cannot be neglected.

In light of these weaknesses in this product-centric approach, it is important to revisit the path to profitability that starts with the customers rather than end with them (as illustrated in the product-centric approach). Figure 1.2 illustrates a customer engagement approach to profitability.

The focus on customers pertains to their level of engagement with the firms and how the engagement can be harnessed to grow the bottom line of companies. As shown in Figure 1.2, the customer engagement approach begins with the firm engaging with its customers in four different ways. First, customers can engage with the firm by buying the various product/service offerings and thereby contributing to the firm's profitability. The breadth and

Figure 1.2 Customer Engagement Approach to Profitability

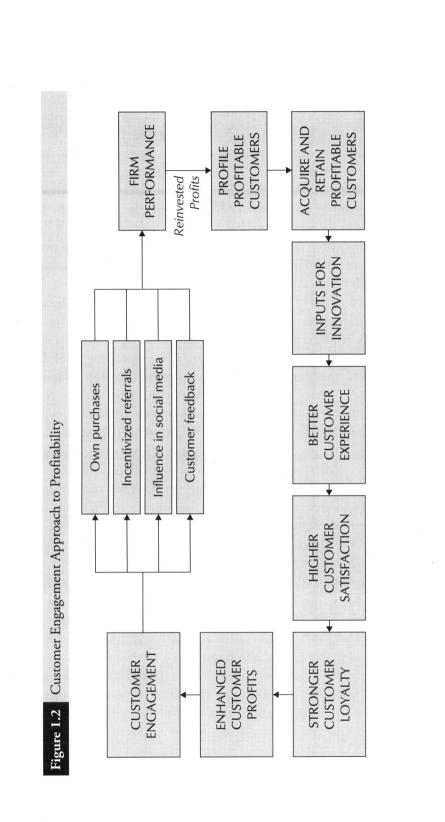

depth of their purchases indicates the level of customer engagement. The breadth of purchases pertains to the various product/service categories that a customer has bought or owns, and the depth of purchases refers to variants of a single product/service category that a customer has bought or owns. Naturally, the broader and deeper a customer's purchases, the more engaged he/she is with the firm. Second, the number of incentivized referrals that a customer promotes also indicates his/her level of engagement with the firm. That is, when customers refer other customers (for a reward) to try the firm's offerings, this action indicates that it is unlikely these customers would not like the firm and also indicates the intent of these customers to continuously interact with the firm/brand.

Third, the extent of influence a customer has on others in social media portals indicates a customer's level of engagement with the firm. Influencing users on social media to buy a firm's offerings can be viewed as a sign of a highly engaged customer. These voluntary actions speak highly of their engagement with the firm/brand, and in turn, get the firm more customers. Finally, firms can create customer engagement by encouraging them to provide feedback about the product usage, product improvement efforts, and/or ideas for new products. Customer feedback is of great value to firms because it allows firms to learn what their customers know. When firms truly understand what their customers want and how to deliver on their customers' expectations, they have an edge over their competition. When companies engage with their customers in one or all of the four ways, it results in an enhanced financial performance of the firm.

Based on the superior performance of the firm, it can reinvest the profits into the firm that can be used toward managing profitable customers. This involves creating profiles of profitable customers that describe the characteristics and features that make them profitable. These profiles can also be used to find "look-alikes" from the prospect pool to aid in acquiring profitable customers. They can be used in customer retention initiatives as well, wherein the firm ensures that profitable customers are retained from churning. With such a "profitable" customer pool in place, the firm can then seek inputs for innovation from their customers that will lead to a better customer experience. This superior customer experience is bound to ensure customer satisfaction, increase customer loyalty, and finally lead to enhanced profits. The book will focus on this customer engagement approach to profitability, and in particular, the five ways to engage with customers profitably.

Increasingly, companies have been trying to understand and measure both the purchase behavior and non-purchase behavior of their customers through various channels. Companies understand that they can increase their profitability by actively engaging with customers and tracking their purchase and non-purchase behavior data. Traditionally, to drive up profits, companies have focused on encouraging customers to purchase more from them. But recently companies not only encourage their customers to buy more from them but also encourage their customers to actively refer other customers, influence customers and prospects through social media, and encourage the customers to provide active feedback to the company, to drive up profits. In order to accomplish this, there has been no comprehensive framework till now. The CEV framework fills this gap. CEV is a set of values provided by customers who value the brand and contribute to the firm through purchase and non-purchase behavior. This book will focus on the CEV framework, focusing on the five ways to engage with customers profitably—customer brand value (CBV), customer lifetime value (CLV), customer referral value (CRV), customer influence value (CIV), and customer knowledge value (CKV). The subsequent chapters elaborate on the CEV framework (CEV framework; Chapter 2) and these five core dimensions in detail as they relate to the crucial business functions that are ideally suited to cultivate and maximize customer engagement: (*a*) customer perception of the brand (CBV metric; Chapter 3); (*b*) direct customer purchases (CLV metric; Chapter 4); (*c*) linking brand value to customer value (CBV metric and CLV metric; Chapter 5); (*d*) purchases through WOM referrals and references (CRV metric/BRV metric; Chapter 6); (*e*) purchases driven by customer influences through social media outlets (CIV metric; Chapter 7); and (*f*) customer feedback/review (CKV metric; Chapter 8). The concluding chapter addresses the organizational challenges encountered in implementing CEV and the strategies involved in maximizing CEV components.

NOTES AND REFERENCES

1. L. Gary, "Diamonds in the Data Mine," *Harvard Business Review, 81*(5), (2003): 109–113.
2. R. Nelson, "Sprint may Cancel Your Service if You Call Customer Service Too Often," (2007) Message posted to http://www.gadgetell.com/tech/comment/sprint-may-cancel-your-service-if-you-call-customer-service-to-often/ (retrieved on April 1, 2013).

3. L. Selden and G. Colvin, *Angel Customers & Demon Customers* (London, England: Penguin Books Ltd., 2003).

4. A. Joyner, "When the Customer Is Wrong—Deciding to Fire a Client," *INC Magazine, 31*(8), (2009): 102–104.

5. Mooball, "Will It Blend? A Viral Marketing Case Study," http://www.mooball.com/blog/will-it-blend-a-viral-marketing-case-study (retrieved on June 1, 2012).

6. Hip2Save, "Hot Domino's: Free Artisan Pizza – first 25,000 (Facebook)," http://hip-2save.com/2012/04/30/hot-dominos-free-artisan-pizza-1st-25000-facebook/ (retrieved on June 1, 2012).

7. The Spin Within, "Maker's Mark Ambassador? Sign Me Up!," http://forza-marketing.com/blog/makers_mark_ambassador_sign_me_up (retrieved on September 9, 2013).

8. Skiddle, "Tell Us What You Think of Our New Homepage, and Be in with a Chance of Winning Tickets to Your Favourite Festival This Summer," http://www.skiddle.com/news/all/Give-us-your-feedback-and-win-tickets-to-a-festival-of-your-choice-/11784/ (retrieved on June 1, 2012).

9. Socialicity, "Social Media and Customer Engagement: A Tale of Two Experiences (Part I)," http://patperdue.com/social-media-and-customer-engagement-a-tale-of-two-experiences-part-1/ (retrieved on June 1, 2012).

10. Toop 582, "Donate a Friend," http://www.t582.org/BloodDrive.aspx (retrieved on June 1, 2012).

11. March of Dimes, http://www.marchofdimes.com/ (retrieved on June 1, 2012).

12. V. Kumar, L. Aksoy, B. Donkers, R. Venkatesan, T. Wiesel, and S. Tillmanns, "Undervalued or Overvalued Customers: Capturing Total Customer Engagement Value," *Journal of Service Research, 13*(3), (2010): 297–310.

13. W. Reinartz and V. Kumar, "The Impact of Customer Relationship Characteristics on Profitable Lifetime Duration," *Journal of Marketing, 67*(1), (2003): 77–99.

14. V. Kumar, J.A. Petersen, and R.P. Leone, "How Valuable Is Word of Mouth?" *Harvard Business Review, 85*(10) (2007): 139–146.

15. V. Kumar, J.A. Petersen, and R.P. Leone, "Defining, Measuring, and Managing Business Reference Value." *Journal of Marketing, 77*(1), (2013): 68–86.

16. V. Kumar, et al. "Undervalued Customers," *Journal of Service Research, 13*(3), (2010): 297–310.

17. S. Hill, F. Provost, and C. Volinsky, "Network-Based Marketing: Identifying Likely Adopters via Consumer Networks," *Statistical Science, 21*(2), (2006): 256–276.

18. A.W. Joshi and S. Sharma, "Customer Knowledge Development: Antecedents and Impact on New Product Performance," *Journal of Marketing, 68*(4), (2004): 47–59.

19. S.L. Vargo and R.F. Lusch, "Evolving to a New Dominant Logic for Marketing," *Journal of Marketing, 68*(1), (2004): 1–17.

20. A. Parasuraman, V.A. Zeithaml, and L.L. Berry, "A Conceptual Model of Service Quality and Its Implications for Future Research," *Journal of Marketing, 49*(3), (1985): 41–50.

21. W. Reinartz and V. Kumar, "On the Profitability of Long-Life Customers in a Non-Contractual Setting: An Empirical Investigation and Implications for Marketing," *Journal of Marketing, 64*(4), (2000): 17–35. Also see W. Reinartz and V. Kumar, "The Mismanagement of Customer Loyalty," *Harvard Business Review, 80*(7), (2002): 86–94.

22. W. Eugene Anderson and Vikas Mittal, "Strengthening the Satisfaction-Profit Chain," *Journal of Service Research, 3*, (2000): 107–120.

Chapter 2

Metrics for Engaging Customers

Find answers for...

- How do firms engage with their customers and derive value out of that engagement?
- What is customer engagement value (CEV)?
- What are the components of the CEV framework?
- How does the CEV framework help organizations?

A FIRM'S APPROACH TO CUSTOMER ENGAGEMENT

In the previous chapter, we discussed the need for firms to quantify the value derived from the customer engagement process. From a firm's standpoint, engaging with customers to derive tangible value out of the interaction is a tough task. However, many firms are successfully doing this today. How do firms actually engage their customers in today's competitive business world? The following paragraphs will discuss how firms engage with their customers through various examples from different firms.

Microsoft, in an independent study of nearly 1,000 Internet users, found that people prefer Bing's search results to Google's, two-to-one in blind comparison tests.[1] Capitalizing on this result, thereby spreading the news in the market, Microsoft launched the "Bing It On" challenge in October 2012. The "Bing It On" challenge was essentially an online and in-store promotion that involved customers comparing any five search results for Bing and Google side by side without knowing which is which, and picked the results that were the most relevant. Consumers who took the challenge in-store received a $25 gift voucher, which they could redeem for any product in the Microsoft store. As a follow-up to the promotion, Microsoft fielded a survey with approximately 4,700 consumers asking for their impressions of Bing before and after taking the challenge. The results showed that around 64 percent of people were surprised by the quality of Bing's Web search results. Over half of the people surveyed indicated that their impression of Bing improved after seeing Bing's Web search results next to Google's. Additionally, of people who identified Google as their primary search engine, 33 percent said they would use Bing more often after taking the Challenge.[2] Google undoubtedly still dominates the search engine market; however, with the "Bing It On" challenge, Microsoft is trying to engage customers and derive value out of this engagement.

Apple Inc. is engaging children through their education-related product offerings. The iPad's popularity among the younger age groups forced the acceptance of iPads as an effective learning tool for schools and colleges. As a step forward, Apple launched its interactive iBooks textbooks for iPad in January 2012.[3] With the world becoming increasingly digitized, children are the quickest to adapt to these technological changes. iBooks textbooks on the iPad offer an engaging solution for experiencing diagrams, photos, and videos for students. Students can dive into an image with interactive captions, rotate a 3D object, or have the answer spring to life in a chapter review. They can flip through a book by simply sliding a finger along the bottom of the screen; highlight text, take notes, search for content, and find definitions in the glossary. Also, carrying all their books on a single iPad is a convenient option for students. Phillip Schiller, senior vice president of worldwide marketing at Apple, said the iBooks provide a "more dynamic, engaging, and interactive" way for students to learn.[4] In addition to this, Apple's iBooks Author app enables anyone with a Mac to create and self-publish a range of books, including textbooks, cookbooks, history books, and picture books, and add engaging features to them. Apple engages their customers in a manner that creates a unique experience for its customers, which in return provides value to Apple with an increased appeal and user-base of the iPad and other Apple products.

While companies are increasingly participating in customer engagement activities to derive value for themselves, these activities provide a clear benefit to the customer as well. One of the leading consumer packaged goods (CPG) companies, Procter & Gamble (P&G) has been successfully running the "Have You Tried This Yet?" campaign for two years. This campaign is designed to highlight innovative products for self, family, and home.[5] In 2012, under the same campaign, P&G launched another leg—"The Great Try

Out," where 15 upcoming tastemakers in the categories of beauty, family, and home competed for a spot. They were called the "Trend Trio," earning the opportunity to be one of three program experts. This competition provided customers with a chance to be a part of selecting the Trend Trio. The Trend Trio acted like a brand ambassador for the various P&G brands, blogging and sharing tips to make customers' everyday life a little easier. The campaign enabled P&G to engage with its customers at a deeper level by providing the story behind their brand innovations. Customer interaction with the Trend Trio, selected by the popular votes of the customers themselves, built up trust and laid the foundation for a long-term engagement with the brand. P&G's attempt to bring their brands closer to their customers, through these third-party experts, is an excellent example of customer engagement with mutual benefits to the firm and the customer.

As seen in the above examples, firms spend a lot of time and resources in customer engagement activities, with an aim to convert a buyer's propensity to buy a product/service into an actual purchase. Customers' future purchases are dependent on their previous experience with the brand in question. As a result of a customer experience (good or bad), a customer is likely to form a perception about the brand (good or bad), talk about the brand to others (in positive or negative context), refer or not refer the brand to their close circle of people, and create a positive or negative influence on potential buyers to convert them into actual customers. All of these activities, in addition to the actual purchase, are of great importance to marketers. Hence, in addition to tracking purchase behavior of customers, marketers need to pay close attention to indirect forms of customer interactions like the ones mentioned above. Also, it is important for marketers to know that not all customers are equal. For instance, a customer may like a product and could make a purchase. However, does such a purchase obligate him/her to talk about the brand, in a sense, spread the word? Many customers may not engage in detailed conversations about the brands they buy or the services they use. So for a marketer, the real questions are (*a*) will customers refer the product to their close friends, (*b*) will they write about the product on their blog/social network, and (*c*) will they actively participate in product improvement initiatives offered by the firm? Even if the answer to all the above questions is yes, not all customers will end up contributing equally to the profits of the firm. Every customer is different and firms require a technique to identify and differentiate customers based on their differences. So, how does one maximize profits and identify this group of customers who not only directly contribute to the firm profits by their purchase but also make an indirect contribution to the firm profits by acting as brand ambassadors for the brand? Customer engagement principles have been studied for a long time but haven't been quantified yet and hence objective measurement and evaluation of customer engagement metrics is challenging. This chapter discusses a comprehensive, quantifiable, and forward-looking framework that will enable such measurement and evaluation of the value of a customer based on all aspects of customer behavior, i.e., purchase- and non-purchase–related contributions to the profit of the firm.

CONCEPTUALIZING CEV: AN INTEGRATED FRAMEWORK

Customer contribution to firm profitability occurs in two ways: (*a*) directly—through their purchases, and (*b*) indirectly—through their non-purchase reactions, i.e., by making referrals to potential customers, by influencing current and potential customers in their network, or by using their own experiences to provide review/feedback for improvements. Identifying the right set of customers who create value for the firm can be useful in trying to maximize profits. The CEV framework can be used to identify and evaluate the right customer, who is successfully engaged with the firm, and who generates value and positively contributes to the profits of the firm.

As discussed in Chapter 1, CEV is managed as a set of four dollar metrics, i.e., CLV, CRV or BRV, CIV and CKV, and one attitudinal metric—CBV. The conceptual approach for measuring customer engagement is comprised of five core dimensions and is shown in Figure 2.1. The framework incorporates recent trends in social media and the influence it has on marketing strategies, thus providing an effective and comprehensive tool to understand the value of a customer and his or her impact on the firm's future profitability. As seen in Figure 2.2, each component in the CEV framework can be applied to business-to-consumer (B2C) as well as business-to-business (B2B) settings. The following paragraphs will explain the CEV framework. For ease in understanding, the framework is discussed from bottom up.

In the business world, customers and businesses are interdependent. Customer actions, in terms of behavior, attitude, and network metrics, have an

Figure 2.1 The CEV Framework

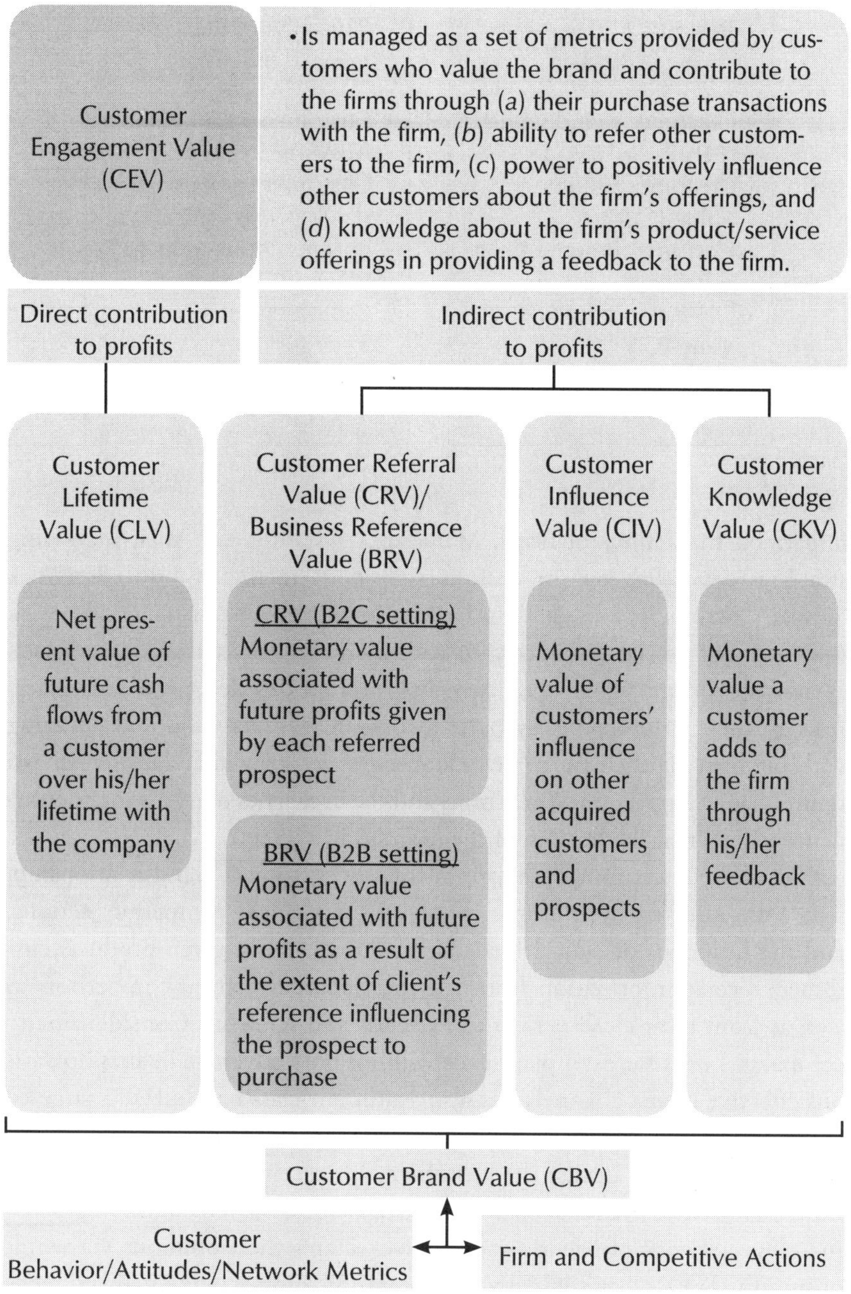

| Customer Engagement Value (CEV) | • Is managed as a set of metrics provided by customers who value the brand and contribute to the firms through (a) their purchase transactions with the firm, (b) ability to refer other customers to the firm, (c) power to positively influence other customers about the firm's offerings, and (d) knowledge about the firm's product/service offerings in providing a feedback to the firm. |

| Direct contribution to profits | Indirect contribution to profits |

Customer Lifetime Value (CLV)	Customer Referral Value (CRV)/ Business Reference Value (BRV)	Customer Influence Value (CIV)	Customer Knowledge Value (CKV)
Net present value of future cash flows from a customer over his/her lifetime with the company	**CRV (B2C setting)** Monetary value associated with future profits given by each referred prospect **BRV (B2B setting)** Monetary value associated with future profits as a result of the extent of client's reference influencing the prospect to purchase	Monetary value of customers' influence on other acquired customers and prospects	Monetary value a customer adds to the firm through his/her feedback

Customer Brand Value (CBV)

Customer Behavior/Attitudes/Network Metrics ↔ Firm and Competitive Actions

Figure 2.2 Five Core Dimensions of CEV Framework

Business to Consumer (B2C)	Business to Business (B2B)
• Customer Brand Value (CBV) • Customer Lifetime Value (CLV) • Customer Referral Value (CRV) • Customer Influence Vaue (CIV) • Customer Knowledge Value (CKV)	• Customer Brand Value (CBV) • Customer Lifetime Value (CLV) • Business Reference Value (BRV) • Customer Influence Vaue (CIV) • Customer Knowledge Value (CKV)

impact on the actions of firms. Managers constantly alter their marketing strategies depending on the customer reactions to their products/services. Similarly, firm or business actions have an impact on customers, i.e., (*a*) with the quality of products/services, (*b*) with the firm's marketing activities such as awareness campaigns, advertisements, promotions/deals, etc. Customers react to these firm actions by participating in firm activities and engaging with the firm via their purchase or non-purchase–related actions, which, in return, has an impact on firm actions and the cycle goes on. This interdependence is shown at the bottom of the diagram in Figure 2.1.

Customer perception is important for any customer–brand relationship. These are affected by multiple forces—firm actions, competitor actions, and the influence of close friends and relatives. For a given product, customers receive information from the focal company, from competitors as well as from their close network of friends and relatives. Consider luxury car maker Lexus for example; Lexus will not only advertise its cars on various effective media channels but also send high-class brochures to targeted customers to build on that perception of the brand. In addition to information received from Lexus, the customer also receives marketing messages from competitive brands such as Mercedes-Benz, BMW, or Audi. Moreover, the close network of friends and relatives shares their opinions via word-of-mouth (WOM) or social media communication channels to influence these customer perceptions. All these different forces act on the customer perception together. Customer brand value (CBV) captured under the CEV framework measures the value that the customer attaches to the brand as a result of all the marketing and communication messages delivered via different media. CBV is a multi-dimensional composite metric that measures the customer's brand knowledge, brand attitude, brand behavior intention, and brand behavior. It enables companies to devise appropriate strategies depending on where the problem exists—awareness, trust, or loyalty?

Based on the perceptions formed, a customer can engage with a firm in a myriad of ways. All these are captured under the CEV framework. The most important way a customer can engage with a firm is via his or her own purchase of a product/service. Customer engagement through their own transactions with the firm is captured under CLV. As seen in Figure 2.1, CLV is the metric that directly contributes to the profitability of the firm. The companies can use CLV to get the net present value of a customer based on his or her future transactions with the firm. The concept of CLV aids in understanding the quality of the length of stay of a customer with the firm during his or her lifetime.

A firm can encourage customers to buy more and more, which will increase the customer's CLV and thereby increase his or her contribution to profits. However, there are other levels of engagement that can indirectly contribute to the profits of a firm. The other three metrics—customer referral value (CRV) or business reference value (BRV), customer influence value (CIV), and customer knowledge value (CKV)—measure the indirect contribution of a customer to the firm profitability.

The customers can engage with a firm via firm-generated referrals programs. Referrals are a form of engaging customers with the firm in a B2C setup. Referral programs enable current customers to influence prospects via these firm-generated, incentivized referral programs. CRV within the CEV framework assists in quantitatively understanding the value generated through referrals and its impact on a firm's profitability. CRV measures the net present value a customer creates for a firm via his or her referrals, i.e., the value a customer generates by referring the firm's products to its potential customers. While referrals work in a B2C setting, B2B companies follow a different reference mechanism. In a B2B setting, client firms provide references to the seller firm, which influence the prospective client firms to purchase the product/service from the seller firm. BRV is the ability of the client firm to influence prospects to purchase. Since B2B reference functions differently from B2C referrals, the CEV framework captures them separately as BRV.

Are referrals the only way current customers can engage and influence potential customers? What about situations when there are no company-sponsored referral programs? Do customers stop talking about the brand within their close network of people? Obviously, customers talk about the good and the bad aspects of their experience with the brand, even if there are no incentivized referral programs. Today, customers influence each other via various social media platforms. A customer's interaction and influence on each other via social media channels such as Facebook, Twitter, MySpace, Foursquare, etc., have increased dramatically in recent years. The CEV framework captures this engagement—the influence of current customers on current customers as well as prospects via social media channels under CIV.

Another level of customer engagement is achieved when a current customer actively involves himself or herself in improving a company's product/service by providing feedback or suggestions. Customer review and feedback add great value to a firm. Moreover, from a firm's standpoint, knowledge and understanding of customer preferences is highly beneficial. It enables them to customize their product offering in line with the customer expectations. When a company implements the feedback or suggestion provided by a customer, that customer indirectly contributes to the profits of the firm as the improved product/service is expected to appeal to a lot more customers than before, thereby bringing more profits to the firm. The CEV framework captures this customer engagement under CKV. CKV is a metric that measures the value of this communication between customers and firms to improve their existing or potential products or services.

CBV is the attitudinal metric under the CEV framework that has an impact on the other four dollar metrics, i.e., CLV, CRV or BRV, CIV, and CKV, as illustrated in Figure 2.1. Customer perceptions of the brand (i.e., CBV) have an impact on the way customers purchase the product/service in the future, refer the brand to their close network of people, engage in social media channels to influence other customers, and get involved in providing feedback. These interactions between CBV and the other four metrics (CLV, CRV/BRV, CIV, and CKV) can be seen in Figure 2.1. These interrelationships will be explored in greater detail in subsequent chapters.

While there are methods and/or conceptual models for measuring the five metrics discussed in the previous paragraphs, an integrated approach to measure the CEV is still in its evolutionary stage. This is because CEV is not merely an aggregate of the four components (CLV, CRV, CIV, and CKV), but a metric that is correlated and constantly interacting within the four metrics. For instance, though CLV and CRV are separate metrics, they cannot be added up across all customers. An understanding of these five components of the framework and the interaction among these components will help senior level leaders in any business to understand and value customers for their contribution in the customer engagement process. The following sections of this chapter will explain the significance of each component of the CEV framework.

CUSTOMER BRAND VALUE (CBV)

In a firm, managers are often faced with a situation where they have to decide if they want to go down the path of selling their brand with the highest margin or treat customers as a valuable asset and focus on building and maintaining this asset. The actual question concerning managers is: which of these routes will result in maximum profitability for the firm? Building a strong brand would develop loyalty amongst customers, while a weak brand would drive customers to the competition.[6] Also, it may be difficult to evaluate the effect of brand building efforts on the customer base. In an ideal world, managers would work on brand building and customer building simultaneously. This balance can be made possible by establishing a link between brand and customer value. One way of looking at this would be "customer-based brand equity." Customer-based brand equity is defined as "the differential effect of brand knowledge on consumer response to the marketing of the brand."[7] In other words, customer-based brand equity is the summation of the customer's individual brand value (CBV). Conceptually, CBV refers to the total value a customer attaches to a brand through his or her experiences with the brand over time.[8]

Brand perceptions are built over a period of time, through various marketing activities that firms carry out to engage customers. From a company's standpoint, brand building activities are often used to increase brand presence in the minds of current and potential customers and thereby enter their consideration set for future purchases. CBV recognizes the attitudinal value of a customer based on his or her perception of the brand. It is a dynamic, multi-dimensional construct, which measures the contribution of each aspect of brand value, i.e., brand knowledge, brand attitude, brand behavior intention, and brand behavior to the lifetime value of that customer. According to this view, brand knowledge is not just the facts about the brand—it includes all the thoughts, feelings, perceptions, images, experiences, etc., that get linked to the brand in the minds of the customers (actual or potential, individuals or organizations).[9] CBV can thus be understood as a set of associations that customers make with the brand.

The starting point for any customer association with a brand can be attributed to brand awareness and brand image. These two metrics form the basic "Brand Knowledge" that creates a sense of trust and impacts the brand attitude of a customer. By influencing customer attitudes, firms can influence the brand behavior intentions and as a result, influence the brand behavior of that customer. A key aspect of brand behavior is "Brand Loyalty," which thereby impacts the brand advocacy and premium price behavior from a customer. In a day and age where customization is the buzzword around marketing of any kind of product, CBV provides managers with a tool to gain an in-depth understanding of the customer level metrics of brand awareness, brand image, brand trust, brand affect, purchase intention, and brand loyalty.

Sustained brand image and strong brand loyalty are key factors to the success of any brand in the long run. A brand like Harley Davidson is an excellent

Brand Perception

Source: Printed with permission from http://tomfishburne.com/ (retrieved on January 03, 2013).

example of the creation of a strong image. The brand enjoys a strong cult status in society. Its motto "Live to Ride, Ride to Live" echoes in the minds of its customers who are seeking to experience the adrenaline rush while riding their machines. Harley Davidson enjoys a strong image owing to the strong brand loyalty and brand advocacy by its loyal customers. With a clear vision to target the customer base seeking adventure and individuality, Harley Davidson does a good job of satisfying the needs of its customer base.

Companies like Samsung have walked the path of building brand value for their customers. Samsung's recent success in the United States has been a result of building brand awareness and positive brand image in the minds of current and potential customers. Having achieved initial success, Samsung's future profitability depends on (*a*) maintaining the current positive buzz around the brand, and (*b*) successfully influencing customers in the next two phases, i.e., brand attitude and brand behavior.

The concept of CBV can be applied to B2B and B2C companies. In B2C companies, the concept is more dynamic and companies are constantly tracking changes happening in the customer portfolio to effectively take appropriate measures. CBV, i.e., the customer's perceived value of the brand is what drives companies such as Apple, Google, Microsoft, and many others. The buzz around every new launch by Apple in recent times can be attributed to the high awareness and positive brand image of the brand. Thus, non-buyers of the brand also have a great amount of information about upcoming Apple products, which only amplifies the buzz around this brand. Oldsmobile, the General Motors (GM) brand, can shed some more light on this concept. Allen Adamson, a managing director at the corporate identity firm Landor Associates mentioned once that "what Oldsmobile ran into was an advertising problem. It failed to clearly define what is different about the brand." In the GM hierarchy of brands, Oldsmobile was supposed to be a sporty, upper-middle-priced division, a touch less expensive and less conservative than Buick and a bit pricier, more sophisticated than Pontiac brand. Such marketing gradations were more effective decades ago, when the US car market was less competitive. GM embarked on a campaign to shrink its cars to match what the company's leaders envisioned would be an era of $3-a-gallon gas and diminished expectations. The Oldsmobile division's reputation for innovative engineering took several hits ranging from quality problems with diesel engines to ineptly handled product decisions, such as putting Chevrolet engines in certain Oldsmobile models. It was a negative brand image that caused GM to park its Oldsmobile vehicle for good in 2000.[10] In spite of expenditures on promotions and advertising, a successful brand image could not be built, which forced GM to eventually stop production.

CBV in B2B companies will have to be looked at a little differently. In a B2B setting, brand value creates an image of the seller in the minds of the client. Hence, a lot of B2B companies use online websites as a tool to build an image which can aid in converting prospects into actual customers. Also, B2B companies have long-standing relationships with their customers and this relationship is built over time based on the perceived brand value. Many firms in a B2B setting say that they are not influenced by advertisements but data and client spending suggest otherwise. In the early to mid-1980s, IBM did not have a leading position in computer systems or pricing. In time, IBM built a strong brand image of quality, assurance, and sustainability. Once the image was formed, IBM could reap the benefits of this strong brand image in terms of stronger business in the future. "Big Blue" soon became the enterprise systems market leader because *you never got fired for buying IBM* (same with Cisco today).[11] IT Directors "bought" a relationship, company, reputation, service, people, and assurance. In other words, they bought the goodwill of the brand. The client firm most often weighs the benefits of doing business with the seller firm based on its reputation in the market, quality of its products and services, etc. This is the precise reason why big consulting firms have long-term client relationships, which last for over a decade. Once a brand value is established in the minds of the client firm, the relationship is expected to last longer when compared to a B2C firm.

Within the CEV framework, CBV offers a quantitative view of the customer perceptions of the brand. CBV interacts with the other components of the CEV framework to develop a good customer–firm relationship with high engagement value. This interaction effect of CBV with all the other four metrics is explored in the respective chapters of the book in greater detail.

CUSTOMER LIFETIME VALUE (CLV)

CLV is the fundamental metric under the CEV framework which directly contributes to firm profitability. CLV is a forward-looking metric that not only accounts for the contribution to profit, based on past purchase behavior of a customer, but also predicts the future value of the current customer as well as profits from prospective customers. In its simplest terms, CLV is a formula that helps marketing managers arrive at a dollar value associated with the long-term relationship with any given customer, revealing just how much a customer relationship is worth over a period of time. CLV helps marketers adopt the right marketing activities today to increase profitability tomorrow. It rewards not those who have been the best customers, but those who will be the best customers in the foreseeable future. Conceptually, CLV refers to the net present value of the monetary contribution of the profits associated with a customer's future purchases.[12]

Essentially, CLV enables a firm to treat individual customers differently and exclusively from each other, based on his or her contribution to the firm. By being able to quantify this value, firms are able to discern how much they can and should invest in a customer in order to achieve a positive return on investment (ROI) or maximized profitability. In addition to calculating CLV for a customer, firms can optimally allocate their resources to gain maximum returns using strategies that can help them maximize the CLV of a customer and ensure long-term profitable customer engagement. These strategies called "Wheel of Fortune" strategies will be discussed in greater detail in Chapter 4. CLV creates value not only for firms but also for customers. Customers get better products and services that are tailor-made to their needs as firms comprehend their needs better than ever before. In other words, customers have an incentive to remain loyal because their relationship with the firm is mutually beneficial.

The concept of CLV can be applied to both B2B and B2C companies. IBM, a leading multinational high-technology firm providing hardware, software, and services to B2B customers, implemented the CLV-based framework with an aim to maximize their profits. IBM used to measure customer profitability using a metric called Customer Spending Score (CSS), which was defined as the total revenue that can be expected from a customer in the next year.[13] Since CSS focused primarily on customer revenues and ignored the variable cost of servicing customers; in 2004, IBM felt the need to move to a better indicator for customer value measurement than CSS. IBM especially wanted to test the following belief, "when all the other drivers remain unchanged, can an increase in the level of contact with the right customers create higher value from the low-value customers?" A CLV-based framework allowed IBM to refine and improve their customer contact strategy. Using the CLV-based approach, IBM could (*a*) increase the return on their marketing investment by allocating resources toward customers who were most likely to provide value in the next year, (*b*) identify products to sell as bundles, and (*c*) reallocate the excess resources (after targeting the most likely customers who would buy in a given time period) to other prospects (acquiring new customers or reactivating dormant customers). Two major initiatives that were being considered based on the CLV management framework included (*a*) segmentation and profiling and (*b*) understanding customer migration.[14] They identified the right customers to target and optimally reallocated resources to profitable customers and saw a tenfold increase in their revenues in the following year.

Consider a B2C example of a fashion retailer wanting to maximize profitability not only at the store level but also at a customer level.[15] The retailer was seeking answers to the following questions: (*a*) What is the right metric to manage customer programs, for example customer loyalty programs? Can CLV outperform traditional metrics? (*b*) How can the CLV concept be applied to measure and manage customer value? (*c*) How can the CLV concept be applied to manage store performance? The CLV framework was implemented with an objective to maximize a customer's lifetime value, thus profits at the store level. After taking a step-by-step approach of the framework, it was observed that (*a*) at a customer level, the top 20 percent of their customers accounted for 95 percent of their profits. Careful analyses of results had indicated that the retailer was losing money with the bottom 30 percent of the customers. (*b*) At a store level, by implementing CLV-based strategies, this B2C firm realized a 42 percent increase in store revenue for the bottom 10 stores in one year and a 30 percent increase in the stock price or shareholder value compared to other B2C firms in this industry. This framework also recommended the firm to shift their management focus from managing customer relationship to managing customer value.

A firm can have customers with positive or negative CLV scores. After having realized their contribution to profit, firms might have the urge to fire customers with a negative CLV. Chapter 1 mentioned Sprint firing 1,000 customers from its pool of 53 million customers for calling the call center too often. AT&T also cancelled service to customers who made most of their calls while in roaming. Given the fact that the cost of acquiring a customer is significantly higher than retaining him or her; is firing a customer a good strategy for any firm aiming to maximize profits? Does one have the information regarding the future value of the present customer to effectively take such a decision? CLV allows firms to predict customer churn/attrition effectively by evaluating the two approaches, i.e., the "always a share" approach and the "lost for good" approach. Chapter 4 will discuss the CLV metric that can be used to optimally allocate resources, predict future purchases of customers, and reach the right customers with the right message through the most apt channels in detail.

CLV provides an excellent framework for managers who aim to maximize profits using a customer-centric approach to marketing. While CLV can measure direct and indirect components and can include all aspects of value creation by a customer; in practice and in academic literature, it is often identified only with the actual purchase behavior. A limitation of the CLV metric is that it fails to measure data on customer attitudes. The CEV framework provides a more robust understanding of customer value for firms to effectively manage customers, build loyalty among the core customer base and maximize profits for the firm. For a firm aiming to maximize profits, it is imperative to consider all levels of customer engagement. By calculating the CLV for all customers, firms can rank the customers on the basis of their contribution to the firm's profit.[16] This forms an important step under the CEV framework to evaluate the value of a customer and the direct contribution made by the customer to the firm profitability. By linking CLV to CBV, managers can (*a*) monitor the overall performance of the brand, (*b*) manage the brand at the segment level, and (*c*) manage the brand at the individual level.

CUSTOMER REFERRAL VALUE (CRV)

Do customers engage with the firm and impact profitability only with their own purchase? The answer is "no." As discussed in the earlier paragraphs, customers not only contribute directly through their purchase, but also contribute through indirect actions; one such action is referrals. The next step in the CEV framework is to look at a metric that deals with the indirect contributions made by a customer through their referrals. The concepts of WOM communication and customer referrals have been around for a while now. Researchers have conducted extensive studies to understand the implications of referrals on customer behavior. Depending on the level of engagement, customers are seen to be at different stages of contact with the firm. Companies spend a lot of resources in devising incentive-generated referral programs to increase penetration of their brand/product. Customer referral, especially WOM communication has been a widely accepted concept and is known to have an impact on the purchase of a product or service by potential customers. For a company spending a part of its marketing budget in referral programs, it is extremely important to know customers who have a high impact amongst prospects. Not all customers are willing to engage with a firm at a level where they not only contribute to profits of the firm by their purchase, but also communicate and refer potential customers to turn prospects into customers for the firm. An effective metric to measure this aspect of consumer behavior and its impact on profitability of the firm did not exist for practical use by companies. CRV was conceptualized with an aim to provide just that. CRV is the quantifiable measure of the type, quantity, and effectiveness of referrals or recommendations that an individual customer provides to others with regard to a particular product. Conceptually, CRV of a customer is the monetary value associated with the future profits given by each referred prospect, discounted to the present value.[17]

CRV enables managers to measure and manage each customer based on his ability to generate indirect profits to the firm.[18] CRV focuses on current customers turning potential customers in their social network into actual customers for the firm via firm-initiated incentivized referral programs. Customers are rewarded for the conversion of potential customers to actual customers as they indirectly contribute to the profit of the firm. The referrals are extrinsically motivated and hence customers can be looked at as nonemployee sales

The Power of "Word of Mouth"

Source: Printed with permission from http://tomfishburne.com/ (retrieved on January 03, 2013).

people who are compensated for contributing to the profit of the firm. CRV enables managers to value customers based on their indirect impact on the firm's profits from both the savings in acquisition costs and the growth of new customers who were referred to by a current customer.

Referrals can be successful or unsuccessful. Therefore, depending on the impact of referrals, CRV can be negative, positive, or zero, i.e., no impact on profits of the firm. A customer with a high CRV contributes to the profits in multiple ways (*a*) by his or her own transaction with the firm, (*b*) by converting prospects into actual customers and thereby the contribution to profit through that transaction, and (*c*) by savings in the customer acquisition cost of the prospect. Every action taken by the firm has an impact on the customer behavior toward the brand as well as the brand perception that the customers have. Negative actions by the firm promote bad referrals and can deter prospects from entering into any transaction with the firm in the future. It is important for firms to ensure that their brand equity is not diluted in the process of achieving maximized profits.

Over the years, many startups have been using referrals as their mode to create awareness and build the user base. Dropbox is one such startup that relied on referrals as their initial strategy. Drew Houston, cofounder and CEO of Dropbox, initiated a two-sided incentive program wherein the referrer and the referee both gain additional space in their account. Bank of America too had a similar referral program where they rewarded the referee and the referrer with $25.[19] Bank of America provided $25 for customer referral, $10 for a student referral and $50 for a business referral. After the referral program has been implemented, it is the key to identifying high impact customers who are influential or who have medium to high CRV, to be able to maximize their indirect contributions to the profits of the firm.

Customers who refer new customers to earn rewards on successful referrals are extrinsically motivated. That aids them to not only talk about their experience with the firm within their social network but also try and convert this WOM communication into an actual transaction. This generates value for the firms as well as customers. Hence, it is important to include the probability of conversion of prospects into actual customers and the cost savings due to each successful referral in the CRV framework. Also, it is important to factor in the possibility of the prospect having turned into an actual customer regardless of the referral and the partial impact of multiple referrals to the same potential customer.

In a B2C context, referrals are often a go-to strategy for marketing managers to increase the reach of their brand. Referrals are a great way to spread awareness for a brand in case of budget constraints in marketing and promotional activities. We see small brands using referrals increasingly to raise their user base and gain potential customers. For example, a small firm called Keku, headquartered in New York, provides cheap international calling services to its users. This company uses referrals to increase its user base. The referee and the referrer are awarded with additional talk time on their international calling plan as an incentive. Customers are happy to be rewarded and the company rejoices with every increase in penetration for the brand. Referrals are not only used by small companies but are successfully implemented by the big players in every industry depending on their marketing strategy.

CRV is definitely an important metric under consideration for any profit-maximizing firm. By linking CRV to CLV, companies can launch successful referral programs that also ensure customer profitability. It is critical for managers to understand the limitations of CRV to be able to effectively use the metric in their business. We will discuss a few important factors managers should keep in mind while incorporating CRV in the CEV framework[20]:

- Measuring CRV is only one method of finding out whether a customer can impact profitability by bringing in new customers to the firm and might not be applicable to all firms or industries.
- It is difficult for every business to have the ability to track referral behavior. If they do, managers should ensure that the systems in place have a reasonably long history of tracking customer referral behavior to estimate the customer value accurately.
- The method suggested under the CEV framework for measuring CRV only takes into account the extrinsic motivation of a customer to make referrals (i.e., through incentives) and does not try to determine which customers generate referrals through an intrinsic motivation.

Chapter 6 discusses the details of measurement, application and future of CRV in greater detail. For a company aiming to understand the value of a customer, measuring CRV and linking this to CLV of that customer is the next step. CRV captures the indirect aspect of the customer behavior through referrals under the CEV framework.

BUSINESS REFERENCE VALUE (BRV)

The purchase decision in a B2B setting is far more complex when compared to a B2C setting. Similarly, the reference in a B2B setting works differently from referrals in a B2C setting. For B2B businesses, in most cases, the use of client references is often the only tool seller firms have to build their business.[21] In a B2B client's words, "[the] list of references provided by the seller helps us to shortlist the seller firms. However, to decide on whom to buy from, we check at least a couple of references provided by the seller." Many companies have a database of customer reference cases on their website for potential customers. Some encourage customers to create "video success stories," which they use as references for potential customers. We often see most B2B companies incorporating testimonials on their website to provide confidence to potential customers. For instance, McKinsey mentions testimonials and video references on their website to encourage potential customers to use their consulting services. Although companies have adopted these measures for a long time now, they have not been able to measure the impact of such referrals to the profits of the firm. With this in mind, the concept of Brand Reference Value, i.e., BRV was conceptualized to be able to appropriately capture the value created by such references for the seller firm. Conceptually, BRV for a client is the monetary value associated with future profits as a result of the extent of a client's reference influencing the prospects to purchase, discounted to present value.[22]

BRV is guided by the following three components: (*a*) How much influence, in general, do references have on the prospect's adoption? (*b*) How much influence does a particular client firm's reference have on the prospect's adoption? (*c*) How profitable is the prospective client post adoption? BRV is an effective tool for managers to select the right references that can indirectly contribute to the profits of the firm. The drivers of BRV are discussed in greater detail in Chapter 6.

CUSTOMER INFLUENCE VALUE (CIV)

Referrals are not the only way current customers influence prospect behavior. By now we know that customers can have an impact on firm's revenue and profits based on what they feel and what they are prepared to communicate to others about the brand. This impact is, at times, more valuable for the company than just the purchase, as this influence brings in prospects for the firm. Researchers in the past have established the influence an individual can have on prospects and the significant role of WOM communication in a firm's marketing efforts.[23] However, firms do not have a metric to evaluate the impact of WOM in social media platforms pertaining to the return on marketing investments. Conceptually, CIV refers to the monetary value of the profits associated with the purchases generated by a customer's social media influence on other acquired customers and prospects, discounted to present value.[24]

The customer influences are usually intrinsically motivated by WOM activities that persuade and convert prospects to customers, minimize buyer remorse (to reduce defections), and encourage an increased share of wallet (SOW) of the existing customers. With an ever increasing social media network, customers are provided with a platform to openly communicate about customer experiences and thereby exchange views and reviews about a product or service. Companies need to value customers with high CIV who can bring in additional revenue to the firm by influencing current as well as potential customers. The CIV under the CEV framework provides a platform to measure this behavioral aspect of customer behavior.

The existing customer base is as important to a firm as acquiring new customers. Customer retention has been a key focus for many companies as the value created by existing customers over a period can have a huge impact on the profits of a firm. Rennlist, an international online community for Porsche, Audi, and BMW enthusiasts founded in 1998, is an example of customers engaging in an online world to share their views with other customers having similar interests.[25] Members of this group actively engage in discussions and share opinions on very specific aspects of the brand. These customers consider themselves a part of the company and evaluate the products offered by the company in great detail. There is an increase in the number of such forums in the online world today. Brand enthusiasts break the space barriers and openly discuss and influence other potential customers in an online community. Traditionally, customers consulted their close circle of family and friends for advice; today the social media and the Internet have drastically widened the consumer's network. Consumers are increasingly seeking reviews of products and services online before making that purchase decision. A firm needs to identify influential customers and evaluate the degree to which these customers are able to influence potential customers to enter into a transaction with the firm.

Social media marketing has taken center stage for most marketers today. With innumerable options and the abundance of information, it is tough for managers to optimally use social media marketing platforms to influence potential customers. CIV provides a straightforward step-by-step model to evaluate and measure the effectiveness of the influence a current customer has on customers in the social media setting. Chapter 7 discusses the quantifiable aspect of the CIV, its implications, and the linkage of CIV with other related metrics in greater detail.

Like CRV, CIV too involves WOM communication to influence prospects. Then, how different is CIV from CRV? The concepts of CRV and CIV are distinct. Hence, it is critical to understand the differences between them clearly, to be able to evaluate each metric individually.[26] These are illustrated in Table 2.1.

Table 2.1 Comparison between CRV and CKV

CRV	CIV
CRV measures the value a current customer brings to a firm by referring prospects and converting them into actual customers using traceable official communication channels like email or text message with individually identified codes.	CIV measures the value a current customer brings to a firm by influencing current and prospective customers in a social media setting.
Customers are extrinsically motivated through firm-generated incentive programs.	Customers are intrinsically motivated. Customers are engaged with a brand to the extent where they feel motivated enough to talk about the brand and thereby influence people in their social network who may or may not be current customers of the firm.
Customers are monetarily compensated. These are tangible compensations provided for the referrals.	Customers are not monetarily compensated but are given prizes (intangible or experiential).

(Table 2.1 Continued)

(Table 2.1 Continued)

CRV	CIV
The value can be positive, negative or zero. The marketing and servicing costs can be higher for the referred prospect than the revenue from the referred prospect, resulting in a negative CRV.	The value can be negative but these occurrences are less. CIV assumes negative values when a firm is dealing with deal-prone customers who buy only when offered a deal/promotion, which impacts firm profitability negatively.
A customer can be referred only once in his or her lifetime with the firm.	A customer can be influenced multiple times during his/her lifetime.
Generally, the total number of referrals made by a customer is fewer.	Total number of influences, on the other hand is much more.

Source: Printed with permission from V. Kumar, L. Aksoy, B. Donkers, R. Venkatesan, T. Wiesel, and S. Tillmanns, "Undervalued or Overvalued Customers: Capturing Total Customer Engagement Value," *Journal of Service Research*, *13*(3), (2010): 297–310.

CUSTOMER KNOWLEDGE VALUE (CKV)

"Customization" is a key term in marketing today. Customers value a brand that can customize a product to their needs. Given that the failure rate of new products is between 40 percent and 75 percent,[27] firms should be particularly concerned about what their customers say they want and need. Highly engaged customers are more than willing to provide feedback to the firm for improvements or changes in their product offering. Similarly, from a company's standpoint, customer feedback provides great value to a company as firms gather knowledge about what their customers understand about their product and/or service offerings. This feedback can play a vital role in a company's new product development processes. If the companies listen to their customers, they can reduce the failure rate of products and also improve the service quality.[28] Delivering value to customers by understanding and incorporating their feedback gives companies an edge over their competitors.

Let us consider the example of Atlanta-based Delta Air Lines.[29] In 2011, they created an online forum called "Ideas in Flight" on a social media site (Facebook) to gain feedback from customers on how the airlines could improve the travel experience for its customers. According to the airlines, about one-fourth of the suggestions were small ideas that could be examined immediately, although the actual execution of the suggestions would still depend on many aspects. However, the fact that customers provided directions to the company for improvement increases the value of such customers for the firm. Several companies are now coming up with similar initiatives. However, companies are not able to assign a value for this feedback from customers and correlate it to the company's goal of profit maximization. CKV under the CEV framework provides a model to measure this customer knowledge and feedback and link it to the profits of a firm. Conceptually, CKV is the monetary value associated with the profits generated by a customer's feedback, suggestion or an idea to the firm over a period of time.[30]

In both physical and viral communities, customers leave traces of behavior and opinions (intentionally and unintentionally), which can be analyzed to improve a product and service as well as the various processes and methods that go into bringing it to the customer. Customers with a strong interest in the brand usually have extensive product knowledge and are actively engaging in discussions and forums to share their opinions.

An important component of obtaining customer feedback is to be able to utilize customer knowledge efficiently. In order to achieve this, firms need to establish a quick and easy medium of communication. Providing feedback should be natural, interactive, and effortless. For these reasons, social media is a particularly useful tool to maximize CKV.[31] We notice the increasing use of social media and such forums in business-to-customer companies involving customers in the new product development process across product categories; although, CKV extends its merit to not only new product development ideas but also to service creation and innovation. With customers spending 10 percent of their time online on social networking sites, engaging customers in a conversation through various platforms (such as the Facebook fan pages) is a great option for companies to explore.[32]

There are recent examples in companies who have failed to capitalize on the knowledge provided by customers. Two of the most innovative companies in the world today, Google and Apple, have failed in one of their attempts to be innovative and ignore the customer taste and preference and feedback. Let us explore Google first. "Google Buzz," a social network pitched against Facebook, focused on making the sharing experience very rich by integrating photos, videos, and links was launched in February 2010. It offered an easy solution to flip through photos and experience them the way they were meant to be seen: big and full resolution. And videos play online so you can watch them without opening a new window.[33] However, soon after its launch

Google buzz faced privacy nightmares.[34] Customers clearly did not want consolidation due to privacy concerns and hence this initiative did not take off as intended by its makers. As a result, Google decided to shut down Google Buzz.[35] Another technology giant, Apple, had a similar experience. Apple's "Mobile Me" service was intended to consolidate all mobile apps in one, but it did not get the reaction Apple desired from its loyal customer base.[36] In spite of having great visuals and usability features, the change was too drastic for customers to accept. However, there have been companies who have deployed marketing strategies based on customer feedback and achieved success in the market. Dominos was able to capitalize on the feedback provided to reinvent its brand after the drop in sales in 2009.[37] They took customer feedback and followed cues to drastically improve their product offering.

Customers with interest in the brand provide valuable feedback and suggestions from time to time. They are constantly communicating with the firm. It is the marketers who need to listen to the customer voice and thereby devise strategies to incorporate this feedback. Take an example of the Telecommunication industry, which is an extremely competitive industry for firms to operate in. AT&T faces stiff competition from other leading players like Verizon, Sprint, and T Mobile. Customers have often expressed their feedback in customer satisfaction surveys regarding AT&T's poor voice service and phone-based customer care. However, AT&T has failed to capitalize on this feedback attaining the last position in the satisfaction survey while its competitor Verizon attains the No. 1 ranking.[38] Companies have various ways of engaging customers to utilize customer knowledge of their product and service. Apple, for instance, has shared their software development kit to the common user to create his or her own application. With this, Apple stimulates cocreation amongst its customer base. Customers with appropriate knowledge are able to make useful applications, which create value for Apple as well as the entire customer base. The University of Texas, Austin recently launched a university wide program called "Ideas of Texas" to promote "creative problem solving" on the campus.[39] Members have been asked to "contribute ideas to enhance teaching, research, student life and the alumni experience, increase productivity, reduce costs and improve effectiveness. The members are also asked to review and vote on submitted suggestions so that at the end of the term, the administration can implement the winning and feasible ideas. The program received an overwhelming response with around 700 submissions, of which over 50 were implementable ideas.[40]

The top ideas are in the implementation phase. Once implemented, these are expected to enhance the overall experience and effectiveness, as per the program objective.

B2B companies have been a slow adopter of this feedback process from customers. However, the recent trend is encouraging. B2B companies are increasingly using social media to understand their core customer needs and are seeking feedback to improve their services. Some consulting companies, for example, have a feedback process built in at the end of the each project to gain insights to improve their service and better understand the gaps.

By consolidating all feedback data received from customers into a single centralized system and using that system across the organization, companies can gain valuable insights into what customers need, want and value most, as well as identify important trends and patterns in the data that contributes to the success of the business. As a result, the total value from a customer's engagement could evolve from the measurement of CLV, CBV, CRV or BRV, CIV, and CKV of that customer. This ensemble of metrics helps firms assess the degree (in value terms) to which a customer directly or indirectly impacts a firm or its product, with the goal of increasing the profitability of the firm.

By means of case studies and examples, Chapter 8 shall discuss the concept, measurement, and applications of CKV in greater detail.

Customer Feedback

Source: Printed with permission from http://tomfishburne.com/ (retrieved on January 03, 2013).

HOW DOES IT HELP ORGANIZATIONS?

Before we look at how the CEV framework assists organizations, it is important to understand the current economic environment and how it is impacting the consumer decision-making process. The economy today plays a crucial part in day-to-day decisions. With consumers being extremely cautious about their purchases, companies have an increasingly tough task to gain and retain customers, which affects their profit margins. With the added pressure of plunging sales, it is easier for companies to release coupons and distribute those using social media channels like Facebook, Twitter, Pinterest, etc. Companies fail to understand that although many customers may respond positively to such initiatives, the initiatives have a different impact on different customers. It is important to identify the right customer—existing or potential—who can add value to the firm by contributing to the profits over a period of time. Understanding and providing value to customers can help companies overcome the challenges posed by the economy by devising strategies that are targeted to the right customer who will not only add value by their purchase, but will also be a marketer for the brand and will spread a positive word about the brand to influence future prospects.

Companies now have a forward-looking approach, which enables them to understand the current value of a customer based on his or her current purchase behavior, the impact of this current behavior on future profitability for the firm, and the future contribution of prospective customers to the profit of the firm. Companies can continue to reward its loyal customers but now managers will have a better hold on which customer should be rewarded based on the customer value calculated using the proposed framework. This is an effective tool that can equip managers to be better informed about the customers they are dealing with and their contribution to the profit of the firm. The interconnected nature of these five key metrics make it that much more interesting for a manager to evaluate the value of a customer. Managers can use these concepts and frameworks to further their objectives for the brand, product, or service.

In addition to evaluating these metrics, companies can now maximize the profit for the firm and make customers market their product on the company's behalf in an efficient and cost effective manner. When companies understand the exact nature of each of these various elements, it is possible to develop and implement effective marketing strategies and ensure the efficient allocation of resources. Companies need to understand that customers are not only purchasing a product or service but are also increasingly partnering with the firm in creating a valuable brand for themselves.

CONCLUSION

The components that make up CEV can be determined by considering: (*a*) value of a customer's own transactions and corresponding CLV, (*b*) CRV generated by bringing in new customers via referrals thereby aiding in the acquisition process, (*c*) CIV generated by primarily influencing and encouraging existing customers to continue and/or expand usage post acquisition as well as encouraging prospects (individuals the firm is trying to acquire) to buy, (*d*) CKV created by providing knowledge and feedback to aid in the process of innovation, and (*e*) CBV created by the perception of the brand in minds of customers that helps in maximizing the CLV of the customer. The following chapters discusses each metric, details how they can be defined, and how they are different from one another so that managers can understand and apply the proposed concept in real-world situations to solve business problems faced by the brand/product or service.

NOTES AND REFERENCES

1. S. Fiegerman (2012), "Microsoft Asks Consumers to Compare Bing to Google Via a Pepsi Challenge," Message posted to http://mashable.com/2012/09/06/microsoft-bing-it-on-challenge/ (retrieved on January 03, 2013).
2. The Bing Team (2012), "Over 5 Million Have Visited the Bing It On challenge," Message posted to http://www.bing.com/community/site_blogs/b/search/archive/2012/10/02/over-5-million-have-visited-the-bing-it-on-challenge-35-of-google-primary-users-say-they-would-use-bing-more-after-taking-the-challenge.aspx (retrieved on January 03, 2013).
3. Apple, "iBooks Textbooks for iPad," http://www.apple.com/education/ibooks-textbooks/ (retrieved on January 03, 2013).
4. S. Shearman (2012), "Apple Launches Interactive Textbooks for iPad," Message posted to http://www.marketingmagazine.co.uk/news/1113101/Apple-launches-interactive-textbooks-iPad/ (retrieved on January 03, 2013).
5. Proctor & Gamble (2012), "Have You Tried This Yet? Returns to Showcase Innovative P&G Brands," http://news.pg.com/press-release/pg-corporate-announcements/have-you-tried-yet-returns-showcase-innovative-pg-brands (retrieved on January 03, 2013).

6. V. Kumar, A.M. Luo, and V.R. Rao, Connecting brands with customers: An integrated framework. Working Paper (as of 2013), Georgia State University.

7. K.L. Keller, "Conceptualizing, Measuring, and Managing Customer-Based Brand Equity," *Journal of Marketing*, 57(1), (1993): 1–22.

8. Kumar, Luo, and Rao, Connecting brands with customers: An integrated framework.

9. R.P. Leone, V.R. Rao, K.L. Keller, A.M. Luo, L. McAllister, and R. Srivastava, "Linking Brand Equity to Customer Equity," *Journal of Service Research*, 9(2), (2006): 125–138.

10. V. O'Connell and J. White, (December 13, 2000). "After decades of brand bodywork, GM parks Oldsmobile: for good," *The Wall Street Journal* http://online.wsj.com/article/SB97666277082301184.html (retrieved on January 03, 2013).

11. K. Randall, It's a fact: Strong brands drive B2B Markets. http://www.brandchannel.com/papers_review.asp?sp_id=1235 (retrieved on January 03, 2013).

12. V. Kumar, *Managing Customers for Profit: Strategies to Increase Profits and Build Loyalty* (Upper Saddle River, New Jersey: Pearson Education, 2008).

13. V. Kumar and J.A. Petersen, *Statistical Methods in Customer Relationship Management* (West Sussex, United Kingdom: John Wiley & Sons, 2012).

14. V. Kumar, R. Venkatesan, T. Bohling, and D. Beckmann, "The Power of CLV: Managing Customer Lifetime Value at IBM," *Marketing Science*, 27(4), (2008): 585–599.

15. Kumar and Petersen, *Statistical Methods in Customer Relationship Management* (2012).

16. V. Kumar, *Customer Lifetime Value: The Path to Profitability* (Hanover, MA: Now Publishers, 2008).

17. V. Kumar, J.A. Petersen, and R.P. Leone, "Driving Profitability by Encouraging Customer Referrals: Who, When, and How," *Journal of Marketing*, 74(5), (2010): 1–17.

18. V. Kumar, L. Aksoy, B. Donkers, R. Venkatesan, T. Wiesel, and S. Tillmanns, "Undervalued or Overvalued Customers: Capturing Total Customer Engagement Value," *Journal of Service Research*, 13(3), (2010): 297–310.

19. Bank of America Referral Program, http://www.maximizingmoney.com/banking-bonus-deals/bank-of-america-referral-program-25-personal-and-50-business-checking-bonuses/ (retrieved on January 03, 2013).

20. Kumar et al., "Undervalued or Overvalued Customers: Capturing Total Customer Engagement Value."

21. V. Kumar, J.A. Petersen, and R.P. Leone, "Defining, Measuring, and Managing Business Reference Value," *Journal of Marketing*, 77(1), (2013): 68–86.

22. Ibid.

23. Kumar et al., "Undervalued or Overvalued Customers."

24. V. Kumar, V. Bhaskaran, R. Mirchandani, and M. Shah, "Creating a Measurable Social Media Marketing Strategy for HokeyPokey: Increasing the Value and ROI of Intangibles & Tangibles," *Marketing Science* (Forthcoming).

25. Rennlist is a site for high-end sports car enthusiasts. http://www.rennlist.com (retrieved on January 03, 2013).

26. Kumar et al., "Undervalued or Overvalued Customers."

27. G.A. Stevens and J. Burley, "Piloting the Rocket of Radical Innovation," *Research-Technology Management*, 46(2), (2003): 16–25.

28. V. Kumar and Y. Bhagwat, "Listen to the Customer," *Marketing Research*, 22(2), (2010): 14–19.

29. Atlanta Journal Constitution. 25 December, 2011, *The Atlanta Journal Constitution*, Business section; December 8, 2011.

30. V. Kumar and Y. Bhagwat, "Listen to the Customer."

31. Ibid.
32. The Nielsen Company Global Faces and Networked Places: A Nielsen Report on Social Networking's New Global Footprint; March 2009.
33. E. Ho (2010), Google Buzz in Gmail. Message posted to http://gmailblog.blogspot.com/2010/02/google-buzz-in-gmail.html (retrieved on January 3, 2013).
34. M, Wood, (2010), "Google Buzz: Privacy Nightmare," Message posted to http://news.cnet.com/8301-31322_3-10451428-256.html (retrieved on January 03, 2013).
35. https://support.google.com/mail/bin/answer.py?hl=en&answer=1698228&ctx=mail (retrieved on January 23, 2013).
36. Apple's 'Mobile me', http://www.apple.com/support/mobileme/ (retrieved on January 28, 2013).
37. Domino's, (2009), "Domino's Pizza: Celebrating 50th Year Domino's Gives Itself a Makeover." http://phx.corporate-ir.net/phoenix.zhtml?c=135383&p=irol-newsArticle&ID=1366561&highlight= (retrieved on November 13, 2012).
38. Atlanta Journal Constitution. (December 8, 2011).
39. W. Powers, Jr. (2010). Letter to the University of Texas at Austin Community.
40. "Ideas of Texas," http://www.utexas.edu/president/ideas/ (retrieved on January 28, 2013).

Chapter 3

Brand: "Is That What You Think of Me?"

Find answers for...

- What is the role of branding?
- How to connect brand with customers?
- What is customer brand value (CBV) framework and what are its components?
- What are the predicted behavioral outcomes of the CBV framework?

---

ustomer brand value (CBV) and its contribution to the overall customer engagement value (CEV) framework have been explained in the previous chapter. In this chapter, we will explore the fundamentals behind the concept of CBV in greater detail. Before delving deeply into the CBV framework, it is essential to understand the importance of branding and how it affects the growth of companies. Exhibit 3.1 is a perfect example to understand the role of branding.

Exhibit 3.1: Role of Branding

From 2005 till date (2012), Hyundai is ranked amongst the top 100 global brands with its brand value increasing by the year.[1] Between 2000 and 2005, Hyundai was the fastest growing car maker in the United States. In a J.D. Power's Initial Quality Study, Hyundai was ahead of Toyota, lagging behind only Lexus and Porsche. Hyundai's new crossover SUV–Veracruz claimed to be better than Lexus and was priced $10K cheaper. Hyundai's offering in the market was an attractive product at a competitive price point. However, Hyundai's sales

---

(Exhibit 3.1 Continued)

(Exhibit 3.1 Continued)

growth flattened between 2005 and 2007 while the sales of Toyota soared in the same period. So, when Hyundai experimented with a representative sample of 200 people where customers were shown the new Veracruz SUV (Figure 3.1), Hyundai became conscious of the role of branding in customer decision-making process. Table 3.1 summarizes the results from this survey.[2] As seen in the table, the same product offering with Hyundai logo versus Toyota logo elicits a significantly different response from the respondents; branding played a key role in altering consumer perception. Learning a lesson from this experiment, Hyundai renewed their advertisement and spent around $400 million on this branding initiative to strengthen their brand.

Figure 3.1 2012 Hyundai Veracruz

Source: Hyundai (2012); Picture from https://www.hyundaiusa.com/chinese/pdf/Hyundai_Veracruz_eBrochure.pdf (retrieved on March 14, 2013).

Table 3.1 Experiment Results

Experiment	Intent to purchase (%)
Without the Hyundai logo	71
With Hyundai logo	52
With Toyota logo	92

Source: Adapted from David Kiley (May 21, 2007). At Hyundai branding is job 2. Message posted on http://davidkiley.com/pages/starchive-auto-2007-05-21.html (retrieved on March 14, 2013).

CONNECTING BRANDS WITH CUSTOMERS

For companies, customers and their preference in brands and products have been extremely important components to consider during the branding process. In-depth customer understanding is an integral part of any customer-centric company. One key reason for Hyundai's continued success till date can be attributed to its customer-centric approach. Hyundai introduced products in the market to cater to the needs of its loyal customer base so that they are connected with the customer at every stage. So, as a Hyundai customer moved up the value chain, Hyundai aimed to offer an appropriate product for that customer. Over time, Hyundai has therefore ventured into all key segments including the luxury car segment. Table 3.2 provides a comparison of various top luxury cars across different dimensions.[3] If a Mercedes-Benz E-Class (Figure 3.2) customer was asked to consider buying a Hyundai Genesis (Figure 3.3) despite Hyundai matching the performance and safety metrics of the E-Class, and the Genesis being available at a cheaper price, the answer in all probability would be negative. Some might say this is bad for Hyundai as they are losing out on these set of customers, but in reality this is not bad news for Hyundai at all. The target customer for a Hyundai Genesis is not the Mercedes-Benz customer but the customer who would upgrade and consider Hyundai for its good quality at a competitive price.

Hyundai's Genesis brand provides an example of companies catering to customers as they move up the value chain. What would happen if the customer moves down the value chain? Should companies still strive to retain that customer? Let us look at Starbucks for example. Like many other

Table 3.2	Summary of Key Metrics across Top Luxury Brands			
	Hyundai Genesis	**Mercedes-Benz E-Class**	**2012 Audi A6**	**2012 Infiniti M**
Price	$32,847–$44,075	$45,584–$53,855	$39,559–$47,229	$47,700–$61,700
Performance	8.2/10	8.3/10	8.4/10	8.8/10
Safety	10	10	9.9	9.4

Source: US News (2012). Retrieved from http://usnews.rankingsandreviews.com/cars-trucks/rankings/Luxury-Large-Cars/ (retrieved on March 14, 2013).

Figure 3.2   Mercedes-Benz E-Class

Source: Mercedes-Benz (2013). Picture fromhttp://www.mbusa.com/mercedes/vehicles/family/ class-E (retrieved on March 14, 2013).

Figure 3.3   Hyundai Genesis

Source: Hyundai (2013). Picture from https://www.hyundaiusa.com/vehicles/2013/genesis/ (retrieved on March 14, 2013).

companies, the recent global recession has hit Starbucks hard.[4] McDonalds stole some of its market share with their high-quality, yet affordably priced coffee beverages. As a result, non-performing Starbucks stores shut down. Since many customers downgraded to the cheaper priced coffee at McDonalds, Starbucks had to change its tactics to win back the losing segment. After spending millions to build the Starbucks brand, Starbucks decided to open an unbranded store, 15th Avenue Coffee and Tea, one of the several stores in Seattle. Starbucks positioned this store as a local community hangout where they served alcohol, espresso from a manual machine, and hosted book readings and music performances. Starbucks managed to continue servicing the customers who they would have otherwise lost due to customer concerns centering on affordability of coffee. Companies try to connect brands with customers at every level and provide products/services that move along the value chain with those customers.

Another company that focuses on customer needs and moves along the value chain with customers is Abercrombie & Fitch. The company—also known as A&F—is an American retailer focusing on selling to youth in the age group of 14 to 22 through their brands Abercrombie & Fitch, Hollister Co., Abercrombie, Ruehl No 924, and Gilly Hicks.[5] Each of these brands was created in order to ensure customer focus and thereby better customer engagement. Abercrombie & Fitch operates in different segments to cater to the customers at different stages. Each brand has a discrete image and operates under that to cater to its core customer group.

- *Abercrombie & Fitch:* Abercrombie & Fitch targets college students in the 18 to 22 age group. With its distinct positioning, the customers have a clear image of the brand.
- *Hollister Co.:* Hollister Co. is aimed at adolescents from 14 to 18. The product line features colorful sportswear infused with a West Coast feel. Again, the distinct identity clearly separates the target audience from Abercrombie & Fitch.
- *Abercrombie:* While Abercrombie & Fitch is targeted toward college students in the age group of 18–22, Abercrombie is specifically targeted toward children in the age group of 7 through 14.
- *Ruehl No 925:* Once a customer moves from college life to post-college life, he is expected to switch brands from Abercrombie & Fitch to Ruehl No 925. Ruehl No 925 is targeted toward post-college customer, featuring fashions inspired by New York City's Greenwich Village.
- *Gilly Hicks:* Gilly Hicks is a brand inspired by Sydney, Australia and it features underwear and loungewear for men and women on that theme.

With a diverse and targeted product offering, Abercrombie & Fitch capitalizes on the brand equity generated for each of the above mentioned brands under its umbrella. Moreover, the brand-customer alignment enables them to have strong customer equity as well.

NEED TO MEASURE BRAND VALUE

As seen in Chapter 2, a firm can work on building the brand and customer simultaneously by establishing a link between brand value and customer value, i.e., "customer-based brand equity." Traditionally, brand equity and customer equity have been regarded as two distinct marketing assets. Therefore, this approach does not always guarantee growth in the customer value. Traditionally, the effect of the brand was measured through the immediate change in sales after implementing a marketing initiative. However, since brand building seeks to influence customer behavior in the long run, measuring the effect of a brand through immediate changes in sales alone is not sufficient.

From the CEV framework illustrated in Chapter 2, it is clear that brand value affects a customer's behavioral as well as attitudinal response to a brand. Hence, any brand evaluation measure should incorporate all these factors to obtain a comprehensive picture. It is often a tough choice for managers to select between brand building activities and customer building activities. However, it is crucial to understand how a customer's behavior and attitude changes based on the brand value perceptions. A positive attitude toward a brand drives a customer's future purchase and potential recommendations to prospects. So, it is crucial to not only measure and interpret the financial value generated by the brand for the customer but also to consider the customer's perception of the brand.

Consider a set of sales data of two brands of a company, i.e., Brand A and Brand B for a specific period of time. Looking at Figure 3.4, which brand would you invest in? If one looks backwards from today, then, the answer probably would be "Brand A." However, a forward-looking outlook would be to investigate the scenario further and base the decision on the expected future performance. The evaluation of the customer franchise in terms of the expected size of the target segment and the expected spending of each segment in the future will guide the managers to take decisions which can have a higher impact on the profitability of the firm in the long run. Consider the following details for both brands for the purpose of illustration: (*a*) Brand A's target segment is 45- to 60-year-old customers and (*b*) Brand B's target segment

| Figure 3.4 | Sales Data for Brands A and B |

is 18- to 30-year-old customers. In addition to the future contribution of these segments for respective brands, the firm should evaluate the customer franchise in terms of (*a*) future size of the segment and (*b*) future spending power. The size of the age group of 45- to 60-year-olds might decrease while the size of the 18- to 30-year-olds is expected to increase. Similarly, the 45- to 60-year-olds might see a reduction in their spending power due to the age as well as other factors such as retirement. On the other hand, the 18–30-year age group's spending power is going to be on the rise. Using both conditions, Brand B shows more promise in terms of future growth and hence it is important for firms to carefully evaluate these factors before taking conclusive decisions.

While it is clear that firms need to base their decisions on a forward-looking approach, how does this approach result in higher profitability for the firm? Consider an example of two leading electronics manufacturers, Samsung and Nokia. The change in brand value and the net income for Samsung and Nokia (2001 through 2005) is shown in Figures 3.5 and 3.6, respectively. As seen in Figure 3.5, Samsung's brand value and net income is steadily increasing over the given period. The correlation points toward a possible relationship between a firm's brand value and its net income. Figure 3.6 displays Nokia's figures on the same two variables, i.e., brand value and net income. Based on the trend, it is clear that Nokia's brand value is declining between 2001 and 2005 with a stagnant net income over the same period. This correlation points toward a declining brand value affecting a firm's overall performance. These trends clearly demonstrate the importance of building brand

Figure 3.5	The Change in Brand Value and Net Income for Samsung (2001–2005)

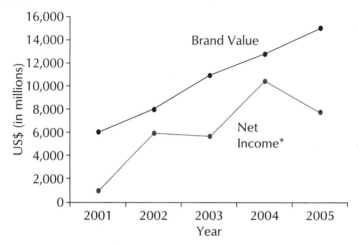

Sources: Samsung (2005) www.samsung.com; and *Businessweek* (2005). Retrieved from http://bwnt.businessweek.com/ (retrieved on March 14, 2013).
Note: *The net income has been scaled by a factor of 1,000 to make it comparable.

Figure 3.6	The Change in Brand Value and Net Income for Nokia (2001–2005)

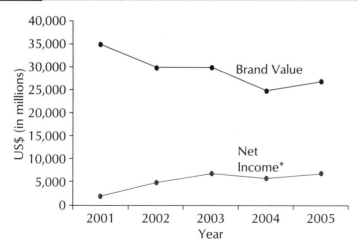

Sources: Nokia (2005) www.nokia.com; and *Businessweek* (2005). Retrieved from http://bwnt. businessweek.com/) (retrieved on March 14, 2013).
Note: *The original values of net income in euros (million) have been converted to US dollars (million).

value and its correlation with a company's bottom line. However, firms do not have a clear set of guidelines as to how to structure their marketing and brand investment strategies to boost their brand value. Usually firms have the aggregate-level brand value perception of their customers. To design and execute effective brand management strategies, firms need to understand exactly how each of their actions will affect the customer's brand perception. Customer brand value (CBV) provides the value a customer attaches to a brand through his or her experiences with the brand over time.

AGGREGATE VERSUS INDIVIDUAL BRAND VALUE

To understand the customer's reaction to each action of the firm and thereby the customer's brand perception, it is important to comprehend the alterations in the reactions of customers to the brand messages. Traditionally, this customer–brand relationship was studied at the aggregate (or collective) level. The reasoning behind this was that customer reactions would be similar if marketers successfully launched a strong brand idea in the market. However, in reality this is not entirely true. The brand perceptions differ from customer to customer. Hence it cannot be looked at as a collective measure and should be measured at the individual level. Variations in customer perceptions need to be given importance and firms should ensure that each unique perspective is identified and measured accurately. Concentrating on managing the brand value at the aggregate level confines the firm's ability to reach its customers and satisfy their needs efficiently. Since customers' brand perceptions are affected by various factors, targeting a heterogeneous crowd with a homogenous message would not be an efficient use of the available marketing resources from a firm's standpoint. Since not all customers are equally profitable, firms will lose out on the opportunity to allocate extra resources to the profitable lot of customers. Calculations made at the individual customer level will enable firms to target profitable customers and send specialized brand messages to communicate efficiently.

THE CBV FRAMEWORK

As discussed in Chapter 2, CBV is the attitudinal metric in the CEV framework interacting with the four dollar components: CLV, CRV/BRV, CIV, and

CKV. CBV refers to the attitudinal value a customer derives from the brand through his/her experiences.

CBV is defined as "the net effect of a customer's brand knowledge, brand attitude, brand purchase intention, and brand behavior formed due to prior brand experience and the marketing of a brand."[6]

A conceptual framework as suggested in Figure 3.7 shows the dynamic process of transferring a customer's brand knowledge to his or her brand attitude, brand purchase intention, and brand behavior, and then ultimately to his or her lifetime value to a firm the outcomes are associated with. The framework includes (*a*) *Brand Knowledge* which consists of brand awareness and brand image, (*b*) *Brand Attitude* which consists of brand trust and brand affect, (*c*) *Brand Behavior Intention* which is measured as purchase intention, and (*d*) *Brand Behavior* which consists of brand loyalty, brand advocacy and brand premium price behavior.

Brand Knowledge

Customer perceptions are the key to any brand. A brand has an identity based only on the customer perceptions and hence it is important to know that the true value of a brand lies in how customers perceive the brand, not in the brand itself. A customer's positive brand knowledge positively impacts the brand value. The two components of brand knowledge are (*a*) brand awareness and (*b*) brand image:

- *Brand awareness:* Awareness is always the first step in the relationship between a brand and a customer. It is an important metric that enables firms to understand the level of a customer's knowledge of a particular brand. It is a gateway for customers to purchase any particular product/ service. Customer purchase behavior differs based on the level of awareness. Moreover, future purchase decisions too are driven by awareness. Thus, it can be inferred that an increase in an awareness of the brand could increase the purchase probability. We see that firms often make frequent efforts to make the brand a part of the customer's consideration set. Firms anticipate that such a repeated exposure to the brand will evoke a favorable outlook in the mind of the customer. Therefore, the greater the brand awareness for a customer, the greater his/her brand value.

Figure 3.7 CBV Framework

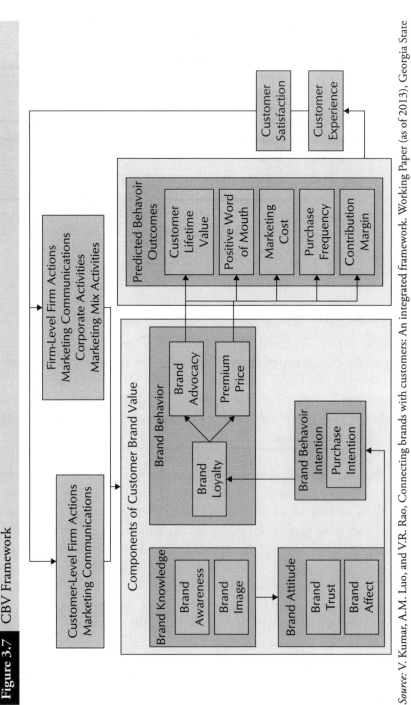

Source: V. Kumar, A.M. Luo, and V.R. Rao, Connecting brands with customers: An integrated framework. Working Paper (as of 2013), Georgia State University.

Coca-Cola is a great example of a firm that enjoys astonishing brand awareness throughout the world. Coke's products are sold in more than 200 countries, and Coke has almost 100 percent brand recognition in the Western world. The brand is over 125 years old and still successfully maintains its awareness levels around the world. The company has been smart in terms of keeping the brand youthful and fresh while connecting with generations of Coke lovers.[7]

- *Brand image:* While brand awareness forms the first level of brand knowledge, brand image builds on that awareness and the two together, i.e., awareness and the image contribute to the overall brand knowledge for a customer. Perceptions of customers about a brand affect brand image. Hence, brand image is not only influenced by how a firm markets its brand, but also by all other brand-related activities undertaken by the firm. For example, the second most trusted beverage brand in India,[8] Tata Tea, revamped its image in 2007 when it launched the "Jaago Re" (Wake up) campaign integrating all its brands like Agni, Gemini, Kanan Devan, etc., under the parent brand, Tata Tea.[9] The campaign positioned Tata Tea as a brand promoting "social awakening." The company's South Asia Regional President, Sanjiv Sarin, said, "While tea may wake you up, Tata Tea awakens you. The campaign demonstrated Tata Tea's thought leadership in positioning tea as a medium of 'social awakening' and not just 'physical awakening'." A customer's brand image is dynamic and changes with time. As the customer becomes more familiar with the product/brand, his or her perceptions alter. So, a customer can judge the satisfaction levels that he or she could derive out of the interaction with the brand depending on the knowledge he or she has about the product. Brand image assumes an important role in building brand knowledge, and it can lead to a negative brand value if the customer has an unpleasant brand image associated with it. Therefore, the greater the brand's image for a customer, the greater his/her brand value.

Harley Davidson for example has, over the years, created a cult image among its loyalists. As seen in Chapter 2, the brand is associated with adventure, adrenaline and individualism. Four Seasons Hotels & Resorts have a distinct brand image that separates them from their competitors. They are known for their excellent service quality to their customers as well as their employees.[10] A clean brand image establishes a unique connection with the customer and drives the relationship.

Brand Attitude

Brand attitude is the attitude each customer forms about the brand; it is mainly comprised of brand trust and brand affect:

- *Brand trust:* Brand trust refers to a customer's willingness to trust the brand to satisfy his/her needs. Customers trust the makers of the brand to provide them with quality products and services. A customer may not always be fully aware of the details that went into the making of the final product but he trusts the makers with the quality of a product. Trust in general is also gained only over a period of time. Hence, brand trust is developed between the customer and the brand over time. For example, Amul, a dairy giant in India since 1946, was rated India's "Most Trusted" food and beverage brand in 2013, according to *The Brand Trust Report*, India study 2013. Amul has been around for over 50 years and this level of trust which is reflected in *The Brand Trust Report* has been a result of Amul's long-term commitment in providing high-quality products to their customers. A customer's positive brand knowledge can be attributed to their experience and information they receive from external sources about the brand. As the customer becomes more familiar with the brand, brand trust moves into the next level of brand intimacy. Brand intimacy is an important factor in order to cultivate attitudinal loyalty with the customers. Therefore, the greater the brand's trust for a customer, the greater his/her brand value.

  In December 2012, Instagram, a photo sharing application bought by Facebook, changed their Terms of Service by adding convoluted language that appeared to greatly broaden the company's photo usage rights and narrow these rights for the user.[11] Due to the use of social media like Twitter, the news spread far and wide about how Instagram was changing their privacy settings to sell users' pictures with no compensation to the users themselves. Backlash from its active user base made Instagram backtrack on the language used in the Terms of Service regarding the ownership of the images. It is essential for a firm to be consistent in practices to build brand trust.

- *Brand affect:* Brand affect is a customer's positive emotional response toward a brand. While brand trust generates a positive rational response toward a brand, brand affect tries to generate a positive emotion toward the usage of the brand. Brand affect indicates a deeper relationship between the brand and the customer and can be revealed via different levels of the relationship between the firm and the customer. Past experiences aid in evoking a positive emotional response toward the brand. Hence for a customer, the greater the brand affect, greater is his/her brand value.

One standout example of brand affect is the strong negative reaction incited among customers when Google Maps was not a part of Apple iPhone 5 and the iOs 6 upgrade. Google Maps has been a highly popular and widely used product. With bad reviews about Apple's own Maps application on the rise, Apple eventually had to include Google Maps in the product offering.[12]

Brand Behavior Intention

Brand behavior intentions reflect the actual effect of the marketing actions on the brand behavior of the customers. Purchase intention influences the brand behavior intentions of the customer.

- *Purchase intention:* Purchase intention is basically the behavioral outcome of a customer's perception and interaction with the brand. A customer decides to make a purchase based on the product offering. In a highly competitive category, the intent to purchase gives the focal company an edge over its competitors if its customers express high purchase intention. Therefore, the greater the brand purchase intention of a customer, the greater his/her brand value.

  Walmart is a good example of a company that takes the initiative to create high purchase intention among its customers with their low prices. Everyone is aware of their popular slogan "everyday low prices," which attracts shoppers from around the world. In 2003, 138 million shoppers visited Walmart stores every week. In 2002, 82 percent of all American households made at least one purchase at Walmart.[13] These numbers indicate the successful implementation of strategies by Walmart in creating purchase intention among its customers.

Brand Behavior

- *Brand loyalty:* A loyal customer is one who makes repeated purchases of a preferred brand and shows both attitudinal and behavioral loyalty to the brand. She/he does not respond to the constant fluctuations in the market. The higher the brand loyalty toward a brand for a customer, the higher his/her brand value. Google is one example of brand loyalty. Google has been the top search engine for years now and continues to be the market leader.[14] Its dominant position in the market is a result of loyal customers using the service over and over again. Another example of brand loyalty would be Nestle's Nespresso. Nestle has been able to build strong loyal customer base by making sure high quality coffee reaches its customers through its exclusive Nespresso clubs. Nespresso clubs help Nestle to build direct and exclusive client relationship which paves the way for a long-term commitment in the relationship from both the consumer and the firm side.[15]

- *Brand advocacy:* Brand advocacy refers to the customer establishing a relationship (through joining a brand community and encouraging other customers to do so) with other customers who use the brand. As seen in Chapter 2, Rennlist is a good example of brand advocacy. Being an international online community for Porsche, Audi, and BMW enthusiasts founded in 1998, it allows patrons to engage in an online world to share their views with other customers having similar interests (www.rennlist.com). Such brand communities share information, promote a subculture, and provide assistance to other customers. Therefore, the greater the brand advocacy for a customer, the greater his/her brand value.

- *Brand price premium behavior:* Brand price premium behavior captures a customer's willingness to pay a premium price to buy a preferred brand over other products. This behavior reveals the customer's brand loyalty and a willingness to pay extra to maintain the quality. This also reduces the chances of a brand switch, i.e., a customer switching to a competitor's brand. Therefore, the greater the brand price premium behavior of a customer, the greater his/her brand value. For example, customers of Ferrari are willing to pay the extra price for the product they get in return. Ferrari resonates with affluence, speed, success and glamor. The brand price premium behavior depicts that customers are willing to go the extra mile for the product. The higher a customer's willingness to pay a premium on the price, the higher is the brand value of that customer. Micromax India, a consumer electronics company, created history for their company with the launch of their new phone—Canvas

HD.[16] Unlike many companies who would reduce the price after the launch, Micromax did the opposite; they increased the price of their Canvas HD mobile phone after the launch. The product that was initially priced at ₹13,999 (approximately $260) and was sold out within a week of its launch. To be able to meet the supply needs, they increased the price by ₹1,000 to ₹14,999. This did not affect the demand or the sale. Customers in this case, were willing to pay a slight premium for a product they desired.

Predicted Behavior Outcomes

It is observed that customers with greater brand value are more likely to engage in activities that result in an increase in customer value when compared to customers with low brand value. The various factors that constitute the individual's brand value, such as brand knowledge, attitude, and behavior intentions, affect the behavior of customers. The consequences of these behaviors can be established through the following customer behavior outcomes:

- *Customer lifetime value:* The factors that are used to measure the lifetime value of a customer are the purchase frequency, profitable lifetime duration, and contribution margin in every purchase occasion. Moreover, the word-of-mouth behavior of customers is also factored when the CLV is calculated. The factors affecting CBV such as brand knowledge, attitude, and behavior intentions affect the CLV also. Therefore, the greater a customer's individual brand value, the greater his/her lifetime value. Chapter 4 will provide a more in depth explanation of CLV.
- *Positive word of mouth:* Awareness of a product enables customers to recommend a brand to others. Greater satisfaction with the brand and trust gained over time play a role in generating a positive word of mouth. Brand satisfaction and brand advocacy are factors that directly and positively influence customer word-of-mouth behavior. Propagating information about the brand is one of the main functions of brand advocacy. It directly contributes to a positive word-of-mouth behavior.
- *Marketing cost:* Customer perceptions have an impact on the marketing costs associated with a product/service. Using targeted marketing communications, firms can make the marketing costs more efficient for the firm. Bombarding new communication messages centered on building

awareness to a customer with high awareness levels is not the best approach for a firm. Instead, firms can ensure these highly aware customers are reached out to with messages that propel them to make the purchase and further, recommend the brand to others.

- *Purchase frequency:* A customer purchases a product more frequently if he/she is highly engaged with the brand. Moreover, more frequent purchases also reflect the high utility value seen by the customer in the product. A customer's purchase frequency is affected by his or her brand knowledge. Customer recall of the brand and its attributes are also linked to the purchase frequency. A highly engaged customer who is familiar with the brand also seeks additional product information, which generates opportunities for the firm to sell more. Loyal customers refrain from getting affected by competition products or service thereby keeping the business with the focal company which indirectly increases the purchase frequency.

- *Contribution margin:* Contribution margin is raised highly for customers who pay a premium price for a brand. Contribution margin on the entire portfolio can be increased by building on brand extensions for a product/service. In brand extensions, firms can capitalize on the parent brand image and build on the same to introduce new products/ services in the market. Since the customer's knowledge about the brand already exists, it reduces the cost of introduction and brand building which further aides the increase in contribution margin. The greater the brand value of a customer, the greater his/her contribution margin.

All the above-discussed factors contribute to the overall customer experience, thereby satisfying the customer with the product or the service. The customer experience and customer satisfaction in a way dictates future actions of the firm and this information is used in deciding marketing budgets and communication strategies. These firm strategies, in turn, impact a customer's perception and the relationship continues.

MEASURING CBV

In order to measure a customer's CBV, we need to collect customer scores on the eight components of CBV. Customers are surveyed for their Brand Awareness, Brand Image, Brand Trust, Brand Affect, Brand Purchase Intention,

Brand Loyalty, Premium Price Behavior, and Brand Advocacy. Brand Awareness is measured based on (*a*) a customer's ability to recognize the brand and (*b*) a customer's ability to recall the brand. A customer's perception of the Brand Image is measured based on (*a*) quality perception, (*b*) customer expectation, and (*c*) company perception. Brand Trust is measured based on (*a*) trust, (*b*) brand honesty, and (*c*) brand reliability. Similarly, Brand Affect can be measured based on (*a*) feel good factor, (*b*) product satisfaction, and (*c*) brand affinity. Brand Purchase Intention is measured by (*a*) purchase intention and (*b*) purchase intention over competition. Brand Loyalty is measured based on (*a*) loyalty and (*b*) brand preference. Premium Price Behavior of the brand is measured based on their (*a*) value perception, (*b*) willingness to pay slightly more, and (*c*) willingness to pay a higher price over competition. Brand Advocacy is evaluated based on customers (*a*) interaction with other customers in social media, (*b*) word-of-mouth communication, and (*c*) brand advocacy. We arrive at the CBV score for a customer by summing up all the averages of individual components. For example, brand awareness comprises two components and hence the brand awareness score would be the sum of the two items' scores divided by two. The same is repeated for the other constructs of CBV and finally all the individual values are added to arrive at a single CBV score for a customer. All questions asked to customers are on a 10-point scale. The minimum score a brand can get is 8 and the maximum score is 80. Based on our research, we have found most companies' scores to be between 35 and 50.

MAXIMIZING CBV

CBV can be maximized by linking the CBV score of a customer to his/her CLV score. The calculation of CLV for a customer will be discussed in Chapter 4. Once a CLV score is calculated, firms can look at the components of CBV by segmenting customers based on their CLV scores, i.e., high, medium, and low CLV segments. The segmentation is discussed in Chapter 5.

CONCLUSION

In this chapter, we introduced the CBV framework and the predicted behavioral outcomes of the framework. By measuring customer perceptions of the brand, firms can clearly strategize ways to engage current customers and to attract new customers. As the foundation of the CEV Framework, CBV plays a vital role in helping firms to effectively engage customers through its interrelationship with the other customer engagement metrics. In subsequent chapters, the link between CBV and CLV, CRV/BRV, CIV, and CKV will be elaborated upon. After garnering a clear understanding of how each metric works, the connections between the metrics will demonstrate how firms can improve customer engagement and maximize overall profitability of the firm.

NOTES AND REFERENCES

1. Interbrand (2012), "Best Global Brands 2012," http://www.interbrand.com/en/best-global-brands/2012/Hyundai (retrieved on December 7, 2012).
2. David Kiley (May 21, 2007), "At Hyundai Branding is Job 2," Message posted on http://davidkiley.com/pages/starchive-auto-2007-05-21.html
3. US News, "Luxury Large Car Ranking 2012," http://usnews.rankingsandreviews.com/cars-trucks/rankings/Luxury-Large-Cars/ (retrieved on November 9, 2012).
4. Jennifer Bassett (July 20, 2009). Starbucks new concept: No name "Local" coffeehouse. Message posted on http://www.interbrand.com/en/knowledge/blog/post/2009-07-20/Starbucks-New-Concept-No-Name-Local-Coffeehouse.aspx (retrieved on March 14, 2013).
5. Four Iconic Businesses ONE brand. http://library.corporate-ir.net/library/61/617/61701/items/249197/Piper_June_2007.pdf (retrieved on November 9, 2012).
6. V. Kumar, A.M. Luo, and V.R. Rao, Connecting brands with customers: An integrated framework. Working Paper (as of 2013), Georgia State University.
7. Interbrand—Coco-Cola (2012), http://www.interbrand.com/en/best-global-brands/2012/Coca-Cola (retrieved on Nov 9, 2012).
8. Tata Global Beverages Limited, http://www.tataglobalbeverages.com/our-brands/brands-overview/brand-detail?brandid=d85b273d-23d7-421c-96e6-be56bae63cae (retrieved on April 1, 2013).
9. *Forbes India*, http://forbesindia.com/printcontent/34249 (retrieved on April 1, 2013).
10. Roger Hallowell, David Bowen, and Carin-Isabel Knoop, "Four Seasons Goes to Paris" *Harvard Business Review*, *16*(4), (2002): 7–24.
11. Huffingtonpost, "Instagram Privacy Policy and Terms of Service Update," www.huffingtonpost.com/2012/12/18/instagram-privacy-policy-terms-of-service_n_2324128.html (retrieved on November 14, 2012).
12. Huffingtonpost, "Google Maps Return to Apple," www.huffingtonpost.com/2012/12/13/google-maps-iphone-app_n_2290035.html (retrieved on January 24, 2012).
13. Anthony Bianco and Wendy Zeller, "Is Wal-Mart too Powerful?" *Businessweek*, *3852* (October 5), (2003): 100–110.

14. Netmarketshare, "Search Engine Market Share," http://www.netmarketshare.com/search-engine-market-share.aspx?qprid=4 (retrieved on January 24, 2013).

15. "The Unique Nespresso Experience Drove Once Again the Company to Strong Performance," http://www.nestle-nespresso.com/newsandfeatures/the-unique-nespresso-experience-drove-once-again-the-company-to-strong-performance (retrieved on April 8, 2013).

16. *Indiatimes*, http://www.indiatimes.com/technology/mobile/micromax-raises-canvas-hd-price-68350.html (retrieved as on April 4, 2013).

Chapter 4

Valuing Customer Contributions:
The Future Looks Green!

Find answers for...
• How can we measure a customer's worth?   • How can we maximize profitable customer contributions to the firm?   • What is the right metric to segment the customers?

INTRODUCTION: WHY MEASURE CUSTOMER VALUE?

Not all customers are equal. This simple fact is the premise upon which the measurement of customer value is based. As a crucial component of customer relationship management (CRM), measuring and managing customer value is critical in effectively engaging customers to achieve their full profit potential from them. The notion that different customers should be managed and satisfied differently is central to a CRM strategy, which focuses on customer engagement and profitability. Customer-focused metrics are a vital component to any corporate culture as they provide firms with the ability to rank customers based on key data to determine which customers provide the most value to the company; and, therefore, should receive the most customer engagement.

Most firms would have observed the Pareto Principle in operation when measuring customer value. Also known as the 80/20 rule, the Pareto Principle asserts that 80 percent of the total value to the firm is usually provided by 20 percent of customers. In this case, it is beneficial for a firm to measure customer value at the individual level in order to capture the differences in customer behavior. Measuring customer value is an essential metric for any firm to understand. Identifying the profitable customers and knowing how long they will remain profitable customers is critical in maximizing the overall profitability. In doing so, a firm must ask important questions regarding the behavior of its customers and seek to predict the future behavior of its customers. Securing answers to these questions allows firms to develop strategic plans that focus on profitability, return on investment (ROI), and optimal resource management.

Firms that capitalize on quantifying the value of their customers are able to more efficiently allocate resources and increase their profitability. Measuring customer value dictates that a firm calculates the expected profits from all its customers. This information can prove vital to organizations in efficiently managing customers and the resources allocated for those customers while developing customer-oriented marketing initiatives. In terms of customer management, it has been observed that managing customers based on their profitability is the most effective approach. This approach defies conventional wisdom, which suggests that enhancing customer loyalty and increasing customer acquisition would be the most effective strategy. It is demonstrated that loyal customers are not always profitable, and not all profitable customers are loyal. The key finding is that customers should be managed based on their profitability, and not on their loyalty.[1]

The profit-based strategy to assessing customer value is rooted in CRM findings that show the magnitude of the benefits to an organization. The adage states "you can't manage what you can't measure." Therefore measuring customer value is paramount to a firm for effectively and efficiently managing its resources. As introduced in Chapter 2, this chapter will further explain the concept of customer lifetime value (CLV) that can help firms align the net present value (NPV) of the monetary contribution of a customer's future purchase transactions with the cost incurred in serving them, thereby identifying ways to profitably engage with the customer.[2]

TRADITIONAL MEASURES OF CUSTOMER VALUE: BACKWARD-LOOKING METRICS

Traditionally, metrics such as Recency-Frequency-Monetary Value (RFM), Past Customer Value (PCV), Share of Wallet (SOW), and Tenure/Duration are used to help companies to measure the value of customers and prioritize them based on their contribution to overall profits. Subsequently, the insights on customer value are used in decisions pertaining to the allocation of marketing resources. However, many of the traditional metrics focus on a backward-looking approach that only takes into consideration the past activity of a customer, which leads to outdated information being used for customer selection.

Due to this limitation, these metrics misjudge a customer's value and duration with the firm and present an incomplete picture of the customer's relationship with the firm. This incomplete view and misallocation causes managers to implement suboptimal marketing campaigns that drain the firm's limited marketing resources and ignore the opportunity to invest in more profitable customers. Further, the traditional metrics assume that past customer behavior will be replicated in the future. In reality, this is not the case. Finally, the traditional metrics also lack the ability to provide managers with recommendations about the marketing strategies which should be implemented in order to maintain a customer's relationship and maximize the profitability of that customer. Subsequently, firms choose the wrong customers to engage, and make ill-informed marketing decisions based on these outdated metrics. The subsequent sections take a closer look at the traditional metrics to further highlight their ineffectiveness in predicting future customer value.

Receny-Frequency-Monetary (RFM) Value

The RFM metric is a composite score of the recency, frequency, and monetary value. Recency value measures the time since a customer last placed an order with the firm; frequency value measures how often a customer purchases from the firm in a particular time period; and monetary value refers to the value of purchases made by a customer in an average transaction. Popularly used by mail-order firms and retailers, the RFM metric uses past customer information to designate a relative weight to each of the three variables—how recent were the purchases, how frequent are the purchases being made, and what is the monetary value of all the purchases. The values are then added based on the relative weights of the metrics. The relative weights can be determined directly by managers or by using simple regression techniques.

The RFM metric is a relational measure. In other words, a higher ranking means that a customer is better for targeting with its marketing resources. The company will select the customers with the highest RFM scores for its marketing campaign as these customers are deemed to be the most profitable to the company. However, the major shortcoming of this metric lies in its inability to accurately forecast future customer contributions to a firm on all three levels, i.e., profitability, loyalty, and timing.

Share of Wallet

The SOW metric, used widely in retail businesses and financial companies, indicates the degree to which a customer meets their needs in the category with the focal brand or firm. This metric can be estimated either at the individual level or at the aggregate level, but as a customer scoring metric it is used almost exclusively at the individual level. The SOW at the individual level is measured as the proportion of category value accounted for by a focal brand or firm for a buyer from all brands the buyer purchases in that category. Simply put, if a customer spends $500 per month on groceries, and $400 of her purchases is with Supermarket A, then A's SOW for that customer is 80 percent in that month. Measured in percentages, SOW also provides B2B companies with an idea of what portion of the marketing budget is being spent with that firm. For example, if a technology firm identifies that one of its business customers is spending 100 percent of its IT budget with them then that business is behaviorally loyal and relies specifically on that firm for all its IT needs.

Unlike RFM, SOW can uncover the level of loyalty a customer has with the firm by identifying whether or not the consumers shop. With the metric, a firm can classify customers who spend a higher percentage of their wallet with a firm as more likely to be loyal to that firm and to make repeat purchases. On the other hand, customers with a lower SOW are classified as more likely to be brand-switchers. However, this metric lacks the ability to explain when a customer is likely to buy in the future and the profitability of those purchases to the firm. Even though a customer with a low SOW spends most of his or her budget elsewhere, that customer might show great potential for future growth. Using only SOW, the firm would miss the opportunity to communicate with customers who can offer future profitability to the firm. Furthermore, SOW only offers useful information when used in conjunction with other metrics.

Past Customer Value

The PCV metric measures the value of a customer, based on his or her profit contribution in the past, after adjusting for the time value of money. The value of a customer is measured in terms of the total consumption of that customer over different points in time. This metric rests on the assumption that the past spending behavior of the customer is going to continue in the future, and that the past pattern is a good predictor of future behavior. Previous research has proven that this assumption is not a good one for marketers to make, as customer behavior can change over time. Further, apart from not accounting for future purchase behavior, PCV also does not consider the costs in managing future customer relationships.

Tenure/Duration

The Tenure/Duration metric takes into consideration the amount of time a customer remains active with a company. In this sense, active is described as the duration of a customer's relationship with the company. Often thought of in terms of churn and attrition rates, a customer's tenure and duration is an indication of that customer's behavioral loyalty toward the company. The lower the churn or attrition rate of a firm, the higher the number of active years its customers will have with the firm.[3] The disadvantage of the Tenure/Duration metric is that in and of itself, it does not communicate the value of a customer.

As highlighted in the previous sections, the need for a forward-looking metric which could overcome the limitations of the traditional, backward-looking metrics was evident. The remainder of this chapter focuses on introducing one such metric. Known as CLV, this metric bypasses the shortcomings of the previous metrics and equips managers with an effective tool to capture the true value of customers.

DEFINING CLV: THE FORWARD-LOOKING METRIC

In contrast to the traditional metrics, the concept of CLV is a very powerful metric that understands the versatile nature of customer behavior and enables firms to treat individual customers differentially and exclusively from each other based on their contributions to the company.

Defined as "the sum of cumulated future cash flows—discounted using the weighted average cost of capital (WACC)—of a customer over their entire lifetime with the company," this metric tracks the future purchase behavior of a customer and computes his/her value in present-day terms.[4] The application of CLV as a marketing decision support system is a sophisticated process that involves significant development of the metric prior to its implementation. The metric is based on the cumulated cash flow and value coming directly or indirectly from a customer over his or her lifetime with the company. By quantifying this value, firms are able to discern how much they can and should invest in a customer in order to achieve a positive ROI or maximized profitability.

The CLV number can be used by firms in many ways. With regards to customer identification, CLV can be used to identify the most and least profitable customers and can direct marketing efforts at the most valuable ones by classifying customers into high, medium, and low-value segments. The classification provides customer relationship managers with substantial insight for making marketing decisions regarding the allocation of scarce resources toward selling efforts and service levels. Such an exercise goes beyond the traditional mass-marketing approach and employs direct customer communication to grow and nurture the high CLV customers.

In addition to the effective allocation of resources and marketing dollars, CLV can also be used to help companies test alternative marketing strategies to gauge the profit potential of the alternatives versus previously implemented campaigns. The testing of these marketing strategies can include for example, the measurement of loyalty programs to determine whether they are worth implementing based on the value added to CLV, with and without the programs. In addition, forecasting for customer defection and customer satisfaction levels can be performed to determine which customers are worth keeping and what strategies should be used to keep them. Efforts to increase future retention and win-back strategies can also be examined to curtail customer defection and improve satisfaction.

In broader strategic terms, CLV can also help companies define their objectives and assess their market position and the value of their existing customer bases. The knowledge gained from this assessment can aid companies in determining the overall company value, which can be used during mergers, purchases, and sales. As their most important assets, a company's market position and customer base can be measured by quantifying their customer groups' total CLV.

As an essential element to CRM and a key metric in customer-centric organizations, CLV measures the total customer portfolio as the difference between what it costs to acquire, service, and retain a customer and the revenue generated from that customer over the customer's lifetime with a firm. By employing the CLV concept, decision makers are able to think in terms of long-term relationships instead of just transactions. Furthermore, the concept is grounded in the acknowledgement that customers are likely to alter their behavior due to factors such as changes in competition and/or customer lifestyle. Accounting for these changes allows firms to execute product/service differentiation strategies according to a customer's expected value.

This chapter establishes that CLV scores over other traditional metrics in profitable customer engagement and management. In simple terms, CLV denotes the value of future profit contributions by a customer to the firm after making adjustments for costs and time value of money. There are two primary reasons why firms would adopt a metric that provides them with the future worth of a customer. First, with the tremendous growth in information technology, firms are now able to track, record, and analyze customer purchase behavior, and thereby determine his or her profitability. The increased data availability has enabled companies to go beyond the traditional, primary and strategic customer-based value metrics. The problem with such metrics is their inability to determine individual customer-level profitability. In this light, CLV overcomes the inherent drawbacks in those metrics and provides a reliable estimate of customer value. Second, customers have also begun to realize and accept the fact that companies treat high-value buyers differentially from low-value buyers. However, companies should have a forward-looking approach for the differentiation to be successful in the long run. Today, any firm is faced with the challenge of developing an optimal blend of differential levels of treatments in such a fashion that the profits earned by the firm are maximized over each customer's lifetime.

MEASURING CLV

In simple terms, CLV can be denoted as the NPV of future gross contributions minus the NPV of future marketing costs. Figure 4.1 further explains the conceptual approach for measuring CLV.

Figure 4.1 CLV Measurement Approach—A Conceptual Framework

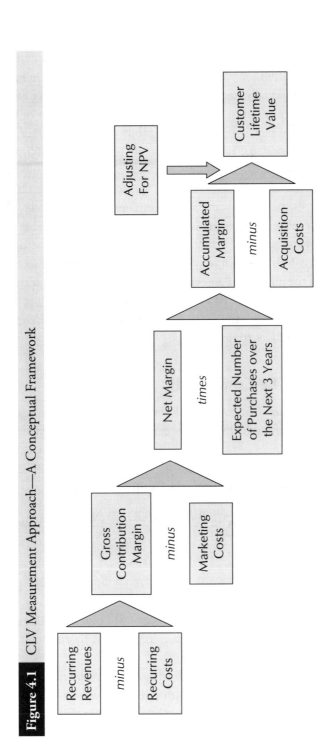

Source: Adapted from V. Kumar, *Managing Customers for Profits* (Upper Saddle River, NJ: Wharton School Publishing, 2008).

As seen from the above framework, the lifetime value of a customer depends, to a great extent, on whether the customer will be active in future time periods. This is especially important in a noncontractual setting because the customer has the freedom to leave the relationship at any point of time. The success of the CLV metric lies in its applicability in both types of customer relationships—contractual (customers who are contractually obligated to be with the firm, such as magazine subscriptions, cellular phone subscriptions, etc.) and noncontractual (customers who are *not* contractually obligated to be with the firm, such as grocery stores, restaurants, etc.). While CLV's applicability in a contractual setting is fairly straight forward, the case of a noncontractual setting presents a different picture. In a noncontractual setting, it may be difficult to ascertain how long a customer has been associated with a firm, due to the absence of an explicit expiry date. In such a scenario, predicting the lifetime duration of a customer by observing buying patterns and other explanatory factors assumes importance. Additionally, CLV can also be used in B2B and B2C settings.

How Can CLV Be Computed?

CLV can be computed in contractual and noncontractual settings. A CLV that would cover contractual situations can be computed using the following equation:

CLV Computation in a Contractual Setting

$$\text{CLV}_i = \sum_{t=1}^{T} \frac{\text{Base GC}}{(1+r)^t} + \sum_{t=1}^{T} \frac{\hat{p}(\text{Buy}_{it}=1)^*\hat{\text{GC}}_{it}}{(1+r)^t} - \frac{\hat{\text{MC}}_{it}}{(1+r)^t} \qquad \text{(Equation 4.1)}$$

where:
CLV_i = lifetime value for customer i
$\hat{p}(\text{Buy}_{it})$ = predicted probability that customer i will purchase in time period t
$\hat{\text{GC}}_{it}$ = predicted gross contribution margin provided by customer i in time period t
$\hat{\text{MC}}_{it}$ = predicted marketing costs directed toward customer i in time period t
t = index for time periods such as months, quarters, years, etc.
T = marks the end of the calibration or observation timeframe
r = monthly discount factor
Base GC = predicted base monthly gross contribution margin

In a contractual setting, the first term $\left(\sum_{t=1}^{T}\dfrac{\text{Base GC}}{(1+r)^{t}}\right)$ corresponds to the constant gross contribution that the customer is going to give to the firm. This could be on a monthly, quarterly or on an annual basis. The second term

$\left(\sum_{t=1}^{T}\dfrac{\hat{p}(\text{Buy}_{it}=1)^{*}\hat{\text{GC}}_{it}}{(1+r)^{t}}\right)$ corresponds to the predicted NPV of future pur-

chases by the customer at a particular time period. The third term $\left(\dfrac{\hat{\text{MC}}_{it}}{(1+r)^{t}}\right)$

corresponds to the NPV of future purchases attributed to the customer at a particular time period. The final value of these three components would yield the CLV in a contractual setting.

In a noncontractual setting, the first term $\left(\sum_{t=1}^{T}\dfrac{\text{Base GC}}{(1+r)^{t}}\right)$ would not be

valid as there is no constant flow of base income from a customer on a periodic basis. In short, there is no assured income due to subscriptions. As with

the previous case, the second term $\left(\sum_{t=1}^{T}\dfrac{\hat{p}(\text{Buy}_{it}=1)^{*}\hat{\text{GC}}_{it}}{(1+r)^{t}}\right)$ corresponds to

the predicted NPV of future purchases by the customer at a particular time

period. The third term $\left(\dfrac{\hat{\text{MC}}_{it}}{(1+r)^{t}}\right)$ corresponds to the NPV of future pur-

chases attributed to the customer at a particular time period. The final value of these three components would yield the CLV in a noncontractual setting. Let us now consider a numerical example in a contractual setting to see how CLV is computed. Equation 4.2 illustrates the computation of CLV in a noncontractual setting.

CLV Computation in a Noncontractual Setting

$$\text{CLV}_{i} = \sum_{t=1}^{T}\dfrac{\hat{p}(\text{Buy}_{it}=1)^{*}\hat{\text{GC}}_{it}}{(1+r)^{t}} - \dfrac{\hat{\text{MC}}_{it}}{(1+r)^{t}} \qquad \text{(Equation 4.2)}$$

Consider the case of Amy, a customer of a mobile phone company. The monthly subscription or the base GC provided by Amy is $40. At the end of May, the company wants to know the value Amy is likely to provide to the company in the next four months (June, July, August, and September).

Table 4.1 provides Amy's probability of buying additional services or $\hat{p}$(Buy) (such as downloads, ringtones, text messaging, etc.) for the next four months, her monthly purchase amount, the percentage of margin for each purchase, and the marketing cost incurred by the company in contacting her.

Assuming an annual discount rate (r) of 12 percent (or 1 percent monthly rate), we can now compute the CLV of Amy for the next four months. First, let us compute the CLV of Amy at the end of June using Equation 4.1.

$$\text{Amy's lifetime value at the end of June} = \frac{40}{(1.01)^1} + \frac{(0.55)*(20*20\%)}{(1.01)^1} - \frac{5}{(1.01)^1}$$

Therefore, $\qquad CLV_{Amy,June} = \$36.83$

Similarly, we can compute the value Amy would give to the company at the end of each subsequent month as follows—July: $33.33, August: $32.80, and September: $29.40. A summation of all the four months' CLV would yield a value of $132.37. In other words, over the next four months Amy would provide $132.37 in value to the company through her subscription and additional purchases.

Table 4.1 can also be used to explain the case of noncontractual purchases. Assume that the table indicates Amy's monthly cappuccino purchases from her nearby café. However, this case will not have the monthly subscription or baseline CLV. Now, let us compute the CLV of Amy at the end of June using Equation 4.2.

$$\text{Amy's lifetime value at the end of June} = \frac{(0.55)*(20*20\%)}{(1.01)^1} - \frac{5}{(1.01)^1}$$

Therefore, $\qquad CLV_{Amy,June} = -\$2.77$

Table 4.1 Transaction Details of Amy

	June	July	August	September
$\hat{p}$(Buy)	0.55	0.50	0.40	0.20
Monthly purchase amount (in $)	20	10	10	15
Profit margin (in %)	20	20	20	20
Marketing cost (in $)	5	7	7	10

In other words, Amy will be costing the café $2.77 in June by receiving communication from the café and by being a part of their customer base. Similarly, we can compute the value Amy would give to the café at the end of each subsequent month as follows—July: –$5.88, August: –$6.01, and September: –$9.03. A summation of all the four months' CLV would yield a value of –$23.70. That is, over the next four months Amy would cost the café $23.70 in value by being their customer. In other words, the amount spent by the café on marketing to Amy will be more than the revenue contributed by her to the café.

DRIVERS OF CLV

Now that we have covered the concept of CLV and how to calculate it, we need to clearly understand the factors that drive a profitable customer relationship with the customer and how they affect CLV. The identification of drivers benefit the firm in providing a better understanding of a profitable customer relationship and in helping managers take proactive measures to maximize a customer's lifetime value. The profitable duration of the customer–firm relationship depends differentially on the exchange characteristics at time t and on customer heterogeneity. The profitable lifetime duration can be expressed as:[5]

Profitable Lifetime Duration$_i$ = f (Exchange Characteristics$_{it}$, Customer Characteristics)

As depicted in the profitable lifetime duration equation, the factors that drive CLV can be classified into two main categories: Exchange Characteristics and Customer Characteristics. Other driver categories include Product Characteristics and Firm's Marketing Actions. The exchange characteristics are predominately the same for the majority of the cases in a B2B and B2C setting. The drivers that reflect customer characteristics, product characteristics, and a firm's marketing actions could vary in these settings. Table 4.2 provides the classification of these drivers in B2B and B2C settings.

As explained in Table 4.2, the drivers of CLV can be thought of as the main factors that affect the lifetime value of a customer. These drivers determine the nature of the relationship between the firm and the customer, and help estimate the level of profitability and the CLV of each customer. The strategies

Table 4.2	Drivers of CLV in B2B and B2C Settings	
Exchange Characteristics	• Spending level • Cross-buying • Purchase frequency and recency • Past purchase activity • Focused buying behavior	• Average inter-purchase time • Participation in loyalty programs • Customer returns • Bidirectional communication
Customer Characteristics	In a B2B firm: Includes variables such as industry, annual revenue and location of the business	In a B2C firm: Includes variables such as age, gender, spatial income and physical location of the customers
Product Characteristics	Consists of the type of products offered, the timing since product acquisition, and the typical lifetime associated with the product	
Firm's Marketing Actions	Constitutes the number of marketing messages, offers, promotions, individual visits by salespersons and so on, and the frequency and timing of these contacts (Frequency of marketing contacts)	

Sources: Printed with permission and adapted from W. Reinartz and V. Kumar, "The Impact of Customer Relationship Characteristics on Profitable Lifetime Duration," *Journal of Marketing*, *67*(1), (2003): 77–99.
R. Venkatesan and V. Kumar, "Customer Lifetime Value Framework for Customer Selection and Resource Allocation Strategy," *Journal of Marketing*, *68*(4), (2004): 106–125.

that can help companies maximize these drivers will ultimately maximize CLV and drive profitable customer engagement. The drivers of CLV also dictate the duration of the customer–firm relationship. A clear understanding of these drivers is essential for building profitable customer loyalty, as this forms the basis of customer management strategies.[6] Having learned how to measure CLV and the drivers of CLV, we need to know how to maximize CLV in order to reap the full benefits of the metric. The next section discusses the popular CLV-based customer engagement strategy that helps firms to maximize CLV and the respective implications of adopting the strategies.

MAXIMIZING CLV TO ENSURE PROFITABLE CUSTOMER ENGAGEMENT

In addition to understanding the concept of CLV, firms should seek to identify how CLV can be maximized. If a company truly understands each customer's lifetime value, it can maximize its own value by increasing the quantity of and improving upon customer relationships that can create value for a firm. This would ultimately result in profitable customer engagement. In terms of marketing implications, CLV enables firms to address marketing issues with greater confidence and make more strategically sound marketing decisions. Some of the areas of cultivating profitable customer engagement through the adoption of the CLV-based approach are provided in Figure 4.2.

Answers to the above set of questions can be found in actionable marketing strategies known as the Wheel of Fortune Strategies. This cycle begins with selecting the right customers based on future profitability. Once the customers are selected, the subsequent strategies then aim at efficiently managing

Figure 4.2	A Sample List of Strategies to Ensure Profitable Customer Engagement

Customer Retention	• Which customers should we retain? How can we retain more customers? • Can we ensure that the customers we retain are profitable or potentially profitable? • What efforts/programs influence customer retention and CLV? • When are customers prone to switch? What are the drivers to switching?
Customer Acquisition	• How can we increase customer acquisition? • Is it possible to acquire profitable customers rather than just any customers? • What acquisition sources are most/least profitable? Which sources are ultimately providing the best customers? • How much to spend on acquiring a customer?
Customer Profitability	• How can we increase our overall profitability? • How to recruit profitable customers who will stay longer? • How long is the customer's actual lifecycle? • Which customers are more prone to specific campaigns (e.g., discounts, deals, etc.)?

and retaining customers. The experience (or information) obtained by implementing these strategies sheds light on future customer selection and profit maximization. Companies have also recognized the need to move beyond the objective of ensuring "behavioral" loyalty (indicated by increased short and long-term customer purchases) to include "attitudinal" loyalty (indicated by short and long-term customer attitudes). This has been reflected in a typical dilemma that many corporate boards face regarding profit maximization. The question then remains whether to invest in building brands or to invest in building the customer base. The probable answer is to invest in both. It would also be difficult to estimate how investing in brand building contributes toward attaining higher profitability. A key to address these issues is to establish a link between brand value and CLV to manage individual customer brand value (CBV). This results in maximizing the CLV. Figure 4.3 illustrates the Wheel of Fortune Strategies for maximizing CLV for the purpose of ensuring profitable customer engagement.

The next sections explain the need for each of Wheel of Fortune strategies and convey how the strategies work and can be implemented to achieve profitable customer engagement.

Customer Selection

Need for the strategy: In the past, firms have used traditional metrics (i.e., RFM, PCV, SOW, Tenure/Duration) to select customers to retain. As traditional metrics are based on past customer behavior, which is a poor indicator of future customer purchase behavior, these metrics fail to identify customers who will be profitable in the future. On the other hand, the CLV metric is forward-looking in nature and focuses on customers who are likely to be profitable in the future.

How it works: Selecting the right customers to manage is critical for two reasons. First, owing to limited marketing budgets, managers have to make choices as to where and on whom they should spend the limited resources. Second, not all customers are equally profitable. This calls for targeting customers with high profitability. By selecting the right customers to manage, CLV enables firms to rank-order customers based on their value to the company and prioritize resources accordingly. Specifically, firms should select up to the top 20 percent of customers as the budget allows. The effectiveness of

Figure 4.3

Wheel of Fortune: Strategies Used for Maximizing CLV

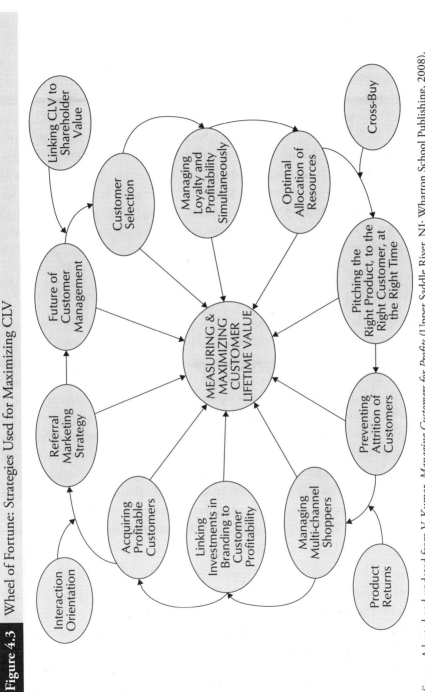

Source: Adapted and updated from V. Kumar, *Managing Customers for Profits* (Upper Saddle River, NJ): Wharton School Publishing, 2008).

CLV versus the traditional metrics in customer selection is superior in offering higher levels of profitability.

Implementation outcome: When the marketing budget of a firm is limited, managers have to make choices as to where and on whom they should spend the limited resources available to them. CLV has been found to meet the needs of managers in this area by identifying customers who provide more profit to the company and therefore should receive the benefits of the firm's limited resources. For instance, it was found that customers of a B2B manufacturer who were selected based on their CLV score, generated about 40 percent greater average revenue, 42 percent more gross margin, and 45 percent more net value than customers selected through other traditional metrics such as RFM, PCV, and SOW.[7] Therefore, selecting the right customers is an important strategy for improving net profits.

Managing Loyalty and Profitability Simultaneously

Need for the strategy: Contrary to popular belief, loyalty is not always the true measure of customer profitability. The relationship between loyalty and profitability is a lot more complex. As such, measures to distinguish between the behavioral and attitudinal loyalty of customers must be taken in order to gain a true measure of customer profitability. In the past, customer loyalty has been defined solely as a behavioral measure with the assumption that the loyalty of a customer is obtained from his purchasing behavior. That is, the more a customer buys, the more loyal that customer is perceived to be; and thus, should be rewarded more. Such a line of approach does not consider the attitudinal loyalty of the customers to the firm. In this regard, how can firms profitably engage with customers who are behaviorally *and* attitudinally loyal toward them? Further, is chasing loyal customers the same as chasing profitable customers?

How it works: The first step in implementing this strategy is to segment customers based on their loyalty and profitability to the firm. Several different measures of loyalty and the profitability of the customer can be used for this purpose. In this approach, customers are segmented into four cells based on their loyalty and profitability levels by rank ordering the loyalty and profitability scores from highest to lowest and then taking the median split of the scores. Once the segments are created, different strategies are directed toward each set of customers to maximize their loyalty and profitability. These segments are identified as Strangers, Butterflies, True Friends, and Barnacles. Figure 4.4 illustrates the relationship between profitability and loyalty.

- *Strangers* (low profitability and short-term customers) are a group of customers that are not loyal to the firm and bring in little to no profits

Figure 4.4 Managing Loyalty and Profitability Simultaneously

	BUTTERFLIES Cell 2	TRUE FRIENDS Cell 3

High Profitability	• Good fit of company offering and customer needs
	• High profit potential
	• Action:
	  – Aim to achieve transactional satisfaction, not attitudinal loyalty
	  – Milk the accounts as long as they are active
	  – Key challenge: cease investment once inflection point is reached
		• Good fit of company offering and customer needs
		• Highest profit potential
		• Action:
		  – Consistent intermittently spaced communication
		  – Achieve attitudinal *and* behavioural loyalty
		  – Delight to nurture/defend/ retain

	STRANGERS Cell 1	BARNACLES Cell 4

Low Profitability	• Little fit of company offering and customer needs
	• Lowest profit potential
	• Action:
	  – No relationship investment
	  – Profitize every transaction
		• Limited fit of company offering and customer needs
		• Low profit potential
		• Action:
		  – Measure size and share of wallet
		  – If share of wallet is low, specific up-selling and cross-selling
		  – If size of wallet is small, strict cost control

	Short-term Customers	Long-term Customers

Source: Printed with permission from W. Reinartz and V. Kumar, "The Mismanagement of Customer Loyalty," *Harvard Business Review*, July (2002): 86.

to the firm. Not only are these customers a poor fit to the company, but they offer very little profit potential to the firm. Identification of such customers at an early stage is critical. Managerially, firms have to avoid any investment toward building a relationship with these customers, and must ensure profits from every transaction.

- *Butterflies* (high profitability and short-term customers) are a group of customers that are transient but highly profitable. These customers do not exhibit traditional behavioral loyalty, tend to buy a lot in a short time period and then move on to other firms, and avoid building a long-term relationship with any single firm. Managerially, firms should enjoy their profits while they last and stop investing in them when they move to competition.

- *True Friends* (high profitability and long-term customers) are a group of customers that are both loyal and profitable. These customers buy steadily and regularly (not too intensively) over time. They are generally satisfied with the firm and are usually comfortable in engaging with the firm's processes. Managerially, firms should take care in building relationships with these customers, since they present the firm with the highest potential to bring long-term profitability.

- *Barnacles* (low profitability and long-term customers) area group of customers that provides poor profits to the firm, despite being loyal. These customers, if managed unwisely, could prove to be a severe drain on the company's resources. Managerially, firms must evaluate the size and the share of their wallet. If the share of wallet is found to be low, firms can up-sell and cross-sell to them to make them profitable. However, if the size of wallet is small, then strict cost-control measures have to be taken in order to prevent losses for the firm.

Implementation outcome: When this strategy was examined with customers at four companies in various industries, results showed that loyal customers know their value to the company and demand premium service, believe they deserve lower prices, and spread positive word of mouth (WOM) only if they feel *and* act loyal. In the case of knowing their value and demanding premium service, the claim that loyal customers cost less to serve was debunked at a high-tech service provider when the firm invested $10 million annually to offer customized websites, sales, and service to its top 200 customers. Instead it was shown that loyal customers exploit their positioning to get premium service and discounts at a high expense to the firm. In addition, loyal customers expect to pay less for products and services. At a mail-order company where its regular customers paid 9 percent less than recent customers, the claim that loyal customers pay more than other customers was refuted. Furthermore, at a grocery retailer it was found that self-reported attitudinally loyal and behaviorally loyal customers were 54 percent more likely to praise the firm than customers with behavioral loyalty only. It is important for a firm to measure its customers' attitude as well as purchasing behavior in order to identify customers who will advocate for the firm.[8]

With this strategy in place, firms can aim to (*a*) build and enhance behavioral loyalty by focusing on each customer's purchase behavior and their respective contributions to firm profit, (*b*) cultivate attitudinal loyalty by studying customers' attitudes toward the firm through customer feedback and focus groups, and (*c*) link loyalty to profitability by using the CLV metric, and ensure a successful customer engagement. This would help companies to identify the high-value customers and spend limited marketing resources on them. In short, this implementation suggests that aiming for *profitable* customer loyalty bodes well for a company rather than just cultivating customer loyalty. As shown in Exhibit 4.1, IBM was able to successfully implement this strategy and ultimately increase its profits, by moving the resources from the Barnacles to the Butterflies.

Exhibit 4.1: Optimal Allocation of Resources at IBM

IBM provides an example of a company that has successfully implemented the CLV metric into a profitable customer engagement strategy. As one of the leading multinational high-technology firms providing hardware, software, and services to B2B customers, IBM chose to harness the advantages of the CLV metric in order to measure customer profitability and decide on the allocation of marketing resources. IBM used CLV to determine the level of marketing contact and outreach efforts through telesales, e-mail, direct mail, and catalogs on an individual customer basis. At the conclusion of this program (based on about 35,000 customers), IBM was able to effectively reallocate resources for about 14 percent of customers as well as increase revenues by

(Exhibit 4.1 Continued)

(Exhibit 4.1 Continued)

about $20 million. All of this was done without increasing the marketing investment by a cent and was accomplished through abandoning ineffective techniques based on the spending history in favor of the CLV metric. An increase in marketing efficiency and productivity derived from this CLV-based implementation are a prime example of the importance of this metric as part of the overall customer engagement strategies.

In the case of IBM, assessing customer value and managing the customer relationship to increase profitability was a primary objective of the firm. Prior to implementing CLV, IBM traditionally used a metric called Customer Spending Score (CSS). CSS was defined as the total revenue that can be expected from a customer in the next year. Based on this metric, IBM classified its customers into 10 deciles and targeted the top one or two deciles for engaging customers. Although the metric aimed to customize the level of contacts to each customer to ensure resource reallocation to their most valuable customers, it lacked in its ability to project future profitability of its customers. As such, IBM felt the need to move to a forward-looking metric such as CLV to overcome the shortcomings of CSS which focused primarily on revenues (top line) and ignored profitability (bottom line).

By implementing the CLV-based management framework, IBM was able to identify which customers to target, how many times to target those customers, and how to reallocate resources to those customers. An optimum contact strategy was developed for each customer using a genetic algorithm to find the optimal level of marketing contacts for each customer that would maximize the sum of expected CLVs of all the customers. Nearly a 160 percent increase in gross value showed that by optimally contacting the low value customers (as decided by the CLV metric), it is possible to derive high value from those customers. Ultimately, the CLV strategy engaged by IBM resulted in the reallocation of resources of about 14 percent of customers within a group of 35,000 customers. This resulted in about a $20 million increase in revenue without changing the level of marketing investment.

Since this strategy evaluated customers based on their future profitability and recommended appropriate marketing initiatives, IBM was able to understand: (a) the response levels of the customers to various channels of contact, and what the optimal contact mix is, and (b) the way to generate the most "bang for the buck" even if a mix of

(Exhibit 4.1 Continued)

(Exhibit 4.1 Continued)

communication strategies was used. Further, by carefully monitoring the customers' purchase frequency, the inter-purchase time, and the contribution of each type of customer toward profits, IBM was able to tailor their marketing initiatives in order to maximize CLV.

Source: Printed with permission and adapted from V. Kumar, Rajkumar Venkatesan, Tim Bohling, and Denise Beckmann, "The Power of CLV: Managing Customer Lifetime Value at IBM," *Marketing Science, 27*(4), July–August, (2008): 585–599.

Optimal Allocation of Resources

Need for the strategy: The optimal allocation of resources is a constant goal of firms as they are often constrained by limited marketing resources. Firms cannot allocate resources equally to all of their customers due to these limitations. As we have discussed previously, not all customers are equal in their loyalty or profitability to a firm. Taking these two facts into consideration, firms should invest their limited marketing resources only on their most loyal and profitable customers. However, many firms are often unable to achieve this balance in resource allocation as they have not successfully identified their most profitable and loyal customers and how resources should be spent on them to maximize their profitability. That is, most firms either invest in customers who are easy to acquire but are not necessarily profitable or try to increase the retention rate of all their customers, thereby leading to wastage of limited resources.

How it works: In order to optimally allocate their resources, firms must first identify their most profitable customers and those who are the most responsive to marketing efforts. Done at the individual customer level, the selection of the best mix of marketing channels to make contact with customers is determined, based on how responsive each customer is to the various channels of communication. The cost-effectiveness of these channels is also considered to measure their return in contacting the customers. The frequency, at which a firm should contact its customers with these channels, and at what intervals, is then decided by the firm in order to develop a contact strategy for its customers. Prior to developing the contact strategy, firms need to analyze the various factors that affect customer behavior such as upgrading to a higher product category and cross-buying in a different category. Analyzing customer behavior in relation to these factors provides firms with valuable information about the preferences and attitudes of its customers. By carefully monitoring the purchase frequency of customers, the inter-purchase time, and the contribution toward profit, managers can determine the frequency of marketing initiatives to maximize CLV through an optimal contact strategy.

Implementation outcome: By implementing an optimal resource allocation strategy, firms can determine how much is to be allocated to each customer and identify an optimal point where CLV is maximized by spending the right amount of marketing dollars and making the right number of contacts for each customer. For instance, should there be an increase in face-to-face meetings and a decrease in the frequency of direct mailers, or vice versa? When a resource allocation strategy that maximizes CLV was implemented in a B2B setting, it resulted in incremental revenue of about $20 million (see Exhibit 4.1).[9] Of the incremental revenue, nearly 40 percent came from high value customers who were actively interacting with firm and nearly 60 percent came from reactivated customers (who were previously "dormant") by allocating more marketing resources that exhibited high profit potential. It is clear that such a strategy is a significant step up from the traditional marketing methods of flooding customers with product promotions. This would not only save the company's valuable resources but will also prevent any customer estrangement due to repeated marketing communications. Exhibit 4.1 provides an example of the optimal allocation of resources.

Cross-buying Behavior

Need for the strategy: In this age of increased retail activity, the impact of cross-buying on firms' bottom line is anything but limited. Cross-buying refers to the degree to which customers buy products from a large number of available products or categories offered by a firm. When customers buy across product categories, they not only contribute to an increase in revenue for the firm, but also engage more with the firm, contribute profits, and increase their own switching costs. Therefore, the impact of cross-selling can be greatly improved if firms can identify and target the right customers who are most likely to cross-buy.

How it works: To identify the right customers who are likely to cross-buy, companies need to (*a*) understand the motivation of customers to cross-buy, (*b*) identify the drivers of cross-buy, and (*c*) observe whether cross-buy helps to improve revenue and other customer-based outcome metrics. In a recent study, we identified the drivers of cross-buy as exchange characteristics (average interpurchase time, ratio of product returns, and focused buying), firm marketing efforts, customer characteristics (demographics), and product characteristics (category of first purchase). Firms that understand the relationship these drivers have with cross-buy will not only be able to select customers who are more likely to cross-buy but also be able to contact them with the right amount of cross promotions and maximize the effectiveness of their marketing communications.

In the study, several key observations were made with regard to cross-buy and its drivers. The effect of the drivers of cross-buy is shown in Table 4.3. As shown, many of the variables have an inverted U-shaped relationship with cross-buy, indicating that customers who have intermediate levels of these variables are more likely to cross-buy.

Of particular interest are the variables of average interpurchase time and the ratio of product returns. In terms of average interpurchase time, it was found that customers who bought at intermediate durations are more likely to purchase from additional categories than customers who bought intensively. Thus, firms should target those customers who purchase at intermediate levels to maximize marketing dollars. Further, the residual dollars can be used to attract "highly profitable but low loyalty" customers (Butterflies) that may turn into attractive candidates for cross-selling or up-selling to remain with the firm longer.

The study also identified that after a certain threshold, product returns have a negative effect on cross-buying. The study suggests that the cause of this negative relationship is the result of a customer's lack of confidence in a firm. Other causes include the possible misuse of the return system by the customers, and/or a possible mismatch between customer expectations and firm offerings. In either case, the study explained that these customers are not attractive options for cross-selling or up-selling.

In addition, the study provides strong support for the effect of marketing efforts on cross-buy. Furthermore, the positive relationship seen with focus buying and cross promotion presents an opportunity for firms to benefit from targeting customers with specific products to encourage cross-buy. The findings

Table 4.3	Effect of the Drivers of Cross-buy	

Variable	Relationship	Effect
Exchange Characteristics		
Average Interpurchase Time	As average interpurchase time increases, cross-buy increases but decreases beyond a certain threshold	∩
Ratio of Product Returns	As the ratio of product returns increases, cross-buy increases but decreases beyond a certain threshold	∩
Focused Buying	As focused buying increases, cross-buy increases	+
Marketing Efforts		
Direct Mail	As the number of direct mailings increases, cross-buy increases but decreases beyond a certain threshold	∩
Cross Promotion	As cross promotion increases, cross-buy increases	+
Customer Characteristics		
Household Income	As the household income increases, cross-buy increases but decreases beyond a certain threshold	∩
Age of Head of Household	As age of head of household increases, cross-buy increases but decreases beyond a certain threshold	∩
Product Characteristics	Cross-buy depends on the category of first purchase	

Source: Printed with permission and adapted from V. Kumar, M. George, and J. Pancras, "Cross-Buying in Retailing: Drivers and Consequences," *Journal of Retailing, 84* (1), (2008): 15–25.

Note: The symbol ∩ shows the variables that have an inverted U-shaped relationship with cross-buy. This symbol represents a positive relationship up to a threshold, beyond which it turns negative.

from this study can help managers to devise strategies that can make high profitability/low loyalty customers remain with the firm for a greater duration.[10]

Implementation outcome: By observing the cross-buy behavior of its customers, a firm can identify its most profitable customers and increase the revenue contributions from existing customers. In the study, we found that customer-based metrics are significantly different for different levels of cross-buy. Observations are made based on (*a*) average revenues per order per customer, (*b*) average contribution margin per order, and (*c*) average orders per month. In terms of the average revenues per order per customer, the following was observed: purchased in one category—122.2, purchased in two categories—190.7 (56 percent increase over one category), purchased in three categories—239.9 (96 percent increase over one category), and purchased in four or more categories—352.9 (188 percent increase over one category). As can be seen, the average revenue per order per customer for any particular level of cross-buy is significantly higher (α = 5 percent) than that for the previous level. Similar differences can be seen with respect to average contribution margin per order and average orders per month. The average orders per month are: purchased from four or more categories—2.97 (significantly higher than three with a 78 percent increase), purchased from three categories—1.67 (significantly higher than two with a 53 percent increase), purchased from two categories—1.09 (significantly higher than one with a 148 percent increase), and purchased from only one category—0.44. These results show that an increase in the number of product categories purchased can positively impact a firm's performance. Therefore, it is essential for a firm to identify the customers to target for cross-sell and to enhance the drivers of cross-buy in order to increase firm profitability.[11]

Although cross-buy has the potential to increase profitability, firms can still encounter unprofitable customers despite taking efforts to promote cross-buying. A higher amount of customer cross-buying does not always result in higher customer profitability. In a recent study, this intriguing issue was raised and the following important research questions were studied: can customers who willingly purchase additional products and/or services of a firm be unprofitable? If so, what factor(s) can potentially characterize customers with unprofitable cross-buy? Can the collective action of such customers substantially impact the firm's bottom-line over time? In such a scenario, what are the implications for the firm's current marketing practices and policies that are typically directed at maximizing cross-buy opportunities across all customers of the firm?[12] This study offered three key insights:

- Customer cross-buy is not necessarily profitable for all customers of the firm and can adversely impact a firm's bottom line. Across the five firms that were studied, about 10 percent to 35 percent of the customers who cross-buy were unprofitable and accounted for 39 percent to 88 percent of the firms' total loss from their customers.

- Persistent adverse customer behavior drives unprofitable customer cross-buying over time. Across all five firms, the study found that customers who exhibited persistent adverse behavioral traits (such as repeatedly spending a limited amount with the firm, excessively returning previously purchased products, persistently demanding a higher level of customer service, and selectively buying products that are steeply discounted) generated more losses as they purchased more products and/or services from the firm over time. In contrast, customers with non-persistent adverse behavioral traits tend to eliminate their initial losses (if any) and generate more profits with an increase in cross-buy over time.
- A company's marketing policies and practices could facilitate (or deter) the persistency of adverse customer behavioral traits associated with unprofitable cross-buying. The study found that the firm with the most liberal product-return policy (amongst the five firms analyzed) had the maximum level of unprofitable cross-buying due to excessive product returns.

These findings have key implications for companies. First, apart from drawing our attention to positive consequences of cross-buying behavior they also highlight the negative consequences of customer cross-buy—an area that has received minimal attention in the marketing literature to date. Second, the findings call for managers to rethink their current managerial practice of maximizing cross-buy opportunities for all customers of the firm. This is imperative given the fact that firms typically hope to increase profits by encouraging customers to cross-buy and thereby engage more with them.

Pitching the Right Product to the Right Customer at the Right Time

Need for the strategy: Cross-selling is an important strategy for firms to increase customer retention and customer value. The impact of cross-selling can be greatly improved if firms can identify and target the right customers who are most likely to cross-buy. As such, identifying the customers who are most likely to cross-buy is the first and most important step in developing a successful cross-selling strategy. Further, the availability of limited resources makes it impossible for firms to target all existing customers for cross-selling.

As not all customers are likely to cross-buy, it is imperative for firms to identify customers who have a higher propensity to cross-buy. Doing so will ultimately maximize a firm's ROI in its various marketing activities, especially cross-selling.

How it works: In order to predict the purchase sequence of each customer, it is important to collect the following pieces of customer purchase information (*a*) in which product category the customer is likely to make a purchase, (*b*) at what intervals and what time periods the customer will make a purchase, and (*c*) how much the customer is likely to spend toward that purchase, or what the likely profit contribution is going to be. Answers to these questions and other customer-level data can then be processed through an advanced likelihood to purchase function to derive the purchases of different products at different times by different customers. This approach is an improvement over the traditional approach, which involves estimating the information regarding purchase timing and product purchase independently and then multiplying them to get the desired outcome. The problem associated with the traditional approach is that the errors associated with each term gets multiplied causing a larger error in the final outcome.

Implementation outcome: By implementing a cross-sell strategy that encourages customers to cross-buy, firms can increase customer engagement with the firm. Customers who engage in cross-buying behavior have a greater scope of interaction with the firm and make more purchases. In terms of interaction, customers who purchase with firms across various product categories demonstrate a high comfort level with the firm's offerings. The result is a strong customer–firm relationship in which the customer is less likely to terminate the relationship with the firm. When this new approach was tested in a B2B setting, 85 percent of the customers predicted by this model to make a purchase actually went on to do so. On the contrary, only 55 percent of the customers predicted by the traditional approach actually made a purchase. Further, the implementation of this strategy resulted in a 160 percent increase in ROI.[13]

While executing a customer-focused sales campaign, we also found that the strategy led to an increase in ROI and profits. By conducting a field study in the telecommunications industry, we found that revenues increased more than 2.5 times ($1,702) and profits increased more than four times ($2,681) with the customer-focused sales campaign. The ROI also doubled (1.9) after implementing the customer-focused sales campaign with the test group.

The magnitude of the improvements in revenue, profits, and ROI can be seen in Table 4.4. Overall, the test group customers provided the firm with more than $500,000 in incremental profits and $2.4 million in total profits. In comparison to the control group, which implemented a product-focused sales campaign, the test group's implementation of a customer-focused sales campaign also lead to a reduction in the marketing investment (–$2,190) and the number of contacts required to induce a purchase (–6). In addition, the relational metrics increased by an average of approximately 3.3 points (more than 63 percent).[14]

The improvements witnessed with the test group are attributed to the firms being able to identify the customers expected to purchase in each product category. Thus, this strategy suggests that efficient management of the purchase sequence not only increases revenue by accurately predicting and preempting a customer purchase, but also minimizes cost by reducing the frequency of customer contacts and promoting profitable customer engagement.

Table 4.4	Sales Campaign Comparison in Telecommunications Industry			
	Test Group: Customer-focused Sales Campaign		**Control Group: Product-focused Sales Campaign**	
Change in Metric	**Change in Metric**	**Base Level**	**Change in Metric**	**Base Level**
Financial Metrics				
Revenue ($)	1,702	13,181	671	13,252
Marketing investment ($)	–2,190	5,288	30	5,206
Contacts before purchase (#)	–6	17	2	18
Profits ($)	2,681	7,401	654	7,284
ROI ($)	1.9	1.4	0.11	1.4
Relational Metrics				
Firm understands my needs	3.58	4.92	–0.9	4.96
Firm provides good value	2.74	5.34	0.12	5.40
Likely to repurchase from the firm	3.52	5.42	0.38	5.36
Likely to recommend the firm	3.23	5.21	0.42	5.47

Source: Printed with permission and adapted from V. Kumar, R. Venkatesan, and W. Reinartz, "Performance Implications of Adopting a Customer-Focused Sales Campaign," *Journal of Marketing, 72*(5), (2008): 50–68.

Preventing Customer Attrition

Need for the strategy: Customer attrition, also known as churn, turnover, defection, is not looked upon favorably by any company. Monitoring customer behavior to predict and prevent attrition is a vital strategic action that firms should undertake to ensure that the most valuable customers are nurtured and retained. Profiling and analyzing customers to formulate effective retention strategies ultimately helps firms to increase their profitability as the old adage still holds true—it is less expensive to retain a current customer than to gain a new one. Further, the calculation of the likelihood to defect enables companies to make informed decisions about intervention offers that would make the customers stay on with the company. Typically, the questions that can be answered after calculating the probability to quit are: (*a*) Should we intervene? (*b*) Which customers to intervene with? (*c*) When to intervene? (*d*) Through which channel to intervene? (*e*) What to offer?

How it works: The above-listed questions can be answered by building a "propensity to quit" model. These models give us the probability of a customer quitting at a particular point in time. Based on when the customer is likely to leave and his/her ability to contribute profits, firms can provide appropriate intervention strategies that will aid retention. For instance let us assume that as of July, the model indicates the likelihood of Customer A to quit in September is 0.5 and in October is 0.8. Then, managers would have to determine whether Customer A is worth retaining. This can be answered by applying the CLV metric. Business wisdom would suggest that only profitable (positive CLV) customers be intervened with offers. In this case, if Customer A is profitable, then she has to be intervened with an offer in the beginning of August. Regarding the details of the intervention offer, managers can again use the CLV metric to guide them. If Customer A has a CLV of $150, it would not be appropriate to intervene with a $200 offer. Therefore, the intervention offer will have to be less than $150.

Implementation outcome: To prevent customer attrition, a proactive intervention strategy is necessary to address those customers who show a strong need for intervention. The use of churn models enables managers to execute timely, customer-specific marketing interventions that result in an increase in ROI. Companies who implement a churn model are able to prevent attrition by identifying customers who are showing signs of leaving. Furthermore, the deployment of customer level strategies to prevent customer attrition can lead to greater cost and profit efficiencies through optimizing resource allocation. For instance, the effect of the customer intervention strategy was studied in a telecom firm using a test group (group on which the intervention strategy was tested) and a control group (group which had no intervention strategy) comprising of 2,601 customers in each group. At the end of the first year, the control group lost 833 customers while the test group lost only 190 customers. In effect, the test group saved 643 customers. At an average revenue contribution per customer of $600, these 643 saved customers translated into a revenue gain of $385,800 for the firm. When the cost of the intervention offer of $40,000 was deducted from this revenue gain, the firm gained an incremental profit of $345,800 with an ROI close to 860 percent.

Product Returns

Need for the strategy: Product returns have long since been regarded as undesirable for an organization. Apart from reflecting the discontent of customers with the firm's offerings, they increase service costs and result in decreased margins. Although companies who employ lenient product return policies can have a competitive advantage, a lenient policy is not always ideal as it can lead to more returns and to customers abusing the policy, which can end up costing the firm instead of being a benefit. Companies must strike a balance in their return policy, which allows customers to freely return unwanted items without the policy being taken advantage of by customers who excessively make returns. In this regard, it is important to identify the optimal amount of product returns to help companies better manage the returns process.

How it works: The optimal amount of product returns can be identified by addressing these three key questions in the firm–customer exchange process: (*a*) What factors affect customers' return behavior? (*b*) How does customers' return behavior influence their future buying behavior and the firm-initiated marketing communication plans? (*c*) Should firms consider product returns as a necessary evil in the exchange process?

This calls for identifying the drivers that lead to product returns. A recent study found empirical support to suggest that (*a*) products received as gifts are less likely to be returned than products not received as gifts, (*b*) products purchased during the holiday season (i.e., November and December) are more likely to be returned than products purchased during the rest of the year, (*c*) products purchased in new categories within the same distribution channel are more likely to be returned than products purchased in familiar categories within the same channel, (*d*) products purchased in new distribution channels within the same product category are less likely to be returned than products purchased in familiar channels within the same product category, (*e*) products purchased in new channels and new categories are more likely to be returned than products purchased in familiar channels and/or familiar product categories, and (*f*) products purchased on sale are less likely to be returned than products purchased at the regular price.

Implementation outcome: While identifying the drivers of product returns are helpful, knowing the consequences of product returns can also be revealing to the companies. The study found evidence to suggest that (*a*) the amount of product returns is positively related to the amount of products purchased in the future, up to a threshold (an inverted U-shaped effect), and (*b*) the amount of product returns is negatively related to the amount of marketing communications a customer receives in the future. The study also showed that although product returns cost the firm in terms of both profits from sales and reverse logistics, up to a threshold, an increase in product return behavior increases future customer purchase behavior.

For instance, for a catalog retailer, the optimal percentage of product returns that maximize firm profits was 13 percent, or a decrease in product returns by 3 percent from the current level of the retailer. It was also found that increases or decreases from the optimal product returns of 13 percent significantly reduced profits. A decrease in product returns beyond 13 percent decreased profits slowly (at 1 percent, or 15 percent below the current amount of product returns, profit is $63,937). In contrast, an increase in product returns significantly decreased profits (at 31 percent, or 15 percent above the current amount of product returns, profit is $20,608). Yet, the results do not imply that a firm should change its return policy as a changing the return policy can also impact customer buying behavior. Instead the firm should seek to implement marketing campaigns to help decrease customer product return behavior by taking into consideration the drivers of product return behavior.[15]

The degree of returns depends on the degree of spending. As such, customers who make returns could be customers who are spending more with the firm. Return policies allow customers to interact and engage with the company. A no-hassle return policy motivates a greater number of customers to get involved with the firm through the return process. Combined with appropriate customer service, this opportunity can be turned into a positive engagement experience for the customer, thereby strengthening the customer–firm relationship and encouraging future purchases. In limited numbers, product returns could indicate a healthy relationship with the customer, because it shows that the customer is willing to communicate with the firm and connect with its channels. Furthermore, marketers can target and manage customers by taking information about both their purchase and return behaviors into account. In effect, up to a threshold, a lenient product return policy is more likely to go a long way in engaging with customers than a strict product return policy.[16]

Managing Multichannel Shoppers

Need for the strategy: Due to the increased complexity of distribution systems and the growth of web-based sales, firms are appealing to diverse customer segments by spreading themselves across various channels. Customers often engage through different channels such as retail stores, brick-and-mortar stores, the Internet, or by mail-order catalogs. Each of these channels services a different set of customers and provides varying levels of service. By reducing service costs, managers can increase a firm's profitability and customer engagement. For instance, Eddie Bauer found that customers who shopped with them through all three channels (brick-and-mortar stores, catalogs, and the Internet) bought five times more than other customers.[17] The multichannel strategy suggested here extends beyond the Eddie Bauer finding and demonstrates that multichannel shoppers initiate more contacts with the firm, stay with the company for a longer duration, purchase more frequently, and are more receptive to contacts through multiple communication channels.

How it works: To effectively manage multiple channels, firms have to first identify who the multichannel shoppers are by studying the drivers associated with purchase behavior across multiple channels. After identifying the drivers, the firms have to determine whether multichannel shoppers are (*a*) more likely to buy in the future, (*b*) spend more money, and (*c*) more profitable than single-channel customers. These answers would help firms determine the profitability of the multichannel customers. Finally, a mere profitability analysis of single-channel versus multichannel customers is not enough. Managers would want to ascertain which channel a customer is likely to adopt next and when this is likely to happen. This information can be obtained by studying (*a*) the travel cost involved in purchasing and immediate product availability, (*b*) the total quantity of items a customer purchases in a single shopping trip, in which product categories, the level of price discounts, and the amount of product returns, (*c*) the customer's purchase frequency and the frequency of marketing communications, and (*d*) customer demographics such as age, gender, and income.

Implementation outcome: Recent research on the topic of multichannel shopping has revealed that identifying the drivers of multichannel shopping can produce important insights in managing this behavior. When this strategy was tested with a large B2B computer hardware and software manufacturer, the customer-specific drivers showed that (*a*) customers who buy across multiple product categories are likely to purchase across multiple channels, (*b*) customers who purchase across multiple product categories are good prospects for adopting new channels, (*c*) up to a certain threshold product returns are positively related to multichannel shopping, beyond which they are negatively related with multichannel shopping, (*d*) customers who initiate contacts with the supplier are more inclined to shop across multiple channels, (*e*) customers who use the online medium are also inclined to shop across multiple channels, (*f*) customers who have been with the firm for a longer period of time are more likely to shop across multiple channels than new customers, and (*g*) customers who have a high purchase frequency are associated with multichannel shopping. With respect to the supplier-specific drivers, the study found that (*a*) the number of different channels used to contact the customer, (*b*) the type of contact channel, and (*c*) the channel mix are strongly associated with multichannel shopping. Regarding customer demographics, variables such as the number of customer-service employees, the annual sales of the company, and the industry category it belongs to can be used to profile customers who are likely to shop across multiple channels.

When the study compared the value of single-channel and multichannel shoppers across various customer-based metrics, the results showed that as a customer shops across more channels (from one channel to four channels), she spends more revenue with your firm, spends a higher proportion on your firm (rather than with a competitor), has a higher past profitability (which is correlated with future profitability), and has a higher likelihood of buying in the future. Table 4.5 shows the results from the study.

The results from the study indicate that for all four of the customer-based metrics—Revenue, SOW, PVC, and Likelihood of Staying Active—the average of at least one of the groups is significantly different from the averages of the other groups.

In terms of revenue, exponential increases are observed as the number of channels a customer shops increases. From customers who shopped in one channel to customers who shopped in two channels, there is a 35 percent increase in average revenue. Yet, from two channels to three channels there is a 131 percent increase and from three channels to four channels an increase of 353 percent in average revenue is observed. Similar increases can be seen in the average PVC—from one channel to two channels: 63 percent, from two channels to three channels: 107 percent, and from three channels to four channels: 320 percent. The figure also clearly indicates that the SOW of multichannel shoppers is much higher compared to the SOW of single-channel shoppers— ranging from 20 percent for single-channel shoppers to 72 percent for shoppers in four channels. The likelihood to stay active also increases as the number of channels shopped increases with the probability ranging from 0.11 for single channel to 0.67 for four channels. These results show that multichannel shoppers are more profitable than single-channel shoppers.[18]

Table 4.5	Average Customer-based Metrics of Single-channel and Multichannel Shoppers			
	Shopped in Single Channel	**Shopped in Two Channels**	**Shopped in Three Channels**	**Shopped in Four Channels**
Revenue ($)	4,262	5,736	13,250	60,076
Share of Wallet	0.20	0.35	0.48	0.72
Past Customer Value	6,671	10,874	22,472	94,456
Likelihood of Staying Active	0.11	0.15	0.38	0.67

Source: Printed with permission from V. Kumar and R. Venkatesan, "Who Are the Multichannel Shoppers and How Do They Perform? Correlates of Multichannel Shopping Behavior," *Journal of Interactive Marketing, 19*(2), (2005): 44–62. Copyright by the Direct Marketing Educational Foundation, Inc., published by Elsevier Inc.

Finally, regarding the choice and timing of channel adoption, a B2C apparel retailer found that the duration to adopt another channel is shorter when (*a*) the travel cost involved in the current channels is higher, (*b*) customers' basket sizes (purchase quantities in a single shopping trip) are either very small or very large, (*c*) the level of buying across product categories is higher, (*d*) the level of price discounts a customer obtains is higher, (*e*) single-channel customers make intermediate levels of returns than customers who make very few or too many returns, (*f*) the purchase frequency is higher, and (*g*) the frequency of marketing communications to the customers is at an intermediate level. However, the duration to adopt another channel is longer when (*a*) the proportion of products the customer is able to consume immediately after purchase in the customer's current channels is higher, and (*b*) the number of returns made by a customer shopping across two channels is higher. With respect to customer demographics, the study found that (*a*) the male customers were found to have shorter channel adoption duration and the female customers took 17 percent longer than the time taken by male customers to adopt a new channel, and (*b*) income is not related to channel adoption behavior.[19]

Linking Investments in Branding to Customer Profitability

Need for the strategy: Brands add value to companies. There are numerous examples of how consumers blindly pursue brand names while they shop. Apple, Samsung, IBM, and Coke, to name a few, are great examples of how brands can influence the buying power of consumers and how brand value can contribute to the sustained success of a business. Why does this happen? Ideally, brands are developed to perform three important roles: (*a*) to draw new customers to the firm, (*b*) to remind existing customers about the products/services it offers, and (*c*) to forge an emotional attachment with its consumers.[20] When brands start to perform poorly on one or more of these roles, the brand starts to lose its sheen and falters. When a brand starts to face such hiccups, the brand manager or the marketing manager, and in some cases the entire corporate board faces some dilemma. Some of these questions include: (*a*) What do we invest on building brands or building the customer base? (*b*) How do we manage the brand? (*c*) What can we do to renew our relationship with our customers? The single answer to all these questions is to strengthen the brand and nurture profitable customer relationships simultaneously. How can we achieve this?

How it works: It is possible to strengthen a brand by ascertaining and increasing the value a customer provides to the brand. This value is referred to as the CBV. The CBV refers to the total value a customer attaches to a brand through his or her experiences with the brand over time.[21] CBV is comprised of a customer's brand knowledge, brand attitude, brand behavior intention, and brand behavior. Eight constructs are introduced within these four measures:

- Brand knowledge is made up of a customer's awareness of the brand (*brand awareness*) and a customer's image of the brand (*brand image*).
- Brand attitude is made up of a customer's trust in the brand (*brand trust*) and a customer's emotional response toward the brand (*brand affect*).
- Brand behavior intention is made up of a customer's intention to purchase a brand (*purchase intention*).
- Brand behavior is made up of a customer's repeat-buying behavior (*brand loyalty*), relationship with other customers of the brand (*brand advocacy*), and willingness to pay a price premium over other brands (*brand price premium behavior*).

Based on these eight constructs, it has been found that customers with greater brand value are more likely to engage in activities that result in an increase of CLV when compared to customers with low brand value. In other words, a customer's brand knowledge, brand attitude and brand behavior intentions affect his/her brand purchase behavior. When this brand purchase behavior of a customer is linked to their lifetime value, a firm can expect to maximize profitability.

The link between CBV and CLV is established using customer-level data and advanced modeling techniques. Earlier sections in this chapter have discussed the CLV computation based on the customer transaction database. To compute CBV, firms can get information regarding the various components of CBV from survey data. A survey that contains questions pertaining to the eight constructs can yield the firm information necessary for computing CBV. Once this information is available, the next step is to estimate how these components affect each other by using sophisticated estimation techniques.

The components of CBV are obtained using a 10-point scale from a sample of customers. For the same customers, CLV is computed at that time. Conceptually, the CLV score is modeled as a function of these eight constructs.

Implementation outcome: Firms that understand the link between CBV and CLV can efficiently allocate resources to generate maximum value. Simultaneous growth in brand equity and customer equity are achieved through the optimization of CLV. Consider the example of a customer, Jessica, whose observed CBV is below average and whose CLV is $15,000 at the time of the observation. When steps are taken to further engage Jessica, the firm is able to see shifts not only in Jessica's CBV, which is optimized to higher scores but also in her CLV, which increases to $18,000. This example of Jessica is analyzed in more detail in the subsequent chapter when the relationship between CLV and CBV is further discussed.

In terms of customer acquisition and retention, firms can prioritize their existing customers based on CLV and analyze the profile of customers with high brand value to target potential customers with similar profiles. When a new customer purchases from the firm, the potential brand value of that customer can be predicted by comparing it to an existing customer with a similar profile. In addition, a firm can redesign its communication strategies to better cater to the needs of its customers once it has identified how its customers value the brand. Chapter 5 discusses, in detail, the relationship between CBV and CLV.

Acquiring Profitable Customers

Need for the strategy: In terms of customer acquisition, the profitability of a customer is an important value for the firm to quantify. Understanding how firms acquire customers and the best metric to use while acquiring those customers is essential for firms to maximize their overall profitability. There are several issues that can plague firms when seeking to acquire new customers. These issues include the (*a*) law of diminishing returns, (*b*) short-term versus long-term outlook, (*c*) treating acquisition and retention strategies independently, and (*d*) relying too much on current customers. Firms that address these issues are able to overcome the pitfalls associated with balancing acquisition and retention efforts in order to attract and keep the most profitable customers. In addition, firms that use customer referral as a strategic tool to acquire new customers are able to capitalize on the value offered through effectively engaging their current customers.

How it works: To overcome the issues surrounding customer acquisition, it is important for managers to realize that (*a*) after a certain point, the cost of acquiring and/or retaining an additional customer outweighs the future stream of profit accrued from that customer, (*b*) focusing on customers who are easy to acquire and easy to retain may improve short-term profitability, but will not hold out in the long run, and (*c*) acquiring all possible customers and retaining all customers will lead to wastage of marketing resources on some customers who will never be profitable. A recent study investigated the following to better understand these issues:[22]

- How do we allocate resources between the different contact modes for acquisition and retention, under a budget constraint?
- Between acquisition and retention expenditures, which is more critical to ensure profitability?
- What is the impact of choices in communication channels on investment effectiveness?

Using the concept of CLV, the study proposed the introduction of an Allocating Resources for Profit (ARPRO) framework that would help firms decide which customers are worth chasing and which dormant customers should be pursued to come back to the firm. Firms using this strategy can use customer profiles to identify customers who are most likely to be profitable and should be acquired and retained.

Implementation outcome: The question of focusing on acquisition versus retention often arises when managers are faced with budget cuts. For instance, when the pharmaceutical company that the study investigated was faced with a 5 percent total marketing budget cut, one way to tackle this would be to cut 5 percent from the acquisition and retention budgets. When both budgets are reduced in such a fashion, the study found that for every $1 underinvested in the relationship, the optimal long-term profitability would be reduced by $1.25.[23] However, if the company chose to cut only the acquisition budget (say, a 25 percent cut) and not touch the retention budget, the study found that every $1 underinvested in the relationship would reduce the customer's optimal long-term profitability by $3.03. Further, the study found that reducing the acquisition and retention budgets by 10 percent (a $2 profit loss for every $1 cost savings) is better than reducing the total budget by reducing acquisition budget only (a $3 profit loss for every $1 acquisition cost savings).[24] While this study shows that the equal decrease in spending for acquisition and retention would result in a higher long-term customer profit (than a budget cut in acquisition spending alone), it is important for companies to perform analysis internally of how deviations in spending affect overall profitability.

Regarding the impact of choices in communication channels on investment effectiveness for a B2B service provider, the study found that if the service provider allocated 80 percent of the number of communication instances to e-mail, 11 percent to telephone contacts, 7 percent to web-based contacts, and 2 percent face-to-face contacts, it would maximize customer profitability. In the case of using multiple channels to communicate, the study also found that in over one-third of the cases (37 percent) when telephone interactions and e-mail messages are used simultaneously profits are maximized. Additionally, the study found that sending email messages and employing face-to-face contact simultaneously would maximize profitability in 67 percent of the cases.

Interaction Orientation

Need for the strategy: Nowadays marketing managers are expected to demonstrate the profitability of their marketing actions down to the level of their individual customers and on an ongoing basis. At the same time, customers expect firms to customize products and services to meet their demands. Although firms still need to produce superior products and offer better services, it will be the ability for firms to better interact with customers that will allow them to differentiate themselves from the competition in the future. From a marketing strategy viewpoint, this boils down to the difference between a product-centric approach and a customer-centric approach.

Traditionally, firms have used a product-centric approach, which focuses on making and selling superior products. With this approach, firms focus entirely on the products ignoring the customer's needs and wants. Evolving from the product-centric approach, firms recognized the need to design products according to customer needs and started implementing the market-centric approach. Although the market-centric approach shifted the focus from products to the customer, there was still a need to further engrain the customer as an integral part of a firm's marketing strategy. As such, a customer-centric approach that employs interaction with customers is imperative for a firm to maintain future profitability.

How it works: A recent research study addressed this under-researched area of marketing-interaction orientation by creating a construct for interaction orientation and identifying the antecedents of interaction orientation.[25] There are several components of the interaction-oriented approach that firms can utilize to increase its impact on a firm's profitability. First, the *customer concept* proposes that the unit of every marketing action or reaction is an individual customer. This firmly places the customer at the top of the hierarchy in the customer-firm relationship. By doing so, firms are able to observe customer behavior and respond appropriately. Second, the *interaction response capacity,* the degree to which a firm can provide successive products or services based on previous feedback from customers, highlights the importance of firms being attentive to and promptly addressing customer needs. Third, the *customer empowerment* component refers to the extent to which a firm allows its customers to (*a*) connect with the firm and design the nature of transaction and (*b*) connect and collaborate with each other by sharing information, praise, and criticism about a firm's product and services. Finally, the *customer value management* component refers to the extent to which a firm can quantify and calculate the individual customer value and use it to reallocate resources to customers who will add higher value in the future.

Implementation outcome: Interaction orientation helps firms develop organizational resources for successful management of customers. By adopting these measures, firms can customize their products and services by better understanding the needs of their customers. This leads to increased customer satisfaction, generates positive WOM, and leads to acquiring and retaining profitable customers. Further, firms are also able to develop the ability to foresee customer response and plan marketing activities for longer periods of time. These customers can be developed into a skilled resource for the firm by helping the firm acquire new customers through referrals and WOM. As a result, firms that implement interaction orientation strategies start exhibiting superior aggregate-level business performance. This is achieved by maximizing the profit of the firm across all customer segments and business units. IBM and American Express have successfully adopted the interaction orientation. Their endorsement of practices, consistent with the elements of interaction orientation and recent business performance, demonstrate the managerial significance of an interaction orientation.

Viral and Referral Marketing Strategies

Need for the strategy: It is evident that not only can customers contribute to the firm through their own transactions (direct profit), but they also have an impact on the transactions of other customers through WOM and referrals (indirect profit), and both can increase the value of that customer to a firm. In this regard, companies should design and implement viral and referral marketing strategies to unlock the "hidden" profit potential of their customers by harnessing the influence and social connections of the customers on their peers.

How it works: The concept of customer referral value (CRV) is ideal for implementing this strategy. As introduced in Chapter 2, CRV is defined as the monetary value associated with the future profits given by each referred prospect, discounted to the present value.[26] This metric enables managers to measure and manage customer referral behavior. This dictates that customers need to be valued based on their indirect impact on the firm's profits, through savings in acquisition costs and the addition of new customers by way of customer referral. This metric and the subsequent referral campaigns that can be developed based on the metric is best suited for B2C settings wherein, customers refer other customers via a referral campaign (usually in an offline format) to join the company.

While the concept of referral programs is popular in the B2C setting, recent research has developed a similar concept that can be applied in the B2B context also. The new metric known as business reference value (BRV) is the monetary value associated with future profits as a result of the extent of a client's reference influencing a prospect to purchase.[27] Using this concept, companies can now design and implement strategies to encourage their clients to provide references to their business partners to engage the services of the focal company and also measure the effectiveness of such campaigns. Chapter 6 discusses in detail the concepts of CRV and BRV and the specific strategies and implications of using them in marketing campaigns.

Companies have also begun realizing the important role that social media platforms can play in connecting with their target consumers and creating an engaging brand experience. Because of this realization many companies are now looking for ways to create and optimize their social media strategies and measure the success of their marketing efforts. In this regard, recent research has proposed a seven-step guide to implement and measure a social media marketing strategy's ROI, and the value of a customer's WOM.[28] With new and innovative metrics that measure customer influence, companies can implement viral online marketing campaigns on social media to assess key performance indicators such as the campaign's ROI, sales revenue generated, and any increases in brand awareness.

One such metric is customer influence effect (CIE), which measures the net influence and quantifies a user's WOM value in a social network and predicts the user's ability to generate the spread of viral information. Taken a step further, customer influence value (CIV) links the WOM measured through CIE to the actual sales generated from a customer's influence. More specifically, CIV refers to the monetary value of a customer's social media influence on other acquired customers and prospects discounted to present value.[29] Chapter 7 discusses, in detail, the concepts of CIE and CIV and the approaches companies can adopt in profitably engaging with customers through social media.

Implementation outcome: In implementing a referral marketing program, a financial services firm and a telecommunications firm found that less behaviorally loyal customers tend to have a stronger impact on referring new customers when compared to more behaviorally loyal customers. They also observed that the referral process is not only able to bring in customers without excessive marketing expenses; it is also able to bring in customers who are not likely to join through traditional advertising and promotions by the company. Across the two industries, it was evident that the campaigns targeted to increase referrals can play a key role in acquiring new customers and increasing profitability. Knowing the drivers of CRV is instrumental in capitalizing on the referral process and can significantly help firms to target the right customers for referral marketing campaigns.

Observed through research with a retail store, the average CRV for low-CRV customers before and after the referral marketing campaign further demonstrated the impact that targeted communication can have on a customer's CRV and CLV. The average CRV of the customers in the control group increased only by 10 percent (from $192 to $212). In contrast, the average CRV of the targeted customer group showed a three times greater increase (30 percent—from $191 to $249) during the test period. In addition, the customers who increased their CRV also on average increased their CLV indicating that when providing referrals customers also in turn increase their purchasing behavior.[30]

When campaigns seeking to promote business references were implemented at a financial services firm and a telecommunications firm, they found that on average over 50 percent of the purchase decisions for both the firms were influenced by the client references. Further, on an average, converted prospects reported only one or two clients as key references in influencing their decisions to adopt the services of the focal firm. Finally, on average the converted prospects who joined during the one-year time period of the field test were profitable customers for both the firms.[31] These results clearly indicate that marketing strategies designed to encourage referrals/references can be successfully implemented at B2C/B2B firms to profitably engage with the customers.

In terms of influence, when an online viral marketing campaign was implemented at an ice-cream retail chain, results indicated that about 23 percent of the total revenue was attributable to conversations on Twitter while about 80 percent was attributable to Facebook (with a 3–8 percent overlap between the two social networks). Overall, the campaign was a huge success with the retailer realizing an increase of 49 percent in brand awareness, 83 percent in ROI, and a 40 percent share of the total growth in sales revenue.[32] These results indicate that businesses can grow sales, profits, brand awareness, and positive WOM when they engage with their customers who are influential on social media platforms.

FUTURE OF CLV

The CLV framework relies on the customers' attitudinal and behavioral information. Based on the richness of the customer transaction data and the demographic and psychographic information, this framework gains even more refinement. The CLV framework is also expected to undergo further sophistication and improvement. Improvements are expected in (*a*) measuring CLV, (*b*) a better understanding of the antecedents or drivers of CLV, and (*c*) emergence of the evidence regarding the importance of using CLV to measure customer engagement. The formula for calculation of CLV has improved in the past years significantly. However, considering the dynamic nature of the purchase behavior of customers more sophisticated models that incorporate the conditional effects of changes in the amount and quality of marketing-mix need to be developed. Development and extension of other meaningful strategies involving CLV in addition to the ones discussed in this chapter and a deeper understanding of their relationships with lifetime value will be of immense help to companies aiming to profitably engage with customers. Though recent studies have shown the impact of using CLV as a better metric for profitable customer engagement, many firms continue to use traditional metrics. One possible reason may be the inertia to move away from the accepted practices while another reason is the lack of empirical evidence supporting the impact of the use of CLV on profitability. With more firms adopting the CLV framework for customer engagement strategies, CLV is expected to gain wide spread acceptability as the preferred metric for valuing customer engagement.

LOOKING BEYOND CLV

The CLV is a direct means to measure the value of a customer to a firm in the future, and thereby a strong indicator of the level of customer engagement with the firm. Taking into account the total financial contribution of a customer, CLV captures the value of a customer in terms of that customer's future profitability to a firm. However, a customer's value to a firm is not limited to the direct impact of that customer. Customers can also affect the profitability of other customers of a firm through their activities and behavior.

In addition to purchase transactions, a customer's ability to refer other customers to the firm, power to positively influence other customers about the firm's offerings, and knowledge about the firm's product/service offerings in providing feedback to the firm need to be considered when measuring the total value of a customer to a firm. As a result, firms should consider the influence of these indirect factors of customer engagement; CRV, CIV, and CKV, and their relationship with CLV which can further quantify the value of a customer to a firm. These elements will be addressed in the upcoming chapters.

In terms of direct influence, the link between CLV and CBV is also an important relationship for a firm to consider. As demonstrated in the previous chapters, CBV is the foundation of the CEV framework and plays a vital role in customer engagement with its interaction with the behavioral metrics, particularly CLV. Given that the interrelationship between CLV and CBV can have such a profound influence on a firm's growth, the next chapter will discuss, in depth, the impact that branding has on customer value and how firms can capitalize on that relationship.

NOTES AND REFERENCES

1. W. Reinartz and V. Kumar, "The Mismanagement of Customer Loyalty," *Harvard Business Review, 80*(7), (2002): 86–94.
2. V. Kumar, *Managing Customers for Profit: Strategies to Increase Profits and Build Loyalty* (Upper Saddle River, NJ: Pearson Education, 2008).
3. Bain & Company Net Promoter System, "How to Calculate Customer Lifetime Value," http://www.netpromotersystem.com/resources/toolkit/customer-lifetime-value.aspx (retrieved on February 15, 2013).
4. V. Kumar, *Managing Customers for Profit* (Philadelphia, PA: Wharton School Publishing, 2008).
5. W. Reinartz and V. Kumar, "The Impact of Customer Relationship Characteristics on Profitable Lifetime Duration," *Journal of Marketing, 67*(1), (2003): 77–99.
6. For a detailed discussion on the drivers of CLV in B2B and B2C settings, please refer to R. Venkatesan and V. Kumar, "A Customer Lifetime Value Framework for Customer Selection and Resource Allocation Strategy," *Journal of Marketing, 68*(4), (2004): 106–125; V. Kumar, D. Shah, and R. Venkatesan, "Managing Retailer Profitability: One Customer at a time!" *Journal of Retailing, 82*(4), (2006): 277–294.
7. R. Venkatesan and V. Kumar, "Customer Lifetime Value Framework for Customer Selection and Resource Allocation Strategy," *Journal of Marketing, 68*(4), (2004): 106–125.
8. Reinartz and Kumar, "The Mismanagement of Customer Loyalty."
9. V. Kumar, R. Venkatesan, T. Bohling, and D. Beckmann, "The Power of CLV: Managing Customer Lifetime Value at IBM," *Marketing Science, 27*(4), (2008): 585–599.
10. V. Kumar, M. George, and J. Pancras, "Cross-Buying in Retailing: Drivers and Consequences," *Journal of Retailing, 84*(1), (2008): 15–25.
11. Ibid.
12. D. Shah, V. Kumar, Y. Qu, and S. Chen, "Unprofitable Cross-buying: Evidence from Consumer & Business Markets," *Journal of Marketing, 76*(3), (2012): 78–95.
13. V. Kumar, R. Venkatesan, and W. Reinartz, "Knowing What to Sell, When, and to Whom," *Harvard Business Review, 84*(3), (2006): 131–137.
14. V. Kumar, R. Venkatesan, and W. Reinartz, "Performance Implications of Adopting a Customer-Focused Sales Campaign," *Journal of Marketing, 72*(5), (2008): 50–68.
15. J.A. Petersen and V. Kumar, "Are Product Returns Necessary Evil? Antecedents and Consequences," *Journal of Marketing, 73*, (2009): 35–51.
16. J.A. Petersen and V. Kumar, "Can Product Returns Make You Money?" *Sloan Management Review, 51*(3), (2009): 85–89.

17. J. Dyché, *The CRM Handbook: A Business Guide to Customer Relationship Management* (1st ed.) (Boston, MA: Addison-Wesley Professional, 2001).

18. V. Kumar and R. Venkatesan, "Who Are the Multichannel Shoppers and How Do They Perform? Correlates of Multichannel Shopping Behavior," *Journal of Interactive Marketing*, *19*(2), (2005): 44–62.

19. R. Venkatesan, V. Kumar, and N. Ravishanker, "Multichannel Shopping: Causes and Consequences," *Journal of Marketing*, *71*(2), (2007): 114–132.

20. R.T. Rust, K.N. Lemon, and D. Narayandas, *Customer Equity Management* (New Jersey: Pearson Education, Inc., 2004).

21. V. Kumar, A.M. Luo, and V.R. Rao, Connecting brands with customers: An integrated framework. Working Paper (as of 2013), Georgia State University.

22. J. Thomas, W. Reinartz, and V. Kumar, "Getting the Most out of All Your Customers," *Harvard Business Review*, July–August, (2004): 116–123.

23. It is important to note that acquisition and retention expenditures represent different proportions of the total budget. For instance, a 10 percent deviation in the acquisition budget from the optimal level would represent only a 2.11 percent deviation from the optimal budget.

24. W. Reinartz, J. Thomas, and V. Kumar. "Balancing Acquisition and Retention Resources to Maximize Profitability," *Journal of Marketing*, *69*, (2005): 63–79.

25. G. Ramani and V. Kumar, "Interaction Orientation and Firm Performance," *Journal of Marketing*, *72*(1), (2008): 27–45.

26. V. Kumar, J.A. Petersen, and R.P. Leone, "Driving Profitability by Encouraging Customer Referrals: Who, When, and How," *Journal of Marketing*, *74*(5), (2010): 1–17.

27. Ibid.

28. V. Kumar, V. Bhaskaran, R. Mirchandani, and M. Shah, "Creating a Measurable Social Media Marketing Strategy for Hokey Pokey: Increasing the Value and ROI of Intangibles & Tangibles," *Marketing Science* (forthcoming).

29. Ibid.

30. Kumar, Petersen, and Leone, "Driving Profitability by Encouraging Customer Referrals," 2010.

31. V. Kumar, J.A. Petersen, and R.P. Leone, "Defining, Measuring, and Managing Business Reference Value," *Journal of Marketing*, *77*(1), (2013): 68–86.

32. V. Kumar and R. Mirchandani, "Can Your Customers Also Be Successful Marketers for You?" *MIT Sloan Management Review* (forthcoming).

Chapter 5

Linking Brand Value to Customer Value

Find answers for...
<ul><li>How to link customer brand value to customer lifetime value?</li><li>What are the effects of linking customer brand value to customer lifetime value?</li><li>How to implement strategies to segment customers based on their customer brand value and customer lifetime value?</li></ul>

In order to focus on growth in brand as well as customer equity, managers need to link the customer brand value (CBV) with the customer lifetime value (CLV). Since not all customers are equally profitable, by linking CBV to CLV, managers can assess the value of the brand in the mind of the customer, thereby targeting the right set of brand messages to achieve higher returns on the marketing investments for that customer.

HOW TO LINK THE BRAND VALUE TO CUSTOMER VALUE

In the previous chapters, we discussed the various components of CBV and CLV. In this chapter, we shall explore the modeling techniques used to link these components. Various components of CBV can be obtained from survey data and the various components of CLV can be obtained from customer transaction data. Sophisticated estimation techniques are used to estimate how these components affect each other. In doing so, the components of CBV are calculated using a five-point scale. The sample customer data and CLV are calculated for the same set of customers. The following equations map out the interactions between these components.[1]

How the Various Components of CBV Are Linked

- Brand Attitude = function of (Brand Knowledge)

$$Trust = f(Awareness, Image) \qquad \text{(Equation 5.1)}$$

$$Affect = f(Awareness, Image) \qquad \text{(Equation 5.2)}$$

- Brand Behavior Intention = function of (Brand Attitude)

$$Pintent = f(Trust, Affect) \qquad \text{(Equation 5.3)}$$

- Brand Behavior = function of (Brand Behavior Intention)

$$Loyalty = f(Pintent) \qquad \text{(Equation 5.4)}$$

$$Pprice = f(Loyalty) \qquad \text{(Equation 5.5)}$$

$$Advocacy = f(Loyalty) \qquad \text{(Equation 5.6)}$$

How CBV and CLV Are Linked

- CLV = function of (Brand Behavior)

$$CLV = f(Pprice, Advocacy) \qquad \text{(Equation 5.7)}$$

These equations explain how an individual's brand knowledge (brand awareness and brand image) translates into brand attitude (brand trust and brand affect), brand purchase intention, brand behavior (brand loyalty, premium price behavior and brand advocacy), and finally to his or her lifetime value to a firm. The Seemingly Unrelated Regression (SUR) methodology is used to estimate these equations. SUR utilizes the correlations amongst the errors in the above-mentioned equations to improve the estimates. Genetic algorithms are then used to achieve the optimal level of CBV based on the coefficients obtained from the above-mentioned equations, so that a customer's lifetime value is maximized under the budgetary constraints of a firm.

Once the equations are estimated, the connection between the CBV and CLV can be further examined. First, the brand behavior (brand advocacy and premium price behavior) needs to be optimized in order to maximize

CLV. Hence, in order to increase a customer's level of brand awareness and to encourage a favorable brand image, appropriate brand messages need to be sent to him or her. Brand trust and brand affect increases with an increase in favorable brand knowledge. In addition, brand purchase intention will be positively affected and revealed through behavioral brand loyalty (increase in purchase frequency). Finally, a truly loyal customer will not only advocate the brand but also be willing to pay a premium price for the quality of the product.

As such, monitoring all the components of CBV becomes important. Brand building is the most important as it eventually leads to brand behavior, which induces favorable behavior outcomes such as longer duration, higher purchase frequency, higher contribution margin, and customer referral. A customer's lifetime value is calculated based on the behavior outcomes, as mentioned earlier. When components of CBV are simultaneously optimized, CLV scores are maximized for that customer. With this understanding, managers can work on optimizing components of CBV so that an individual's CLV score improves.

THE ROLE OF BRAND COMMUNICATION IN LINKING BRAND AND CUSTOMER VALUE

Communication plays a vital role in linking CBV to CLV. Planned and unplanned marketing communications such as word of mouth, product messages, marketing-mix activities, corporate activities, and marketing initiatives all constitute brand communication and contribute to messaging.[2] There are several types of communication that firms can release via various outlets to further promote their brands and encourage customer engagement. For example, corporate events are the best platform to communicate business practices, overall philosophies, and mission statements among other factors. In terms of product messaging, the product performance, price, and choice of distribution channel form the core of what is communicated to the customer. However, exceptional brand communication does not automatically guarantee an increase in CBV. CBV is highly dependent on customer satisfaction and therefore, the actions of a firm must align with the communication that a firm puts out. Ultimately, customer satisfaction (or dissatisfaction) goes a long way in deciding a customer's brand knowledge.

STRATEGIC IMPLEMENTATION OF MANAGING BRANDS AND CUSTOMERS

As discussed in Chapter 2, managing both brands and customers simultaneously can be overwhelming for managers. Hence, we outline a seven step approach in this chapter for streamlining the monitoring of the overall performance of CBV. Each step is carefully evaluated to devise appropriate strategies to achieve positive growth in both CBV and CLV. For instance, if a customer's brand awareness and brand image are known to be low, companies can develop product trail initiatives to build awareness and invest in advertising to build on the brand image. The strategic implementation of managing brands and customers through a seven-step approach is shown in Figure 5.1.

The seven suggested steps are discussed as follows:

Step 1: Measure CLV for the customer base. In the first step, the CLV of each customer is measured to categorize the customer base. The customers put in deciles, rank ordered by their CLV values, so that the resulting sample provides a good variation. The segmentation allows managers to identify the firm's most profitable customers.

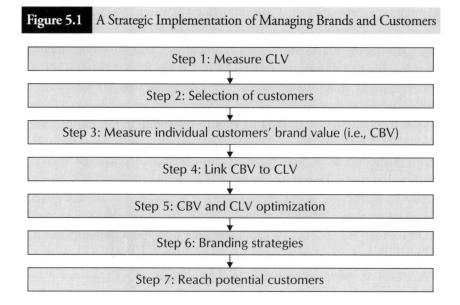

Figure 5.1 A Strategic Implementation of Managing Brands and Customers

Step 1: Measure CLV

Step 2: Selection of customers

Step 3: Measure individual customers' brand value (i.e., CBV)

Step 4: Link CBV to CLV

Step 5: CBV and CLV optimization

Step 6: Branding strategies

Step 7: Reach potential customers

Step 2: Select a sample of customers. In step two, a sample of customers is selected from each decile using a systematic sampling technique wherein 10 percent of customers from each decile are included in the sample.

Step 3: Measure their CBV. Next, a survey is carried out with each customer in the sample to obtain information on the components of his or her brand value (i.e., the components of CBV). The firm can pick the channels through which the survey can be administered.

Step 4: Link CBV to CLV. Following the measurement of CBV, a customer's CBV is linked to their CLV and an importance or weight for each component of brand value is obtained. To obtain this weight and to establish the link with CLV, an analysis is performed on all brand value components and steps are taken to improve their impact.

- First, examine the brand knowledge of each customer to see how much brand knowledge is transferred to the creation of a positive attitude for each customer.

  a. Build brand awareness through product trials.
  b. Build brand image through advertising.

- Then, examine the brand attitude of each customer to see how much brand attitude is transferred to an increase in purchase intention for each customer.

  a. Build brand trust through product trials.
  b. Build brand affect through advertising.

- Then, examine the purchase intention of each customer to see how much brand purchase intention leads to brand loyalty.

  a. Build purchase intention through promotion.

- Lastly, examine the purchase behavior of each customer to see how much brand behavior leads to CLV.

  a. Build brand loyalty through loyalty programs
  b. Build brand advocacy through referral program
  c. Build premium price behavior through advertising

Step 5: Optimize CBV and CLV. After examining the various components of the CBV, companies will be able to comprehend the brand value of each customer. As a next step, companies need to evaluate their branding strategies in order to optimize CBV. By addressing pitfalls that may exist in the current brand communications, companies can further strengthen their brand and eventually maximize the CLV of its customers.

We implemented this framework for a financial services firm. We measured the CBV scores for their customers. One of their customers' (Jessica) score on the various components of CBV is shown in Figure 5.2. The figure suggests that Jessica, with a moderate level of brand awareness and brand image, trusts the brand but has no attachment to it. Moreover, she scores low on brand behavior (due to her low scores on premium price intention, brand loyalty, and brand advocacy). In order to maximize Jessica's CLV, the firm should measure the individual attributes of Jessica's brand value and take steps to optimize various factors of her brand value. Optimized values are shown in Figure 5.3. As a caution, a firm needs to bear in mind its budget constraints in order to optimally allocate resources to optimize the various factors of her brand value.

Figure 5.2 Jessica's Measured Brand Value

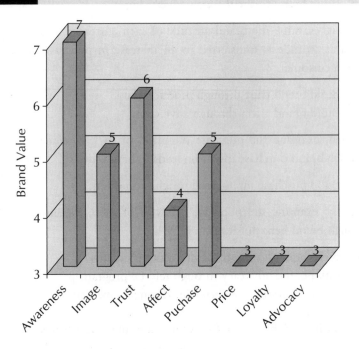

Figure 5.3 Jessica's Estimated and Optimized Brand Value

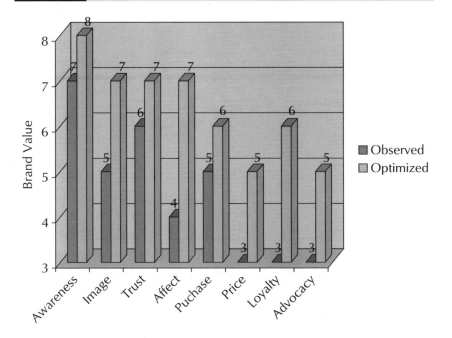

Once the brand value components are optimized, the firm can use these optimized values to devise strategies to better communicate with the customer. If a component increases in the optimized scenario as a result of an increase in another component, the firm can capitalize and develop strategies like sending personalized messages, devising awareness programs, and building a strong brand image depending on the component under consideration.

The focal firm under consideration in this example sent out an invitation for Jessica to join the loyalty program with an aim to build her brand loyalty. Post implementation of the new brand management strategies, the focal firm realized that Jessica's CLV curve improved significantly as shown in Figure 5.4. Such an increase was driven directly by increasing Jessica's brand value. By the firm implementing these brand value strategies, Jessica's CLV score increased from about $12,000 to about $18,000, and the cost of implementing these customized strategies for Jessica was about $600. The ROI on implementing these strategies for Jessica is 10 (on a scale value from 1 to 10), or 1,000

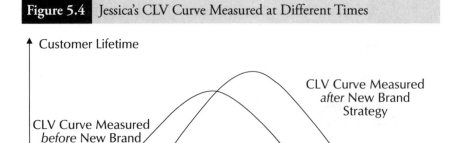

Figure 5.4 Jessica's CLV Curve Measured at Different Times

percent. Hence the approach suggested provides clear step by step guidance in order to maximize CLV by optimizing some of the brand value components.

For any firm, the idea behind successful implementation of brand management strategies is to maximize a customer's lifetime value. This is driven by a brand in all three stages of the customer life cycle: acquisition, retention, and attrition, as shown in Figure 5.5. As the customer moves from acquisition to retention, the firm needs to alter its strategies of dealing with that customer. Similar strategies devised for a customer in the retention phase are different from strategies adopted in the attrition phase. At the acquisition stage, the focus is on building the brand knowledge of that customer, developing a favorable image and encourage positive brand behavior intentions. However, in the retention stage, a firm would focus on maintaining and updating the current brand knowledge by sending repeated personalized brand messages. Loyalty programs and brand communities can be looked at as an example for developing a positive brand image and favorable brand behavior intentions. It is critical for companies to predict when the customer will move to the attrition stage. This can be done by observing the CBV components closely. Appropriate strategies to retain and win back the lost customers should be developed.

There are three main paths for reaching a customer: marketing communications, corporate activities, and marketing-mix activities as shown in Figure 5.5. An optimal allocation of a firm's marketing resources across these three paths should be developed in order to attain maximum value.

Figure 5.5 Customer Life Cycle Brand Management: An Integrated Framework

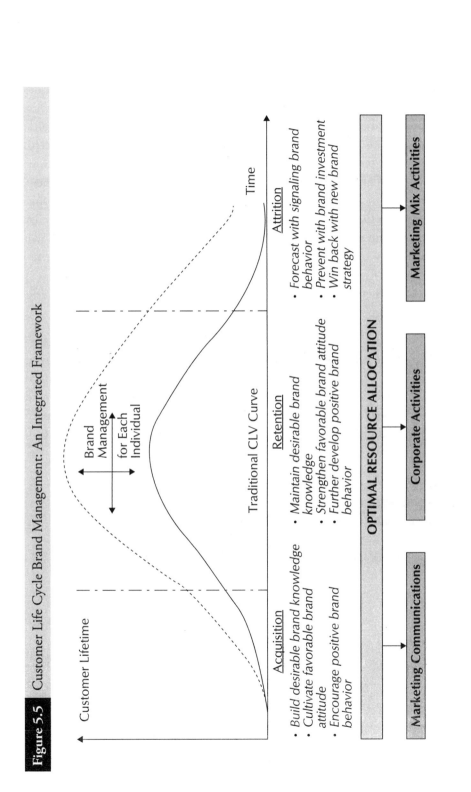

Customer Lifetime

Brand
Management
for Each
Individual

Traditional CLV Curve

Time

Acquisition
- *Build desirable brand knowledge*
- *Cultivate favorable brand attitude*
- *Encourage positive brand behavior*

Retention
- *Maintain desirable brand knowledge*
- *Strengthen favorable brand attitude*
- *Further develop positive brand behavior*

Attrition
- *Forecast with signaling brand behavior*
- *Prevent with brand investment*
- *Win back with new brand strategy*

OPTIMAL RESOURCE ALLOCATION

| Marketing Communications | Corporate Activities | Marketing Mix Activities |

Step 6: Implement branding strategies. In this step, segmentation strategies based on brand value and customer value are implemented. Segmenting customers based on brand value and customer value is very important because it allows firms to see which of their customer segments should be targeted. To segment the customers into a representative sample appropriately, companies can compute customer's CLV and CBV of a sample of customers. Then, rank order the customers by their CLV scores and take a median split to segregate them as high CLV customers and low CLV customers. Similar groupings are made for customers with high CBV and low CBV, as shown in Figure 5.6.

- Customers with a high CLV score and high CBV score are called *True Loyalists*.

  a. These customers are highly engaged with the brand. Their current perception as well as the future contribution is expected to be strong. Therefore, the strategy should be to continue investments to maintain the high brand value and continue to build positive brand knowledge and attitude so that they have high purchase frequency and brand loyalty. This favorable brand behavior is expected to turn into a high CLV score for that customer.

Figure 5.6 Segmentation Strategies to Manage CLV and CBV

ACQUAINTANCES	TRUE LOYALISTS
• Increase Brand Investment • Build Customer Relationships	• Brand Investment to Maintain High Brand Value • Nurture the Customer Relationship
STRANGERS	**POOR PATRONS**
• Kill the Brand if no association • Invest in the Brand if association exists	• Align the Brand with the right customer segment

- Customers with a low CLV score and high CBV score are called *Poor Patrons.*

  a. These customers have high brand value but are not expected to remain loyal to the brand. The strategy here should be to align the brand with the right customer segment. Also, encourage cross-buy and add-on selling to boost the customer's CLV score. In spite of having favorable brand knowledge, attitude, purchase intention, and brand behavior; the potential contribution of these customers to firm profitability is limited.

- Customers with a high CLV score and low CBV score are called *Acquaintances.*

  a. These customers have potential in the future, but are not considering the brand to be high value currently. Their awareness, knowledge, attitude, purchase intention and/or brand behavior is not strong. The strategy here should be to invest in brand management and engagement activities to push these customers into being *True Loyalists* as these customers have a good profitability potential.

- Customers with a low CLV score and low CBV score are called *Strangers.*

  a. These are customers who are not at all engaged with the brand currently. The firm should identify customers who have a potential high value (CLV) within this segment and should invest in brand building efforts for these customers. The firm should also reconsider their investments for customers who neither have any potential value nor value the brand highly at present.

Step 7: Reach potential customers. Understanding the link between CBV and CLV can enable firms to efficiently allocate their resources to generate maximum value by effectively communicating with customers. By linking these factors to the final customer behavior outcomes, firms can thus link the CBV of their customers and their CLV in order to reach the right customers. A clear understanding of the various factors that affect CBV and its link to CLV enables firms to take appropriate corrective measures to simultaneously build both the customer's CBV and CLV.

The following implementations will help to better understand the usefulness of the framework.

Telecommunication

We implemented the framework in one of the firms in the Telecommunication industry. The firm's objective was to target their customers who fall under *Acquaintances* with low advocacy and devise appropriate strategies to migrate these customers from being *Acquaintances* to being *True Loyalists*. Basically, the objective was to increase the CBV score so that customers can contribute more to the profitability of the firm. The firm identified a set of customers with a high CLV score but a low CBV score due to low ratings on advocacy, and initiated a campaign. The campaign involved the following four actions completed by the firm:

- Emphasized the importance of referrals to these customers by providing great incentive programs to participate in.
- Provided the customers with a $20 incentive for each referral.
- Waived a month of service if the referrals further reached out to three to four new customers.
- Improved their communication channel and reached out to customers by using direct-mail, followed by direct-mail communication again after two weeks.

Figure 5.7 summarizes the results from the campaign. As a result of the campaign, out of 29 percent *Acquaintances*, 9 percent of them moved toward *True Loyalists* with an increase in CLV. Moreover, as seen in Table 5.1, the ROI for the campaign was around 9.2 percent.

While the 20 percent out of the 29 percent customers in the *Acquaintances* region remained *Acquaintances,* the results provide clear directions in terms of the strategies to be implemented for each of the two buckets of customers. A firm can segregate its strategies and look at the 20 percent and the 9 percent customers differently to maximize their potential profitability.

Financial Services

A similar study was conducted for one of the firms in the financial services sector. The results are shown in Tables 5.2 and 5.3. These customers received a personal communication in the form of a direct mail that included

Figure 5.7 Migration from Acquaintances toward True Loyalists

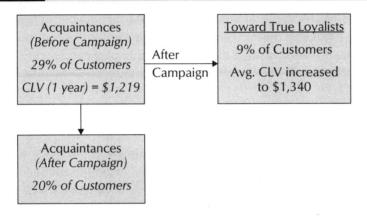

Table 5.1 ROI of the Campaign—Telecommunications

	Profit (CLV)	Cost	ROI
Telecommunications	$248,400	$27,000	9.2

Table 5.2 ROI of the Campaign—Financial Services

	Profit (CLV)	Cost	ROI
Financial Services	$191,250	$22,500	8.5

Table 5.3 Expected Gains in CLV—Financial Services

	1 Million Customers	10 Million Customers
Projected	CLV ($ million)	CLV ($ million)
1 year	6.6	66
3 years	19.9	199

offers for bundling one or more products such as savings accounts, checking accounts, and investment accounts. To follow up and increase the likelihood that the offer was received by the customer, the financial services firm sent an additional piece of direct mail within two weeks; in addition, the company telephoned a sample of these customers to provide answers to any questions regarding the additional services and the value of subscribing to multiple products/services. The projected gains in CLV at the end of Year 1 and Year 3 were attributed to the successful implementation of the CBV framework.

Retailer

A retailer of Brand X approached us to comprehend the reasons for the firm's stagnant growth over a period of time. The profits and the revenues for the retailer had not increased faster than the category which resulted in loss of market share for the retailer. We proposed a solution to alter the marketing mix and devise appropriate strategies at the firm level to impact the customer's perception and thereby their purchase intention. This can bring in additional revenue for the firm. An in-depth customer-level understanding is also extremely critical in this situation to be able to optically allocate the marketing budgets and reap the benefits of customers contributing to the profits of the firm. We suggested the earlier mentioned seven-step process to understand the customer and brand value better. While the store level data was used to calculate the CLV of the customer, in order to understand the CBV, a sample survey was conducted with the decision maker of the household. Each of the eight CBV components was calculated using a series of questions asked to the customer on a 10-point scale. The sample results are explained below. The numbers below are for illustration purposes only. For more details, please contact the author of the book.

Brand Awareness and Image

Tables 5.4 and 5.5 show the results for brand awareness and brand image of Brand X retailer, respectively. From the numbers displayed below, it is clear that while the retailer enjoys a strong brand awareness and positive brand image at the overall level, recognition of the brand and the positive image for the negative to low CLV segment is relatively lower. In such a scenario, the retailer needs to invest in a campaign specifically targeting the negative to low

Table 5.4	Brand Awareness of Brand X Retailer

Customer Segments Based on CLV	Recognition	Recall
Super High	6.35	5.33
Medium to High	5.25	5.05
Negative to Low	4.07	4.25

Table 5.5	Brand Image of Brand X Retailer

Customer Segments Based on CLV	Quality Perception	Customer Expectation	Company Perception
Super High	6.2	6.3	6.4
Medium to High	5.6	5.3	5.3
Negative to Low	4.15	4.1	4.3

CLV segment, to build brand awareness and brand image for the customers in this segment.

Brand Trust and Affect

Tables 5.6 and 5.7 show the results for brand trust and brand affect for Brand X retailer, respectively. Retailer of Brand X is a trusted retailer with encouraging scores across the segments. Reliability perceptions can be improved across the CLV segments as per the data in Table 5.6. Since the lower CLV segments also display a high level of brand trust and brand affect the retailer of Brand X needs to consider up-selling in order to drive profitability.

Brand Purchase Intention

Table 5.8 displays the results for brand purchase intention across the CLV segments. Middle and lower CLV segments display lower intention to purchase and the retailer can consider cross-selling and up-selling strategies to

Table 5.6 Brand Trust of Brand X Retailer

Customer Segments Based on CLV	Trust	Brand Honesty	Brand Reliability
Super High	6.35	6.32	4.1
Medium to High	6.21	5.9	4.1
Negative to Low	6.1	5.8	4.1

Table 5.7 Brand Affect of Brand X Retailer

Customer Segments Based on CLV	Feel Good Factor	Product Satisfaction	Brand Affinity
Super High	6.21	6.1	6.1
Medium to High	5.7	5.9	5.9
Negative to Low	5.1	5.3	5.2

Table 5.8 Brand Purchase Intention of Brand X Retailer

Customer Segments Based on CLV	Purchase Intention	Purchase Intention over Competition
Super High	6.2	6.3
Medium to High	5.12	5.13
Negative to Low	4.57	4.69

build purchase regularity and thereby increase firm profitability. Another way of increasing the regularity of purchase could be by offering deals at regular intervals and keeping up with the purchase cycle.

Brand Loyalty

Table 5.9 displays the results for Brand Loyalty across the CLV segments. Other than the Super High CLV segment, loyalty scores are relatively lower for the rest of the segments. In order to improve the loyalty scores for the lower segments, the retailer can initiate loyalty programs for the customers in

Table 5.9	Brand Loyalty of Brand X Retailer	

Customer Segments Based on CLV	Loyalty	Brand Preference
Super High	6.2	6.3
Medium to High	4.7	4.92
Negative to Low	4.86	4.88

these segments. This can impact the overall loyalty perceptions and thereby build the CLV of that customer.

Premium Price Behavior

Table 5.10 displays the results for premium price behavior for Brand X across the CLV segments. While the price perceptions about Brand X being offered at a reasonable price are steady across segments, customers are not extremely positive about the price increases. This set of customers could be price sensitive and hence the retailer should carefully evaluate their past strategies. The retailer of Brand X is currently not considered a seller of premium brands and hence the retailer should consider branding its products appropriately to improve premium price perceptions.

Brand Advocacy

The results for brand advocacy are shown in Table 5.11. The retailer of Brand X should consider increasing their presence in the social media as the scores for brand community are low across the segments. As the customers

Table 5.10	Premium Price Behavior		

Customer Segments Based on CLV	Value Perception	Willingness to Pay Slightly More	Willingness to Pay a Higher Price over Competition
Super High	6.27	4.8	4.1
Medium to High	5.87	4.49	4.93
Negative to Low	5.82	4.4	4.9

Table 5.11	Brand Advocacy		
Customer Segments Based on CLV	**Interaction with Other Customers in Social Media**	**Word-of-mouth Communication**	**Brand Advocacy**
Super High	4.3	4.3	4.2
Medium to High	3.2	3.51	3.98
Negative to Low	3.2	3.08	3.9

are willing to talk about the brand, the retailer should also consider investing in referral programs for such customers who can bring prospects to the firm.

While the customers across the CLV segments displayed strong brand awareness, brand image, brand trust, and brand affect; the purchase intention, brand loyalty, premium price behavior and brand advocacy scores are relatively lower. Based on all the above scores, the CBV for the customer can be calculated as discussed in Chapter 3. Taking into account the allocation of marketing budgets and the availability of resources, firms can develop appropriate marketing strategies to increase the CBV score and thereby CLV score for a customer.

CONCLUSION

This chapter provided a comprehensive overview of how brand value and customer value can be linked to shed light on the exact segment that the firm needs to build in order to further engage customers and increase the profitability of a firm. The directional results obtained from measuring CBV can help firms to develop strategies to strengthen the relationship that a customer has with a particular brand, which can ultimately enhance the customer-firm relationship. By building upon the customer–firm relationship, firms can positively impact the behavior of its customers to increase transactions and to maximize a firm's profits as seen with the interrelationship of CBV and CLV.

In the upcoming chapters, we will discuss the indirect measures of CRV, CIV, and CKV and their effect on a firm's bottom line. The interrelationship amongst these concepts will also be discussed in order to demonstrate the impact that each metric can have on each other.

NOTES AND REFERENCES

1. V. Kumar, A.M. Luo, and V.R. Rao, Connecting brands with customers: An integrated framework. Working Paper (as of 2013), Georgia State University.
2. Ibid.

Chapter 6

Customer Referrals

Find answers for...

- How do we account for the referral behavior of customers while designing customer specific strategies?
- How do we measure the indirect contribution (referrals, word of mouth) made by customers toward the firm's profits?
- How do we measure this contribution in a business-to-business setting?
- How do we maximize profitability using referrals and recommendations?

INTRODUCTION: VALUING THE WORD THAT GOES AROUND

While the customer lifetime value (CLV) metric has been shown to accurately predict the value a customer is likely to provide in the future, it does have one main limitation as a complete measure of a customer's value—the inability to measure a customer's attitude. Even if modern customer relationship management (CRM) systems collect data on customer attitudes, such as in the form of surveys, these attitude measurements are often excluded from the estimation of CLV. However, it is necessary to consider the customers' attitudes toward a firm and its offerings to obtain a comprehensive view of the customers' value for the firm.

It is clear that not only can customers contribute to the firm through their own transactions (direct profits), but they also have an impact on the transactions of other customers through word of mouth (WOM) and referrals (indirect profits), and both can increase the value of that customer for a firm.

In a recent study,[1] it was shown that less behaviorally loyal customers tend to have a stronger impact on referring new customers when compared to more behaviorally loyal customers. It was also shown that the referral process is not only able to bring customers without excessive marketing expenditure, it is also able to bring customers who were not likely to join because of traditional advertising and promotions by the company. When designing a marketing strategy to target our highest value customers, we need to consider the actual value that each customer can bring to the table in terms of both direct and indirect profits.

In recent years, technology advancements in database implementation have created an innumerable amount of new avenues through which firms can improve their own engagement processes as well as that of their customers. This is particularly true for the customer referral value (CRV) metric, which is the monetary value of a customer associated with the future profits given by each referred prospect, discounted to the present value, as defined in Chapter 2. Compiling information on customers' attitudinal and referral behaviors is fundamentally crucial for CRV as, by compiling this information, firms are able to encapsulate the customers' referral values through demographic profiles based on data collection. What makes these processes both attractive and relevant is that customer attitudes, and the CRV metric, are becoming increasingly important as interconnectedness amongst customers (both potential and existing) increases. Building relationships with customers who serve as "ambassadors" of a firm's brand is an ever-growing tool, implemented with the goal of vicariously entering peer-to-peer conversations.

Companies such as the mobile phone operator, Sprint (Figure 6.1) and online brokerage, Scottrade (Figure 6.2) offer incentives to the referring customer, or both the referring customer and customers who have been referred. Many well-known financial institutions like Citibank India also encourage its home loan customers to refer new customers by offering incentives to the referring customers.[2] Existing home loan customers of Citibank India thus become unpaid salespersons for Citibank India as they promote the brand amidst their friends and relatives. Citibank India benefits in two ways from this: (*a*) customers spread good will and (*b*) though Citibank India pays customers for their referrals, the amount they pay is far less than what they would pay an employee. It is interesting to witness companies incentivizing customers based on the number of successful referrals. HSBC in China, as part of their referral campaign—"2013 Member-Get Member Programme"[3]—are

Figure 6.1   Sample Referral Program by Sprint

Source: Sprint. (2013). Sprint Referral Rewards, https://refer.sprint.com/public/home.pg (retrieved on February 15, 2013).

Figure 6.2   Sample Referral Program by Scottrade

Source: Scottrade. (2013). Free Trades—Referral Program, http://www.scottrade.com/online-brokerage/referall.html (retrieved on February 15, 2013).

rewarding customers depending on the number of successful referrals. With gifts being categorized under three tiers, customers can now win low value to high value items depending on the number and quality of their referrals. For instance, successful referral of two new Advance customers or successful referral of a new Premier customers will receive a gift in B category (i.e., their middle category), whereas a successful referral of four new Advance customers or successful referral of two new Premier customers will receive a gift in A category (i.e., their top category). Thus, promoting positive WOM and CRV through incentive programs is becoming commonplace, and techniques for doing so are becoming progressively differentiated and innovative.

However, the greatest difficulty in implementing the CRV metric lies in optimizing the profitability of the firm's efforts. Although customers may emerge very positively from an experience with the firm and may have the intention to refer, research[4] suggests that most customers will not actively engage in expressing their sentiment with other customers. Of those that do engage in conversations, not all conversations are acted upon by the receiver(s). In light of this, firms must identify those customers who have high CRV and engage them in becoming profitable "ambassadors" for the company/brand.

A classic example of this is Panasonic.[5] In 2009, prior to the important Consumer Electronics show, Panasonic hired the consulting company, Crayon, to provide them with influential bloggers to attend the show. These bloggers, reputable amongst their own fan bases and followers for their candidness, were not urged to write positive reviews, thus eliminating the conflict of interest and skepticism regarding positive commentary. However, by encouraging these hand-selected, high-CRV customers to take control of the brand-oriented conversations and steer them, Panasonic was able to broaden its reach and pitch their product to new customer bases from a neutral party.[6] This approach made customers and prospects of Panasonic respond in a better fashion than they would in a traditional incentive-driven sales pitch.

CONCEPTUAL BACKGROUND

Before defining CRV, it is essential to introduce some concepts on which it builds upon, which include WOM marketing, customer referrals, referral programs, and the referral process.

WOM Marketing

WOM marketing is a way of building active consumer-to-consumer and consumer-to-marketer communications. In WOM marketing, consumers provide information to other consumers, who can become potential customers of the product/service they received the information about. WOM marketing techniques are based on the concepts of customer satisfaction, two-way dialog, and transparent communications. The basic elements are educating the customers about the firm's products/services, and identifying people who are most likely to share their opinions. WOM can be facilitated so firms should encourage their customers to communicate and share information about the firm and its offerings. By carefully monitoring and listening how, where, and when opinions are being shared, firms can find both positive and negative opinions about their products or services and use them constructively. By implementing WOM marketing techniques, they can make it easier for customers to tell their friends, and they can ensure that influential individuals know about the good qualities of their products/services. Customers are sometimes the biggest champions in an overly communicated world, so WOM marketing done by loyal customers is very valuable.

Customer Referrals and Referral Programs

Customer referrals are a type of positive WOM communication by the customers of a firm regarding its products. Since it is generated from people who are using the firm's products or services, it is essentially positive WOM in the form of "this is good, you should try it too!" Given the value of customer referrals, companies should manage, measure, and encourage them through dedicated programs, known as referral programs. In the context of referral programs, a referral is a firm-incentivized recommendation from a current customer (referring customer or referrer) to a prospect (referred customer) about trying the firm's products/services. In contrast to customer-initiated WOM, referral programs are associated with a reward for the customers. The referral process, shown in Figure 6.3, starts when a current customer (customer A) talks to his or her friends, family, coworkers, or other social contacts (customers B, C, and D) about the firm's product or service. When the prospects become customers, the referring person (customer A) receives a reward.

| Figure 6.3 | The Customer Referral Process |

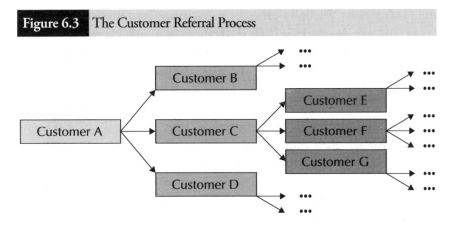

Next, the new customers can participate in the referral program and start referring the company to their own social network (customers E, F, G, etc.), so they eventually become referrers as well. Businesses are able to boost the number of high-quality customers by implementing their own creative customer referral programs and providing incentives for people to recommend their products to others.

Referral programs encourage referral behavior by offering one of many different types of incentives, mainly depending on the firm and its product/service offerings. Some of the most popular incentives include free service, free products, credit, points, vouchers, gifts, discounts, or cash. These rewards are usually extended to either the referring customers or both the referring and the referred customers. According to research, offering rewards to the referring customers is effective in motivating referrals to weak ties in a customer's network, but when the reward is extended to the prospects too, customers are more likely to make referrals to stronger ties in their network as well.[7] Therefore, with the right amount of rewards, firms can expand their customer base for less and, at the same time, increase existing customer satisfaction.

Increasing the testimonials of current, satisfied customers is a highly effective way of gaining more regular customers with a profitable lifetime value. The inputs and outputs are easier to measure because the number of referrals resulting in new customers and the amount spent obtaining those referrals can be tracked and quantified. Microsoft[8] has created "Windows U Crew," a program that sets up a contract with college students to promote the firm's newest Windows products in exchange for prizes that include a laptop and software package. This method can minimize the costs associated with funding customer referral programs and still generate high quality customers. In fact, considering the costs associated with traditional acquisition techniques—like advertising or direct mail—referrals allow firms to acquire new customers for much lower costs than using traditional methods.[9] In addition to lower acquisition costs, the referred customers are a source of future revenue through their future purchases from the firm. Therefore, referrals provide a great opportunity to invest on and derive customer value.

Given all the benefits of referral programs, it is no surprise that they are becoming increasingly popular among many firms in different industries, including education. Ashworth College,[10] a distance learning institute that offers online high school and college degree programs, has implemented a referral program to attract new students through referrals from their current students. Referrers are awarded $50 cash or account credit per new referred customer that successfully enrolls in one of the institute's programs, with a limit of two paid referrals ($100) per year (Figure 6.4).

Figure 6.4	Sample Referral Program by Ashworth College

Source: Ashworth College. (2012). Refer A Friend Make $50. http://www.referashworth.com/ (retrieved on February 15, 2013).

The Value of Referred Customers

A question arises at this point: Are customers who are recruited through referral programs more valuable than customers acquired through traditional methods? A recent study on referral programs[11] attempted to answer this question. In addition, it investigated whether this difference is enough to cover the expenses related to referral programs, where this difference comes from and if it is sustainable. These questions were answered using customer data from a financial services firm that ran a referral program. Specifically, information on all the customers that were acquired through referrals during one year ($n = 5,181$) and a sample of customers acquired traditionally during the same year ($n = 4,633$) was used. From this data, information about each individual's contribution margin, to capture profitability, and retention, to capture loyalty, was obtained for a period of 33 months. The referral program of the bank provided an initiative to referring customers for each referred customer that they recruited. This reward was a €25 voucher that could be redeemed at many retailer stores, and it applied for every new customer account that they brought to the firm. The referral program and its rewards were promoted to the customers in store, through the staff and print information, and by direct mail.

The results of this study support the notion that referred customers are more profitable than non-referred customers. Specifically, the daily contribution margin of referred customers is ¢7.6 higher than that of traditionally acquired customers. This difference amounts to €27.74 per year, and it represents an overall 25 percent increased profitability of customers acquired through referrals compared to other customers. The contribution margin difference is actually higher in the beginning of the customer's relationship with the firm (at ¢19.8 per day), but it gradually decreases. It eventually fades after around 29 months from the time of acquisition. This means that overall, referred customers are more profitable, although this difference is much stronger in the short term and it gradually disappears in the long term. This contribution margin differential is also enough to cover all the costs that are associated with the referral program (incentives and management), so that the overall acquisition cost for each referred customer is around €20 less than the traditional acquisition cost per customer.

Regarding the length of the customers' relationship with the firm, referred customers were found to have higher retention than other customers. In particular, referred customers are 18 percent less likely to leave. Most importantly, the higher retention levels exhibited by customers acquired through referrals remain as high for the entire time. This shows that, due to the referral process, referred customers are more attached and more loyal to the firm. As a consequence of higher margins and loyalty, referred customers' observed value to the firm (based on their purchase activity) is much higher than that of other customers. In particular, referred individuals have an observed value of almost €50 more than traditionally acquired customers, or they are 25 percent more valuable to the firm, based on their actual purchases.

Given that referred customers are more profitable on the short term and have a lower churn on the long term, does their higher value endure throughout their lifetime with the firm? In other words, is their CLV higher? Indeed, the CLV (without acquisition cost savings) of referred customers, for a period of six years after acquisition, was found to be almost €40 higher than the CLV of other customers, which represents a 16 percent higher value. Adding the savings in acquisition costs, which in this case were €20 per customer, the CLV difference becomes 25 percent. Therefore, customers acquired through referral programs are 25 percent more valuable than customers acquired through other methods.

This study shows that a substantial contribution of referral programs to a firm's profitability comes from the fact that referred customers are overall more valuable than customers who are recruited through traditional methods. The findings suggest that referred customers are generating higher profits for the company, through higher contribution margins, than other customers. This effect, combined with the lower acquisition costs, is one of the reasons why referral programs have been embraced by an increasing number of companies during the last few years. In addition, referred customers were found to be more loyal than customers acquired through other methods; that is, they tend to stay with the company for a longer duration. These findings show that, overall, referred customers have a higher customer value in the short as well as the long term. Indeed, when compared to traditionally acquired customers with the same demographic characteristics, referred customers were found to have as much as 25 percent higher CLV.

Referral Intentions

We have seen that many firms use the power of WOM and referrals for acquiring new customers and these customers are more valuable than other customers. Typically, satisfied customers provide referrals and positive WOM to their friends or associates, and some of these referred customers will have the potential to be profitable customers of the firm. Consequently, a customer's value for a firm is not only the profits that he or she generates for the firm but also the profits resulting from the customers he or she brings to the firm. How can we measure these indirect profits that come from referrals? An easy approach would be to ask the customers if they would recommend this product to a friend.[12] However, we cannot assume that this question is the solution to the problem for two important reasons. First, this question only shows correlation, not causation. Second, this question gives results at the aggregate level, so it is unclear to managers exactly which customers are driving this growth and who should be targeted with appropriate communication and incentives in the future to maximize profitability and firm value. We can try to remove the second limitation by analyzing information at the customer level, which shows exactly which customers are willing to refer a product to a friend. Still, can we be sure that the customers who say they would recommend the product actually do talk about it to their friends? Even if they talk about the product, are the prospects willing to listen? Even if the prospects listen, do they become customers? Even if prospects become customers, do they spend enough to be profitable?

Our field study[13] tried to answer these questions for the customers of two firms from two different industries: financial services (n = 6,700) and telecommunications (n = 9,900). After asking about the referral intentions of the sampled customers from the two firms, both the initial customers' and their recruits' behavior was tracked over time, to find out whether their stated intention to recommend was actually acted upon and led to the acquisition of new and profitable customers. The results of the study, presented in Table 6.1, indicate that there is a large gap between stated intentions and following through, as well as in whether a prospect who became a customer is profitable. In the case of the financial services firm, for instance, 68 percent or 4,556 customers intended to make referrals, but only 33 percent or 2,211 actually did. Furthermore, only 14 percent or 938 were successful in bringing customers to the firm, while only 11 percent or 737 ultimately became profitable customers. The results for the telecommunications firm are fairly similar.

It is clear that using a measure for "willingness to recommend" falls short when it comes to actionable strategies to manage customers. However, firms can try to communicate their referral programs to those that are more likely to respond, according to the strategies proposed in Box 6.1.

Table 6.1	Intentions versus Actual Referral Behavior

Item	Financial Services ($n = 6,700$)	Telecommunications ($n = 9,900$)
Stated intention to recommend	68%	81%
Actually referring	33%	30%
Prospects becoming customers	14%	12%
Prospects that are profitable customers	11%	8%

Source: Printed with permission and adapted from V. Kumar, J.A. Petersen, and R.P. Leone, "How Valuable Is Word of Mouth?" *Harvard Business Review*, 85(10), (2007): 139–146.

Box 6.1 Optimal Referral Seeding Strategy—A Research Study

Despite the lower acquisition costs and higher new customer CLV associated with referral programs—as compared to traditional acquisition methods—the investment required for communicating a referral program can still be significant. This is especially true when personal communication, like phone calls and direct mail, is used, as it tends to be more expensive than mass communication. However, personal communication is essential in informing customers about the referral program and persuading them to participate. In light of this, and given the typical budget restrictions, firms can minimize the costs of personal communications by selectively targeting only a part of their customer base. Therefore, it is important to select and target those customers who are more prone to engage in a high degree of referral activities.

REFERRAL SEEDING STRATEGIES

There are a few different approaches in selecting individuals to initiate referral activities which are called seeding strategies. A recent study[14] tried to identify which seeding strategy is the best in terms of referrals generated, as described in the next paragraphs. Considering that the possible referral targets are friends, family, and coworkers, information about the social network of participants can be used to categorize them according to their level and type of connectivity with other

(Box 6.1 Continued)

(Box 6.1 Continued)

individuals. The level of connectivity is measured by the degree centrality scale, which takes higher values for people with more connections and lower values for those with fewer connections. The type of connectivity is captured by the betweenness centrality scale, which takes higher values for people that have more unique connections to others and lower values for those that have fewer unique connections to others. Three distinct groups of people can be identified based on these measures: "hubs," individuals with many connections; "fringes," those with few connections; and "bridges," people with unique connections, connecting groups of others that are otherwise unconnected. Our visual representation of the three types of individuals, according to their position in a social network, is seen in Figure 6.5.

Figure 6.5   Position of Hubs, Fringes, and Bridges in a Social Network

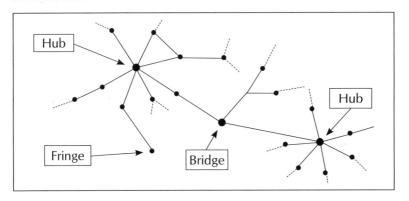

Four seeding strategies are identified, according to the group of individuals that is selected for the initial communication about a referral program. High-degree seeding strategy is used when the initial marketing message (seed) is communicated to hubs, and it relies on their large number of connections. Low-degree seeding strategy is used when the seed is sent to fringes, expecting them to be more easily influenced (and influence others) because they are not overloaded by marketing information. High-betweenness seeding strategy is used when the seed

(Box 6.1 Continued)

(Box 6.1 Continued)

is communicated to bridges, and it relies on their unique position in their social networks. Finally, random seeding strategy is used when the seed is communicated to random people, if there is no available information about the social network of customers. This research study[15] demonstrates how these strategies perform in the context of referrals, comparing them in a controlled setting, through an experiment, and in practice, through a marketing campaign implementation, as presented in the following section.

PERFORMANCE OF REFERRAL SEEDING STRATEGIES

The seeding strategies were first compared using a group of 120 members of an online social networking platform. Based on their connectivity measures, the participants were grouped into hubs, fringes, and bridges, which were used to apply each of the four seeding strategies in succession. A different seed was sent to hubs (high-degree seeding), fringes (low-degree seeding), bridges (high-betweenness seeding), or random individuals (random seeding) every few days through personal messaging, asking them to forward it to friends. Successful referrals were tracked through a website that identified referred individuals, the message they received, and the name of their referrer. To encourage this process, two types of rewards were offered for each successful referral: either a small monetary reward (around ¢40) only for the referred individuals, or a reward for both the referring (¢20) and the referred individuals (¢25).

Even though participation was highly encouraged and reasonably incentivized, 55 percent of all participants were active by referring or being referred, with a total of 1,155 referrals. These activities produced some interesting results regarding the effectiveness of each seeding strategy. In particular, high-degree seeding increased the chance of successful referrals by 53 percent and high-betweenness seeding by 39 percent, as compared to random seeding. In contrast, low-degree seeding considerably lowered the chance of successful referrals by 81 percent less than random seeding. This indicates that low-degree seeding is the least effective, as other strategies are five to eight times more

(Box 6.1 Continued)

(Box 6.1 Continued)

successful, so it is not a recommended strategy. The response difference between high-degree and high-betweenness seeding was not significantly large, which implies that both strategies yield similar results,
so both could be used in practice. However, considering the difficulty
of identifying bridges, which requires information about an individual's
extended social network, the high-degree seeding strategy is the best
practical choice. Regarding the incentives, extending them to both the
referrer and the referred individual increased successful referrals by
more than 37 times, compared to offering them solely to the referred
participants. This supports the common practice in referral programs
for always offering incentives to the referring customers, regardless of
whether an incentive is extended to the prospects as well. In summary,
this experiment showed that it is more effective (i.e., higher successful
referral chances) to seed to hubs and bridges and to offer incentives
to the referrers.

The seeding strategies were also implemented in a marketing campaign for the referral program of a mobile phone service provider,
which rewarded €10 bonus airtime for each referral. The campaign
encouraged customer referral activity through text messages that informed all of the firm's customers ($n = 208,829$) about an increased
referral reward (from €10 to €15) for each new customer they referred
during a one month period. Referrals were recorded in the company
website, where new customers were asked to provide the name of
their referrer. Also, customers' communication data were used to obtain degree centrality measures, which reflected the number of their
contacts that were not customers of the telecommunications firm. Betweenness centrality was not measured in this case, due to the difficulty of obtaining this information.

The referral campaign stimulated a 50 percent increased referral activity, with a total of 4,549 customers making 6,392 referrals to
prospects. Customers that made referrals had almost nine more social
connections than those that did not, so high degree centrality was associated with higher chances of participation in the program. In addition, more connected customers generated more referrals, so high
degree centrality was associated with higher number of referrals. Also,
men and older customers, newly acquired customers, those with high
service usage (both phone calls and texts), and customers who were
recruited online were more likely to participate in the referral program.

(Box 6.1 Continued)

(Box 6.1 Continued)

Combining these findings can help identify customer groups that are more inclined to be actively involved in referral programs and, therefore, viable targets for referral campaigns. Furthermore, dividing the customer base into groups according to their estimated probabilities of participation in the referral program revealed that the top 5,000 group had the highest degree centrality (hubs), while the bottom 5,000 group had the lowest degree centrality (fringes), as illustrated in Table 6.2. Comparing the participation rate, referral rate, and successful referral rate of hubs and fringes shows that high-degree seeding can be almost nine times more effective than low-degree seeding. Comparing these results to the average rates for all customers, (matched to a random seeding strategy) shows that high-degree seeding strategy is expected to be twice as effective. Overall, and in line with the results of the previous experiment, the high-degree seeding strategy is the most effective for encouraging participation in a referral program, maximizing referral generation, and boosting successful referrals.

Table 6.2	Degree Centrality and Referral Rates		
	Top 5,000 (hubs)	**Bottom 5,000 (fringes)**	**Average (random)**
Participation rate	4.4%	0.5%	2.2%
Referral rate	5.8%	0.5%	3.0%
Successful referral rate	3.8%	0.4%	2.0%
Average degree centrality	70.8	18.0	36.5

Source: Adapted from O. Hinz, B. Skiera, C. Barrot, and J. U. Becker, "Seeding Strategies for Viral Marketing: An Empirical Comparison. *Journal of Marketing*, 75(6), (2011): 55–71.

We saw how companies can effectively communicate their referral programs and incentives to achieve the highest possible successful referrals and, therefore, new customer acquisition. It follows that the referring customers that manage to bring more customers are highly valuable to the firm. Therefore, we need a metric such as CRV to determine the value of a customer's ability to spread WOM by building referrals. After quantifying the referral value into the CRV metric, it can be used as a key input in identifying the most valuable customers.

DEFINING CRV

Customer referral value (CRV) of a current customer is defined as the net present value of the future profits of new customers who purchased products/services due to the referral behavior of the current customer. In other words, it captures the value of how firm-initiated and firm-incentivized customer referral programs can improve the profitability of the customer base by cost-effectively acquiring quality prospects. Therefore, CRV is the component of CEV that captures the future value generated by a customer's referral activity.

MEASURING CRV

The indirect value that a customer brings in through his or her referral behavior is measured by the CRV metric. While calculating CRV, it is important to realize that not all referrals that are generated by a customer, contribute the same value. In other words, the value of each referral depends on whether the referred customer would have purchased from the firm even if he or she did not receive the referral. Therefore, CRV has two components, which are summarized in the following equation:

$$CRV = \frac{\text{Value of customers who joined because of the referral}}{\text{Discount rate}} + \frac{\text{Value of customers who would join anyway}}{\text{Discount rate}}$$

The first part refers to the referred customers, who would not have joined otherwise, and it includes both the savings in customer acquisition and the revenue generated from their future purchases. It is important to include the future transactions of these customers in CRV because they would not have purchased without the referral; for that reason, the referring customer should take credit for these sales. However, this is not applicable in the case of the referred customers who would have joined anyway. In this case, it is sufficient to include only the savings in acquisition costs in CRV calculations, considering that the referral is not the reason why they make their future purchases.

This distinction is taken into account in the detailed formula for calculating CRV as follows:

Calculation of CRV

$$CRV_i = \sum_{t=1}^{T} \sum_{y=1}^{n_1} \frac{A_{ty} - a_{ty} - M_{ty} + ACQ1_{ty}}{(1+r)^t}$$

$$+ \sum_{t=1}^{T} \sum_{y=n_1+1}^{n_2} \frac{ACQ2_{ty}}{(1+r)^t} \qquad \text{(Equation 6.1)}$$

where:

T = the number of periods that will be predicted into the future (e.g., years)

n_1 = the number of customers who would not join without the referral

$n_2 - n_1$ = the number of customers who would have joined anyway

A_{ty} = the gross margin contributed by customer y who otherwise would not have bought the product

a_{ty} = the cost of the referral for customer y

M_{ty} = the marketing costs needed to retain the referred customers

$ACQ1_{ty}$ = the savings in acquisition cost from customers who would not join without the referral

$ACQ2_{ty}$ = the savings in acquisition cost from customers who would have joined anyway

r = the discount rate

Note that CRV is a forward-looking metric that predicts a customer's future referral value based on past referral data, much like CLV predicts the future transaction value of a customer. It is measured by summing up the time periods for which we want to predict in the future and during which the existing customer brings new customers to the firm through referrals.

A closer look at the formula for calculating CRV reveals the aspects of the referral process that need to be predicted, which includes the timing of the referrals, the number of the referrals, the associated cost of the referrals, and the savings in acquisition costs. In the case of the referrals to individuals who would not have joined without the recommendation, we also take account of the value of their entire transaction with the firm. In particular, the timing of the referral—i.e., the exact time when the referral was made—determines the time period in which it belongs, so it allows for proper discounting of the future value in today's dollar terms. Further, the number of referrals made within a year is important, as it is clear that we need to know how many new customers are brought to the firm by the original customer to calculate the contribution of each. The cost of the referrals needs to be taken into account as well, since most referral programs are based on the premise of offering incentives to reward and encourage referral behavior; this cost has to be subtracted from the value attached to the referring customer. In addition, the savings in the acquisition cost for referred customers are an integral part of CRV, considering that the firm would have to spend this amount in marketing efforts in order to acquire these customers if not for the referral. These savings are calculated by subtracting the referral cost from the cost associated with traditional customer acquisition. Naturally, this should result in a positive number, provided that the referral cost is lower than the traditional acquisition cost. The acquisition savings are included in the calculations for both groups of customers; those who joined only because of the referral and those who would have joined anyway at some time in the future. As previously described, we differentiate between the two types of referred customers because they contribute differently to the referring customer's CRV. For customers acquired only as a result of the referral, it is important to count their entire transaction value—i.e., their gross contribution margin to the firm minus the marketing costs for retaining them—because the firm would not have made this sale otherwise. This group of customers contributes in all the periods considered when computing the CRV. On the other hand, in the case of the referred customers who would have joined anyway, only the savings in acquisition cost add to the referring customer's value. Accordingly, this group of customers contributes to CRV only once, in the period that the referral was made. After determining these components, a customer's referral value to the firm can be estimated using the formula provided.

The previous description on the value of each customer's referral activity is focused on direct referrals. For example, with reference to Figure 6.3, direct referrals are recommendations made by customer A to customers B, C, and D. However, the CRV for customer A could also include the indirect referrals made from the customers who joined because of him or her (e.g., customers B, C, and D). Those referrals are made by the referred customers after they start purchasing from the firm, so that the referred individual becomes in turn a referrer. It is possible to include these indirect referrals (e.g., from customer C to customer F) in the CRV of the original referring customer (customer A) because the direct referral presented the opportunity for the indirect one. Therefore, credit could be given to the original referrer as well, since this adds to their CRV with the firm. However, our calculations for the

CRV examples and cases that follow in the rest of the chapter will be more conservative, disregarding indirect referrals in CRV calculations.

Calculating CRV—An Example

In order to value customers and see how they truly impact the bottom line of the company, their contributions through referrals should be measured. Tom is a typical customer of a financial services company. Using this customer's referral behavior data for the firm, we will compute his referral value for one year. The data we need for computing the CRV is provided in Table 6.3.

There are four steps in the computation of CRV. They are:

Step 1: In the first step, we determine whether the referred customers would have made purchases in any case. As is evident from Table 6.3, Tom refers four customers per period (six months) and, of those four customers, two would have joined in any case. So, in this case, n_2 is four, n_1 is two, and $n_2 - n_1$ is two. For the sake of illustration, we consider here only the value of those customers who were directly referred to by Tom and who bought something. This approach can also be extended to include the value brought in by customers who were indirectly referred to by Tom (through the referrals of the customers he initially referred) whenever applicable.

Step 2: In the second step, we predict the future value of each referred customer. The future value of each referred customer is based on that customer's gross margin per period ($98), marketing cost per period ($18), acquisition

Table 6.3	Tom's Referral Behavior in a Financial Services Company (Semi-annual Data)	
Total number of referrals per period (n_2)		4
Marketing cost per period (M_{ry})		$18
Average gross margin (A_{ry})		$98
Cost of referral (a_{ty})		$40
Acquisition cost savings (ACQ1$_{ty}$ and ACQ2$_{ty}$)		$5
Number of customers who joined because of the referral (n_1)		2
Number of customers who would have joined anyway ($n_2 - n_1$)		2
Yearly discount rate (r)		15%

cost savings ($5), cost of referral ($40), and discount rate (15 percent annually, so 7.5 percent semi-annually).

Step 3: In the third step, we predict the number of referrals generated. The number of referrals predicted for Tom is four per period. Tom will generate a total of eight referrals because we are measuring the CRV for one year.

Step 4: In the final step, we predict the timing of customer referrals. Tom refers four customers per period, so in terms of timing, this means that four customers are referred in the first half of the year (period 1) and four customers are referred in the second half of the year (period 2).

Applying these steps for the data we have for Tom, we get the following:
For Period 1:

$$\mathrm{CRV}_1 = \sum_{y=1}^{n_1} \frac{A_{1y} - a_{1y} - M_{1y} + \mathrm{ACQ1}_{1y}}{(1+r)^1} + \sum_{y=n_1+1}^{n_2} \frac{\mathrm{ACQ2}_{1y}}{(1+r)^1} \quad \text{(Equation 6.2)}$$

$$\mathrm{CRV}_1 = \sum_{y=1}^{2} \frac{\$98 - \$40 - \$18 + \$5}{(1+0.075)^1} + \sum_{y=3}^{4} \frac{\$5}{(1+0.075)^1} \approx \$93 \quad \text{(Equation 6.3)}$$

For Period 2:

$$\mathrm{CRV}_2 = \sum_{y=1}^{2} \frac{A_{2y} - M_{2y}}{(1+r)^2} + \sum_{y=1}^{n_1} \frac{A_{2y} - a_{2y} - M_{2y} + \mathrm{ACQ1}_{2y}}{(1+r)^2}$$

$$+ \sum_{y=n_1+1}^{n_2} \frac{\mathrm{ACQ2}_{2y}}{(1+r)^2} \quad \text{(Equation 6.4)}$$

$$\mathrm{CRV}_2 = \sum_{y=1}^{2} \frac{\$98 - \$18}{(1+0.075)^2} + \sum_{y=1}^{2} \frac{\$98 - \$40 - \$18 + \$5}{(1+0.075)^2}$$

$$+ \sum_{y=3}^{4} \frac{\$5}{(1+0.075)^2} \approx 225 \quad \text{(Equation 6.5)}$$

$$\text{Total CRV} = \mathrm{CRV}_1 + \mathrm{CRV}_2 \approx \$318 \quad \text{(Equation 6.6)}$$

Therefore, the total CRV for Tom for one year is the sum of CRV_1 and CRV_2, which is around \$318. As the results show, the impact of referral value grows over time. The main reason for this is the growth of the customer base due to additional referrals in each period. In period 1, there were only four new customers, whereas in period 2 there were six customers in the value of the CRV (four new customers and two customers from period 1 who made purchases only because of the referral).

MAXIMIZING CRV

It is clear that the individuals who score high on CRV should not be ignored, seeing that they are an excellent source of new customers for the firm. However, this is not the case with many firms that have been ignoring their high-CRV customers. Neglecting these customers can alienate them from the firm and even drive them to spread negative WOM. To counter this, firms should make use of CRV to find them and invest in providing them with excellent service, fostering a relationship with them, and thus, increasing their satisfaction. This way they can make the most of these customers' potential to make referrals and generate value for the firm through the growth of its customer base.

CRV, when quantified, can be applied in many referral and overall strategies in order to maximize profitability, so firms need to make the most of this metric. The first step in maximizing CRV is to implement creative customer referral programs and provide incentives for customers to recommend the firm's products or services to others. This can increase positive WOM and referrals and, in turn, boost the number of high quality customers. Before this can be accomplished, firms need to optimize some aspects of the referral incentives.

The first issue that should be considered is determining the value of the referral incentive. Traditionally, most referral rewards are fixed for every referred customer, whether they are extended to just the existing customers or to the new customers as well, and they tend to be proportional to the typical customer value of the firm. For instance, Groupon[16] offers a \$10 credit on the account of their customers for each referral they make. Another example would be Tata Sky, a DTH cable operator in India which incentivizes its customers with kids to refer new members with kids. They offer a goodie bag and helicopter rides for the referrer's kids and incentivize the referee with a goodie bag and a free one year subscription of their Fun Learning Package and a free one month subscription of the Supreme Sports Kids package.[17] Alternatively, many companies develop programs that differentiate the value of the referral incentive. One method for varying the rewards is according to the expected purchase behavior of the new customer, considering the customer group this individual belongs to and/or the type of product or service they select. Such is the case of Bank of America, whose past referral program offered $25 for regular personal banking customers, $10 for student customers and $50 for business customers. Its current program[18] increases the amount offered to personal banking customers by $10–$25, depending on whether they opt for a savings account (in addition to a checking account) and the account type they choose. The incentives offered may also depend on the referred customer's actual purchase behavior with the firm. For example, Marriott[19] urges its customers to "Reward Your Friends. Reward Yourself" by making referrals for which both the current and the new customers are granted bonus points toward their Marriott Rewards loyalty program. The awarded points depend on the nights spent in the hotels of the firm, by the newly acquired customers, with a maximum of 10,000 points per customer (5 nights × 2,000 points each). This approach clearly has a high potential for maximizing CRV, especially in the case of customers who join only because of the referral.

In addition to defining the value of the referral incentives, the type of the incentives provided is also a key component in maximizing CRV, as it can highly impact the success of the referral program. Most incentives are usually in the form of a discount on service charges or toward buying more products. There are, however, many products for which this type of rewards is not optimal. For products that are bought rarely, a customer's next purchase extends so far into the future that a discount toward that transaction is probably not that desirable. Firms can overcome this problem by giving rewards that can be applied toward products or services that are linked or complimentary to the referred product. Roku,[20] a best-selling streaming video player for TV, offers a $5 discount on the purchase of a new player to referred customers. Since existing customers are not likely to buy another video player in the near future, a similar discount on the purchase of an additional player would be of little value to most of them. Instead, as shown in Figure 6.6, they are offered a $4 credit on Amazon Instant Video rental, a service they can use through their Roku player, which gives them direct benefits.

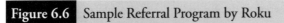

Figure 6.6 Sample Referral Program by Roku

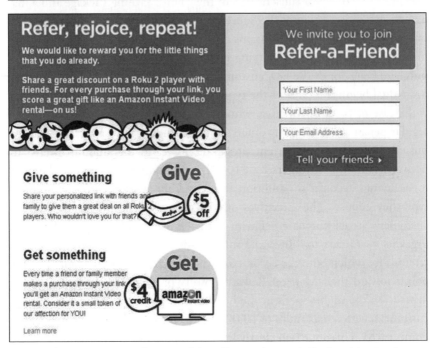

Source: Roku, Inc. (2013). Refer a Friend, http://www.roku.com/referafriend (retrieved on February 15, 2013).

It is also possible, where applicable, to allow customers themselves to choose the type of reward they prefer. The stock image website, iStockphoto[21] has set up its referral program in this way, giving customers the option to choose their preferred reward among the following: $20 per referral, 20 credits per referral, or 20 percent commission on the first purchase of the referred customer. Even though such flexibility is not always easy to offer, firms need to extend referral rewards that are appealing and relevant to their customers, so they are encouraged sufficiently to generate referrals.

LINKING CRV AND CLV

Managers often use CLV as a method to select and target customers for referral campaigns. However, customers who score highly on the CLV measure are not the same customers who score highly on the CRV measure. This happens because CLV does not incorporate data concerning customer attitude toward the firm or customers' tendency of making referrals. This difference between CRV and CLV is illustrated in Table 6.4, which shows the values of both metrics, calculated for the customers of a telecommunications firm based on their transaction and referral behavior data.

As shown in Table 6.4, the customers of the firm were ranked by CLV (from high to low) and divided into ten deciles. When comparing the CLV and CRV for these deciles, it is clear that the customers with the highest CLV are not the customers with the highest CRV. In fact, the top 30 percent of customers based on CLV (deciles 1, 2, and 3) have no overlap with the top 30 percent of customers based on CRV (deciles 5, 6, and 7). We see now that focusing only on customers with high CLV and providing the best service only to them could lead to firms ignoring the customers with high CRV and losing the potential value they can add to the firm. Moreover, this may cause these potentially profitable customers to be alienated from the firm, resulting in reduced customer growth because they would stop their referral activity. Even worse, they might spread negative WOM instead.

Table 6.4	Customer Rankings by CLV and CRV for a Telecommunications Firm	
Deciles (by CLV)	**Customer Lifetime Value ($) (for 1 year)**	**Customer Referral Value ($) (for 1 year)**
1	**1,933**	40
2	**1,067**	52
3	**633**	90
4	360	750
5	313	**930**
6	230	**1,020**
7	190	**870**
8	160	96
9	137	65
10	120	46

Source: Printed with permission from V. Kumar, J.A. Petersen, and R.P. Leone, "How Valuable Is Word of Mouth?" *Harvard Business Review, 85*(10), (2007): 139–146.

Given that high CLV does not mean a high CRV, firms should measure both metrics so they can implement marketing campaigns that focus on customers based on both dimensions. A marketing campaign that focuses on both metrics will allow firms to both increase the profitability of each customer and cash in on the power of positive WOM that enhances their customer base.

Using CRV alongside CLV may enable marketers to implement strategically designed marketing initiatives that can be used to profitably manage customer loyalty. For this purpose, a 2×2 matrix can be used to strategically segment customers based on CLV and CRV. This segmentation may be applied by measuring CLV and CRV scores for the customer base, ordering these scores for each measure, and using the median value to split them into low and high groups for each metric. This process results in the four segments introduced in Figure 6.7.

A brief description and recommended strategies for managing all the four segments is described below.

Figure 6.7	The Relationship between CLV and CRV

	Affluents	**Champions**
High CLV	These customers provide value through their own transactions, but not through referrals. **Strategy:** Work on building CRV.	These customers provide value through referrals and through their own transactions. **Strategy:** Defend, Nurture, and Retain.
	Misers	**Advocates**
Low CLV	These customers do not provide value through their own transactions or through referrals. **Strategy:** Build both CLV and CRV.	These customers do not provide value through their own transactions. Instead, they provide value through referrals. **Strategy:** Work on building CLV.
	Low CRV	High CRV

Source: Printed with permission and adapted from V. Kumar, J.A. Petersen, and R.P. Leone, "How Valuable Is Word of Mouth?" *Harvard Business Review*, 85(10), (2007): 139–146.

- *Affluents:* These customers have a high CLV, which means that they make a lot of purchases from the firm, but they have a low CRV, so they do not refer many new customers to buy products/services. It is recommended to approach them with marketing campaigns that work on building their CRV, since their CLV is already in desired high levels. For example, this may be accomplished by informing them about the referral program through personalized communication, such as emails or phone calls.

- *Misers:* The customers in this segment do not make a lot of purchases, nor do they refer many new customers, which translate to low levels of both CLV and CRV. Therefore, it is recommended to target them with campaigns that aim to enhance both CLV and CRV in order to significantly improve their overall value to the firm. To achieve this, communications to them should combine information about product offerings to initiate purchases, and about the referral program to encourage referrals. Note that, for customers with very low CLV, it may be best to minimize investment in inducing purchases by initiating contacts through inexpensive channels, like email or text messages. This approach minimizes the losses, as they might never purchase too much, or they might be waiting to find out from others whether the product is worth purchasing.

- *Advocates:* Although these customers have a low CLV, which indicates a limited purchase activity, they are active in searching and spreading information to other customers to encourage them to buy products, as is evident from their high CRV. Therefore, the optimal marketing campaign to increase their value is one that is focused on building their CLV. Firms can approach them with special offers, like lower initial prices or product bundles, which are aimed to increase their transactions.

- *Champions:* The customers in this segment are "the best customers" of the firm since they have both high CLV and high CRV. This means that they are more likely to be highly involved with purchasing the product and disseminating information about the product, so marketing campaigns that defend and nurture them are recommended. Personal communication that recognizes their value, while reminding them about the company's offerings and referral programs, is one of the ways to retain them and, at the same time, further enhance their overall value.

It is clear that managers need to move customers from the bottom left of the matrix to the top right, where the customers will impact the company's bottom line not only through their own transactions but also indirectly, through referrals.

Implementing CRV in Business

Consider two of the most popular types of referral offers that are extended to customers. AT&T[22] rewards both the customer who is referred to and the referring customer whenever a referral activates a new, qualifying AT&T wireless service. To incentivize this behavior, both customers get a $25 AT&T gift card each, which can be exchanged for products/services from AT&T. Similarly, DIRECTV[23] provides $100 to both the customer who is referred to and the referring customer. This reward is offered in the form of $10 monthly bill credits for 10 consecutive months. These incentives seem to be in proportion to the typical value brought in by each member in the respective referral groups. How do these programs actually work for a firm? How can they be optimized using CLV and CRV? The benefits in boosting value for the firm by using the CLV and CRV metrics when implementing referral programs are illustrated in the following case study of a telecommunications firm.

Campaign Preparation

Before implementing the referral program, measures of CLV and CRV were obtained in order to segment the telecommunications firm customers according to the 2×2 matrix presented in Figure 6.8. Using the equations provided earlier, the CLV and CRV of each customer were calculated for two different samples (a test sample and a control sample) of 9,900 customers each. The customers in both samples were then divided, matching the four cells of the matrix based on high/low CLV and high/low CRV. The median value for each measure was used as the cutoff point to determine the low and high CLV and the low and high CRV. The results of this segmentation are illustrated in Figure 6.8. It should be noted that both samples (the test sample and the control sample) are summarized together because they contained matched pairs of customers; that is, each group contained 9,900 customers, with almost identical distributions of CLV and CRV scores.

Figure 6.8	Customer Segments (by CLV and CRV) for the Telecommunications Firm

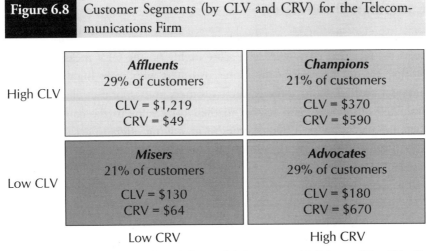

	Affluents 29% of customers CLV = $1,219 CRV = $49	**Champions** 21% of customers CLV = $370 CRV = $590
High CLV		
Low CLV	**Misers** 21% of customers CLV = $130 CRV = $64	**Advocates** 29% of customers CLV = $180 CRV = $670
	Low CRV	High CRV

Source: Printed with permission from V. Kumar, J.A. Petersen, and R.P. Leone, "How Valuable Is Word of Mouth?" *Harvard Business Review, 85*(10), (2007): 139–146.

The segmentation based on the measurements of CLV and CRV resulted in the groups of customers seen in the four matrix cells. We see that these groups have large differences in the values for CLV and CRV, which set them apart from each other. Moreover, there is a significant difference between the customers who are high on the CLV measure and those who are high on the CRV measure, in line with the rankings seen in Table 6.4 earlier. Regarding the high-CLV row, the cell with the highest CLV (upper-left/ Affluents) is found to have a much lower CRV than the adjacent, also high-CLV cell (Champions). Specifically, the value of CRV for Champions is more than ten times greater than that of the Affluents. In addition, looking down the second column, which has the high-CRV customers, we see that the lower-right cell (Advocates) has the highest CRV, but it also has a significantly lower CLV when compared to the other high-CRV cell (Champions). However, if we consider the total value of Advocates as expressed through the sum of CLV and CRV, it is almost as high as the value of Champions. This makes these low-CLV customers almost as valuable to the firm as those with higher CLV, meaning that they should not be neglected. Finally, the Misers cell (lower-left) contains the customers who are low on both CLV and CRV metrics.

Campaign Description

The previous cell values provide strong empirical evidence that further supports the fact that customers who score highly on the CLV measure (direct profits) are not necessarily the same customers who score highly on CRV (indirect profits). Consequently, the customers in each of the cells should be evaluated differently, with respect to their total value to the company, and then approached with different types of marketing offers to get the greatest overall value from them. Based on this, the telecommunications firm of our case launched three different campaigns, one for each segment, in an effort to make customers migrate from low-CLV and/or low-CRV groups to the high CLV and CRV group. Note that there was no campaign for the Champions segment because, according to research,[24] the increases in customer value metrics caused by such communications are negligible, so they do not justify the additional costs. On the other hand, a campaign targeting the Misers makes sense because there is ample room for improvement. The fact that they have scored low on CLV and CRV does not necessarily mean that these customers do not have the potential to be either strong advocates or high-CLV customers. What may be missing is an opportunity to build a relationship. Therefore, this segment was addressed by a separate campaign, as were the Affluents and the Advocates.

Each targeted campaign was carried out on the test sample of customers, with a follow up for each quarter, for the duration of one year. The control sample did not receive any of these marketing communications, to provide a baseline against which the results of the campaign may be compared. Since each segment had different CLV and CRV levels, the respective campaigns were designed with different objectives in mind; that is, each one was aimed to improve the low metrics of the targeted group. Boxes 6.2, 6.3, and 6.4 and the following paragraphs discuss the details and objectives of the three campaigns to illustrate how the combined CLV–CRV approach can be applied in practice.

The first campaign targeted the Affluents, the segment with the highest-CLV customers. However, their CRV is low because they do not refer (or do not succeed in referring) new customers. The goal of this campaign, therefore, was to motivate these customers to increase their referral activity by using referral incentives while ensuring that they kept their high CLV. Successful new referrals from these customers would result in an increased CRV,

---

Box 6.2: The Campaign Targeting the Affluents

These customers were approached with an emphasis on the referral incentive for both of them and the referred customers. They were sent a personal communication in the form of a direct mail, followed by another direct-mail communication within a two-week period. The main goal of the communication was to emphasize a $20 incentive each, for both the referring customer and the referred customer, for signing up for products or services of the firm.

Source: Printed with permission and adapted from V. Kumar, J.A. Petersen, and R.P. Leone, "How Valuable Is Word of Mouth?" *Harvard Business Review*, 85(10), (2007): 139–146.

Box 6.3: The Campaign Targeting the Advocates

These customers received a personal communication in the form of a direct mail that included offers for bundling one or more products. To follow up and raise the opportunity that the offer was received by the customer, the firm sent an additional direct-mail communication within two weeks. In addition, they called a sample of these customers via the telephone to answer any questions regarding the additional services and the value of subscribing to multiple products or services.

Source: Printed with permission and adapted from V. Kumar, J.A. Petersen, and R.P. Leone, "How Valuable Is Word of Mouth?" *Harvard Business Review*, 85(10), (2007): 139–146.

---

leading them to migrate to the Champions cell. In addition, the success of the campaign would mean the average CLV of the Champions cell would increase even more because of the contribution of the Affluents' high CLV.

The second campaign was set up to target the Advocates segment, the customers with the highest CRV. Although they are successful in referring customers, these customers do not spend much on purchasing products and services. Consequently, the goal of this campaign was to encourage them to spend more while, at the same time, maintain their CRV at the highest level. A successful implementation of the campaign would generate a greater amount of direct profit from these customers, moving them from the

---

Box 6.4: The Campaign Targeting the Misers

These customers were targeted with bundled offers for one or more products through a personalized communication sent via direct mail and followed up with another direct-mail communication within two weeks. These customers also received phone calls to address any questions regarding the additional services and the value of obtaining the additional services. In addition, the direct-mail highlighted the value of making referrals to new customers by telling them that a $20 incentive would be given to them and the referred customers following a referral.

Source: Printed with permission and adapted fromV. Kumar, J.A. Petersen, and R.P. Leone, "How Valuable Is Word of Mouth?" *Harvard Business Review,* *85*(10), (2007): 139–146.

Advocates cell to the Champions cell. It could also cause a small increase in the average CRV of the Champions cell because of the contribution of the Advocates' high CRV.

Finally, the third campaign targeted the Misers, the segment with the lowest-CLV and lowest-CRV customers. Since these customers do not make many purchases, nor are they successful in referring customers, the goal of this campaign was to increase both their CLV and their CRV. This was attempted by offering them incentives to buy more products for themselves and, at the same time, encouraging them to refer new customers; thus, trying to create an opportunity to build a relationship. By motivating these customers to increase both their spending with the firm and their referral activity, success of the campaign would make them migrate to one of the other three cells (Affluents, Advocates, or Champions), depending on whether the campaign increased their CLV, their CRV, or both.

Campaign Results

One year after the campaigns were launched, it was clear that they had a significant impact on the customers in each of the three targeted segments. To find out whether the initiative was successful at moving customers toward a higher CLV and/or CRV cell in the matrix from Figure 6.8, the migration patterns of the customers and the change in their CLV and CRV metrics were followed for the three targeted segments (Misers, Affluents, and Advocates). This was done by measuring the CLV and CRV for each customer in the sample set at the end of the one year period and comparing it to the values before the campaign. The changes in CLV and CRV and the resulting migration patterns of the customers in each segment are shown in the three following figures.

Figure 6.9 shows the influence of the first campaign on the Affluents segment (high CLV and low CRV). This campaign was aimed at converting them to Champions (high CLV and high CRV) by increasing their CRV while maintaining their very high CLV. Before the campaign started, 29 percent of the total customers in the sample belonged to this segment. After running the campaign, 4 percent of them increased their CRV by an average of $190 and were, therefore, successfully migrated to the Champions segment. Considering that their initial CRV was $49, the referral value for these customers named "New Champions" in Figure 6.9, grew by 388 percent. The overall impact of this migration of customers is large since 4 percent of the customers increasing their CRV by that much amounts to a total increase of more than $75,000 (4% × 9,900 × $190). It also means that the customer base of the telecommunications firm is growing, providing new revenue sources besides cross-selling and up-selling to their current customers.

Figure 6.9 Campaign Results for Affluents Segment

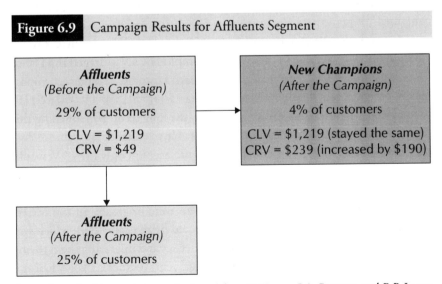

Source: Printed with permission and adapted from V. Kumar, J.A. Petersen, and R.P. Leone, "How Valuable Is Word of Mouth?" *Harvard Business Review*, 85(10), (2007): 139–146.

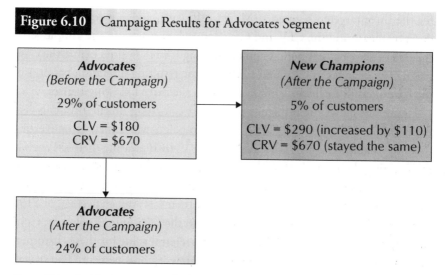

Figure 6.10 Campaign Results for Advocates Segment

Source: Printed with permission and adapted from V. Kumar, J.A. Petersen, and R.P. Leone, "How Valuable Is Word of Mouth?" *Harvard Business Review,* 85(10), (2007): 139–146.

In Figure 6.10, the results of the second campaign for the Advocates segment (low CLV and high CRV) are shown. The campaign was directed at increasing these customers' CLV, while maintaining their high CRV, and thus, upgrade them to Champions (high CLV and high CRV). This segment also contained 29 percent of the customers before the campaign, and after one year, 5 percent of these customers had an increased CLV and moved toward Champions. The increase in these New Champions' CLV averaged at $110 or 61 percent more than the initial value for each customer. The direct impact may not seem as much, but it added more than $54,000 (5% × 9,900 × $110) to total value. Besides, it is still significant in the long term. By launching this campaign, the telecommunications firm was able to enhance the value of customers who otherwise, in the case of taking into account only the CLV, would have been ignored due to their low CLV and thus, to move them to the most desirable segment of the Champions.

Figure 6.11 illustrates how customers who were originally in the Misers segment (low CLV and low CRV) were affected by the campaign, which was targeted at increasing both customer value metrics and migrating them to one of the other three higher-value segments of Affluents (higher CLV), Advocates (higher CRV), or Champions (higher CLV and CRV). Before the campaign

| **Figure 6.11** | Campaign Results for Misers Segment |

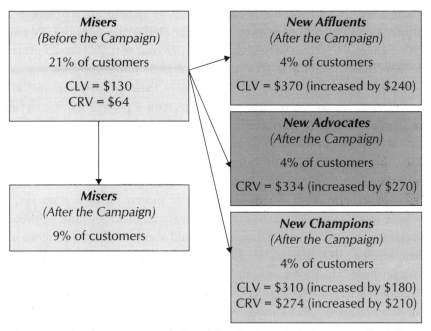

Source: Printed with permission and adapted from V. Kumar, J.A. Petersen, and R.P. Leone, "How Valuable Is Word of Mouth?" *Harvard Business Review*, 85(10), (2007): 139–146.

was launched, this segment was made up of 21 percent of the customers in the sample, yet the campaign was able to shift 12 percent of the customers to the other segments. These "upgraded" customers were shared between the three segments, with 4 percent "New Affluents," 4 percent "New Advocates," and 4 percent "New Champions." Not only did these customers move up to a more desirable segment, but also the gains made on average were substantial. For example, customers who became "New Champions" had an average CLV that was $180 higher and a CRV that was $210 higher than before. This means that these customers increased their CLV scores by 138 percent and their CRV scores by 328 percent, which translates into an increase of more than $71,000 (4% × 9,900 × $180) in total CLV value and more than $83,000 (4% × 9,900 × $210) in total CRV value for the firm. Therefore, of the original sample of customers in this segment, those who moved toward

Champions produced increases of more than $154,000 in total customer value. Although this number might not seem so large, compared to the usual revenues for multimillion-dollar companies, if we were to project them to a sample size of 990,000 customers, rather than 9,900, the gains in CLV and CRV from this 4 percent of total customers (396 out of 9,900) would generate more than $7 million in CLV and more than $8 million in CRV.

The previous results showcase the success of these campaigns in migrating customers to segments with higher value, with 4 percent moving to Affluents (from Misers), 4 percent moving to Advocates (from Misers), and a total of 13 percent moving to Champions (4 percent from Misers, 4 percent from Affluents, and 5 percent from Advocates), the most desirable segment. Even though the migration of customers toward higher-value segments is a highly desirable result and a good measure of success for these campaigns, we have to take into the account the investment required for running them. Therefore, the success of the campaign should also be evaluated in terms of the campaign's ROI, that is, by comparing the added value generated to the costs involved. The total cost of the three campaigns—including direct mail, email, and selected telephone calls—was approximately $31,500. Since the campaign targeted 7,821 customers in the sample (approximately 2,871 Affluents, 2,079 Misers, and 2,871 Advocates), the campaign cost per customer was around $4. Further, the overall gains in value obtained by increasing each customer's CLV, CRV, or both through all three campaigns were $486,090. Therefore, the overall ROI of the campaigns was around 15.5, which means that they were successful from a financial viewpoint as well. Table 6.5 shows

Table 6.5 Campaign ROI for the Telecommunications Firm

	Gains in Customer Value (CLV and CRV)	Cost	ROI
Campaign 1	$75,240 (CRV)		
Campaign 2	$54,450 (CLV)		
Campaign 3	$190,080 (CRV)		
	$166,320 (CLV)		
Campaign totals	**$486,090**	**$31,500**	**15.4**

Source: Adapted from V. Kumar, J.A. Petersen, and R.P. Leone, "How Valuable Is Word of Mouth?" *Harvard Business Review,* 85(10), (2007): 139–146.

a summary of these results. Note that a similar set of campaigns was run with a financial services firm, with a similarly high ROI (13.6).

How can we translate these results for a much larger sample of customers from the telecommunications firm's customer database or for a longer period of time? Table 6.6 illustrates a projection of the campaign outcomes across 1 million and 10 million customers of the telecommunications firm (their customer base has more than 40 million customers), and for a period of measuring CLV and CRV of one year and three years. It becomes clear that there are substantial gains in customer value when running these three customized campaigns on a larger scale. There are a lot of opportunities for firms who traditionally have used only CLV as a metric to increase their profitability by selecting customers for marketing campaigns based on both their CLV and their CRV.

The telecommunications firm case underlined the significance of using CRV in combination with CLV in boosting both CEV and profitability. However, this would not have been achieved if only the CLV metric was used. Targeting only customers that score high on CLV is not an optimal strategy for increasing referral activity because CLV does not coincide with CRV. This happens because not all behaviorally loyal customers provide referrals, and not all customers who provide referrals are behaviorally loyal. Therefore, many low-CLV customers can add great value to the firm, through their high CRV. Implementing the CRV metric enables firms to locate and target these individuals with high referral value, and develop outreach programs and referral programs that maximize profitability.

Even though high-CLV and high-CRV customers are the most valuable, the telecommunications firm case showed how firms can generate value

Table 6.6 Profit Projection for the Telecommunications Firm's Campaign

Period	1 Million Customers		10 Million Customers	
	CLV (in millions)	**CRV** (in millions)	**CLV** (in millions)	**CRV** (in millions)
1 year	$22.3	$26.8	$223	$268
3 years	$66.9	$80.4	$669	$804

Source: Adapted from V. Kumar, J.A. Petersen, and R.P. Leone, "How Valuable Is Word of Mouth?" *Harvard Business Review*, 85(10), (2007): 139–146.

from customers that are low on either or both metrics. Additionally, after running campaigns similar to those described in the previous section, managers can use the results to locate the smaller groups of customers within each of the targeted segments (Affluents, Advocates, and Misers) that are more prone to increase their CLV, CRV, or both. These groups can be identified by examining the differences in characteristics of the customers who showed an increased CLV and/or CRV and those that remained the same after the campaign was run. Knowing what sets those two groups of customers apart, managers can find prospective customers that are similar to those most responsive to the previous campaigns, and then target these individuals through new campaigns. Therefore, whichever marketing campaign is chosen to increase the overall revenue and profit obtained from customers, we have shown the importance of measuring both the value of customers' own transactions and their impact on the transactions of other customers.

LINKING CBV AND CRV

CRV may also be used in conjunction with CBV to optimally design and implement marketing initiatives so as to maximize overall customer value. Combining these two metrics produces a 2×2 matrix that can be used as a framework to strategically segment customers based on their individual CRV and CBV. To apply this framework, measures of CBV and CRV for all customers should first be calculated and ordered, and then the customer base should be split into high and low groups for each metric using the median as a cutoff point. This is how the four segments presented in Figure 6.12 are obtained.

A brief description and recommended strategies for managing each of the four segments is described below.

- *Admirers:* The customers in this segment have a high CBV, which means that they think highly of the brand, but they have a low CRV, so they do not refer many new customers to buy products/services. They may not be aware of the referral program or they may not have enough information about its terms and the rewards. For that reason, it is recommended

Figure 6.12	The Relationship between CBV and CRV

	Low CRV	High CRV
High CBV	**Admirers** These customers place high value to the brand, but they do not generate substantial referrals. **Strategy:** Work on building CRV.	**Enthusiasts** These customers both provide value through referrals and recognize the brand as of high value. **Strategy:** Retain, Support, and Nurture.
Low CBV	**Benchwarmers** The customers in this segment do not value the brand; neither do they make referrals. **Strategy:** Provided that CLV is not low, build both CBV and CRV.	**Opportunists** These customers do not appreciate the brand, although they do generate value through referrals. **Strategy:** Work on building CBV.

to target them with marketing campaigns that are designed to build their CRV, since their CBV is already in the desired high levels. Being specific, these campaigns should mainly include communications, like email or phone calls, with information about the referral program and the related rewards, while reminding these customers how much they value the brand.

- *Benchwarmers:* These customers do not value the brand, nor do they refer many new customers, which lead to low levels of both CBV and CRV. A variety of reasons may explain their low values, such as having little information about the brand, having had a bad experience, and/or being unaware of the referral program. If these customers have a low CLV as well, it is best to stop investing in them. If their CLV is high, they should be approached with marketing campaigns that work on enhancing both their CBV and their CRV, in order to significantly improve their overall value to the firm. This can be achieved through a series of personal communication activities that inform them about both the brand and product offerings and the referral program, with added emphasis on building brand value.

- *Opportunists:* Although the customers in this segment have a low CBV, which indicates that they do not value the brand, they are actively participating in the firm's referral program by recruiting new customers, as is evident from their high CRV. Thus, approaching them with marketing actions that are focused on building their CBV, such as sending out emails with information about the brand and the service or product offerings, is highly recommended. It should be noted that the costs associated with this type of campaign should not be extensive, especially for those customers that have low CLV, since this behavior might indicate that they are trying to exploit the referral program, participating in it only for the rewards.

- *Enthusiasts:* This segment is where most of the customers should ideally belong, as it is characterized by both high CBV and high CRV. This means that not only are these customers highly involved with the brand and spread information about it, but they also expand the firm's customer base. Marketing campaigns that target them should always recognize their value by supporting and nurturing them, while trying to add even more value through both metrics. Personalized messages that recognize and appreciate their relationship with the firm, while reminding them about the brand and the referral program, are examples of activities that would help attain these goals.

Overall, it follows that managers should aim to migrate their customers in the direction from the bottom left segment (Admirers) to the top right segment (Enthusiasts) of this matrix, focusing on the dimensions that suffer for each individual. This would ensure that customers have the highest value on both metrics and, thus, benefit the company through both their brand evaluation and their referrals.

So far we have seen how CRV can be used to enhance the profitability of a firm by recruiting valuable customers through referral programs. The majority of referral programs, however, are applied and relevant in business-to-consumer (B2C) markets, like most examples illustrated in the previous pages. The following section will discuss how to measure the value that stems from recommendations that stimulate purchases in business-to-business (B2B) markets.

THE VALUE OF REFERENCES IN THE B2B SETTING

As this chapter has demonstrated, firms are using WOM and referral marketing campaigns to encourage new customer acquisition. However, in a B2B setting, the purchase decision does not rely on customer referrals or social influences such as WOM. Instead, many B2B firms are influenced to purchase based on references from other businesses. Also known as testimonials, these references play a key role in the decision of a business to purchase and are quantified as a firm's business reference value (BRV).

As stated in Chapter 2, the concept of BRV is defined as the monetary value associated with future profits as a result of the extent of a client's reference influencing a prospect to purchase.[25] In their quest to acquire new customers, many firms are implementing initiatives to capitalize on the power of referencing behavior as part of their general marketing and sales efforts. The use of referencing behavior is often the only alternative for B2B firms to leverage the value of current clients on new customer adoption.

For example, Microsoft and SAS have reference programs to influence prospects to adopt their products and services. As shown in Box 6.5, Microsoft has a Customer Reference Program that uses case studies and white papers from a sample of current clients as the reference source.

Microsoft selects the case studies and white papers to be representative of what its sales executives believe are the best examples of successful implementations of Microsoft products and services. Microsoft then encourages prospects to visit the website that contains the case studies and white papers. In a different approach, SAS encourages its customers to create "video success stories" which will be used as references for future client customers. As shown in Box 6.6, customers are asked to "Tell Your SAS Story."

The above examples showcase how firms use references. Yet, how does a firm determine which firms to seek references from? When firms seek to obtain references they must take into consideration factors about the referencing firm as the source of a reference plays a vital role in the effectiveness of the business reference. The perceived value of a product or service is directly tied to the source of the referral. The client featured in the reference also provides a valuable signal to the prospect about the quality of the products or services offered by the selling firm and the type of firms that currently purchase from the selling firm. The study has also shown that the caliber of the selling firm is elevated by the stature of the referring firm. Now, let us take a look at how BRV is measured and the drivers that influence BRV.

Box 6.5: Microsoft Customer Reference Program

Microsoft takes great pride in demonstrating customer success and in showcasing companies, like yours, that are realizing benefits—for your business and your people—by using Microsoft Dynamics. We invite you, as a valued Microsoft customer, to showcase the real-world results your business and your people have achieved by using Microsoft technologies and services.

Customers who participate in the Reference Program for Microsoft Dynamics are rewarded with unique opportunities to showcase their successes and network with peers and key industry influencers in their communities—and across the world.

HOW YOU CAN BENEFIT

The Reference Program benefits you and your business in a variety of ways. By taking part, you can promote yourself and your business to diverse audiences and influence organizations around the world.

- *Promote Your Brand:* Increase awareness of your brand and extend your existing PR, Marketing, and advertising efforts.
- *Build Industry Networks:* Expand your professional networks and connect with other technology leaders.
- *Enjoy Closer Relationships with Microsoft:* Develop deeper, mutually beneficial relationships with Microsoft and raise the profile of key company executives within your industry.
- *Showcase Business Leadership:* Participate in customer advisory boards and executive briefings. Share your thought leadership and showcase your IT innovations.

Source: Microsoft. Customer reference cases, http://www.microsoft.com/dynamics/customer/en-US/reference-program.aspx (retrieved on April 15, 2013).

MEASURING BRV

The measurement of BRV takes into account three entities: the Seller Firm, the Client Firm, and the Prospect Firm. BRV is computed as the amount of profit the existing client firm can help generate from the prospect firms who purchase products and services as a result of the reference.[26]

Box 6.6: SAS Reference Program

HIGHLIGHTING YOUR ORGANIZATION— AND YOU

For more than 35 years, loyal SAS customers like you have helped us achieve unwavering growth and success. Likewise, we are committed to helping you grow and succeed.

Together, we can explore avenues for sharing your message in ways that are most advantageous to you and your organization. For more information on how we can help you share your story, please contact us at mccenter@sas.com.

WHAT ARE THE BENEFITS?

When you participate in the SAS Reference Program, we can help you:

- Develop and promote yourself and your organization as thought leaders.
- Network with successful peers at government agencies, educational institutions and businesses around the world.
- Build industry recognition.
- Gain unprecedented access to SAS staff well beyond the sales channel, including R&D experts and even our executive management.
- Gain access to technology experts such as analysts and others who provide valuable technical exchanges that keep you abreast of the latest trends and developments.
- Increase visibility for your organization in channels that may otherwise be unavailable to you.

Source: SAS. Customer success, http://www.sas.com/success/ckc/index.html (retrieved on April 15, 2013).

The value of a business reference is proposed as a function of three components: (*a*) the amount of influence that client references (vis-à-vis other marketing elements) had on a prospect's adoption, (*b*) the amount of influence that a given client reference (vis-à-vis other client references) had on the prospect's adoption, and (*c*) the profitability of the prospect after adoption.

Mathematically speaking, BRV of a client reference is represented in the following manner.

Calculation of BRV

$$BRV_i = \sum_{n=1}^{N} \frac{(Ref_n \times DOI_{in} \times CLV_n)}{(1+r)^{t_n}}$$

(Equation 6.7)

where:

BRV_i = business reference value of client reference i

Ref_n = degree that references impacted the prospect n's purchase decision

DOI_{in} = degree of influence of client reference i on converted prospect n

CLV_n = customer lifetime value of converted prospect n

N = total number of converted prospects

r = discount rate (in months)

t_n = month that converted prospect n became a customer after the first month of the observation window

BRV is computed in three steps: (*a*) determine whether the client references influenced adoption, (*b*) determine the influence of each client's reference, and (*c*) compute the CLV of the converted prospect.

- *Step I:* The first step in computing BRV is to determine whether client reference in general (all client references collectively) has any influence on the prospect's decision to adopt. The adoption process is driven by two processes: seller-generated (director mass-marketing efforts initiated by the seller firm) and client-generated (client information used by the seller firm) marketing. It is assumed that the monetary value a firm gains from a client reference is the percentage of the sale that can be attributed to the influence of that client reference.

- *Step II:* Once it is determined that collective client reference has some influence on the prospect's decision to adopt, the second step seeks to determine the influence that each individual client reference has on the prospect's decision to adopt. In this step, the value of each client reference is the proportion of influence that this client reference has on the decision to adopt relative to the total influence of all client references.

- *Step III:* The third step is to compute the expected future profit, or CLV, of the converted prospect. The computation of BRV allows the managers of the selling firm to identify the best references to use in order to influence potential client firms to purchase products and services in the future. In making the reference selection, the selling firm can then assign a monetary value to each of its client firms based on their BRV scores to quantify the impact of the client firm's references. By doing so, the selling firm will be able to optimize the value gained from its client references and ultimately increase its profitability.

Calculating BRV—An Example

Once the three steps of BRV are computed, BRV can be calculated using the formula in Equation 6.7. Let us consider the situation where Classic University is a typical client of a computer software company that provides a learning software tool for students. The software company decides to use Classic University as a reference to showcase the benefits of adopting the learning tool software. Classic University agrees to be a reference and provides a video testimony. Six prospective universities are evaluating the learning tool software and in the process listened to the video testimony of Classic University. It so happens that all of the six universities ended up buying the learning tool software. Now the question is, did the Classic University play a role in converting the prospects to customers? If yes, how much credit should be assigned to Classic University from each of the six new customers? The data we need for computing the BRV of Classic University is provided in Table 6.7.

Based on the three steps of BRV, we have the following information:

- *Step 1:* The degree that references impacted the six prospect universities' decision to adopt (Ref)
- *Step 2:* The degree of influence that the reference of Classic University had on each of the prospect university (DOI)
- *Step 3:* The CLV of the six prospect universities that bought the learning tool software

The time (t) taken for the prospect university to become a new client of the computer software company is also given. The discount rate (r) is given as 15 percent per year.

Table 6.7	Reference Impact of Classic University			
Prospect University	**Ref %**	**DOI %**	**CLV ($)**	**Time of Adoption**
Technical University	85	70	1,000	Year 1
Top-notch University	65	70	2,000	Year 1
Supreme University	25	60	2,500	Year 2
Arts University	55	50	1,000	Year 2
Science University	35	40	2,000	Year 3
Research University	60	50	1,500	Year 3

Applying these steps for the data we have for the universities, we get the following:

For Technical University:

$$\text{University}_1 = \frac{(\text{Ref}_1 \times \text{DOI}_{i1} \times \text{CLV}_1)}{(1+r)^t}$$

$$= \frac{(0.85 \times 0.70 \times 1000)}{(1+0.15)^1} = \$517.39 \qquad \text{(Equation 6.8)}$$

For Top-notch University:

$$\text{University}_2 = \frac{(\text{Ref}_2 \times \text{DOI}_{i2} \times \text{CLV}_2)}{(1+r)^t}$$

$$= \frac{(0.65 \times 0.70 \times 2000)}{(1+0.15)^1} = \$791.30 \qquad \text{(Equation 6.9)}$$

For Supreme University:

$$\text{University}_3 = \frac{(\text{Ref}_3 \times \text{DOI}_{i3} \times \text{CLV}_3)}{(1+r)^t}$$

$$= \frac{(0.25 \times 0.60 \times 2500)}{(1+0.15)^2} = \$283.55 \qquad \text{(Equation 6.10)}$$

For Arts University:

$$\text{University}_4 = \frac{(\text{Ref}_4 \times \text{DOI}_{i4} \times \text{CLV}_4)}{(1+r)^t}$$

$$= \frac{(0.55 \times 0.50 \times 1000)}{(1+0.15)^2} = \$207.94$$

(Equation 6.11)

For Science University:

$$\text{University}_5 = \frac{(\text{Ref}_5 \times \text{DOI}_{i5} \times \text{CLV}_5)}{(1+r)^t}$$

$$= \frac{(0.35 \times 0.40 \times 2000)}{(1+0.15)^3} = \$184.10$$

(Equation 6.12)

For Research University:

$$\text{University}_6 = \frac{(\text{Ref}_6 \times \text{DOI}_{i6} \times \text{CLV}_6)}{(1+r)^t}$$

$$= \frac{(0.60 \times 0.50 \times 1500)}{(1+0.15)^3} = \$295.88$$

(Equation 6.13)

$$\text{BRV}_{\text{Classic University}} = \text{University}_1 + \text{University}_2 + \text{University}_3 + \text{University}_4$$
$$+ \text{University}_5 + \text{University}_6 = \$2,280.18$$

(Equation 6.14)

Using Equation 6.7, we calculate the BRV of Classic University as the sum of each prospect. Therefore, the BRV for Classic University is around $2,280.18.

DRIVERS OF BRV

The purchase decision process in the B2B setting is far more complex in comparison to the transactions between businesses and consumers. Decisions regarding purchases made by organizations are likely to be discussed on many levels with different employees within the organization having input in the purchasing decision. As such, the key drivers of reference selection by the sellers and the drivers of BRV for each client reference are important dimensions to consider. Two arguments are made in regards to identifying the drivers: (*a*) firms strategically select as references, client firms that are more likely to influence the prospect firm's decision to adopt in order to maximize profitability and (*b*) prospect firms make decisions to adopt in order to maximize the benefit they receive from the relationship with the seller firm.

Based on these arguments, four key drivers of reference selection and reference value are identified:

- The degree to which the client firm can be viewed as a trusted informant through the *client firm size.*
- The degree to which the client firm has built a strategic alliance with the seller firm through the *length of client relationship.*
- The ability of the communication to convey information to the potential client firm through the *reference media format.*
- The degree to which the information provided is relatable to the potential client firm through the *reference congruency.*

Drivers of BRV in a Telecommunications Firm and a Financial Services Firm

The drivers of BRV and their impact on reference selection are explained in further detail in the following sections in the context of being implemented at a telecommunications firm and a financial services firm. In order to calculate the BRV for the firms, the influence of each of the drivers is observed as shown in Table 6.8.

The results from the implementation (as shown in Table 6.8) show that the client firm size and the length of the client relationship together account for approximately 31 percent of the change in BRV at a telecommunications firm. The drivers of congruency and reference media format explain 17 percent and 14 percent of the change, respectively. The interaction effects between client firm size and the other three constructs explain approximately 9 percent. Similar results were found for the financial services firm with 31 percent of the change in BRV being attributed to client firm size and the length of the client relationship. Additionally, the drivers of congruency, reference media format, and firm size interaction effects explain approximately 40 percent collectively.

| Table 6.8 | Influence of the Drivers of BRV | | |

Variable	Influence	Telecommunications Firm	Financial Services Firm
Client Firm Size			
Employees	+		
Revenue	+	31%	31%
Length of Client Relationship			
Customer lifetime value	∩		
Tenure	∩		
Reference Media Format			
Video testimonial	+		
Audio testimonial	+	14%	
Written testimonial	+		
Case study/white paper	+		
"Call me"	+		
Reference Congruency			
Industry	+		40%
Product/service	+	17%	
Role	+		
Congruency	+		
Interaction Effects			
Firm size and Relationship length	+		
Firm size and Reference media format	+	9%	
Firm size and Congruency	+		

Source: Printed with permission and adapted from V. Kumar, J.A. Petersen, and R. P. Leone, "Defining, Measuring, and Managing Business Reference Value," *Journal of Marketing, 77*(1), (2013): 68–86.
Note: The ∩ symbol represents a positive relationship up to a threshold, beyond which it turns negative.

Client Firm Size: A firm's size is a determining factor when it comes to the selection of which client firm to use for references. In this context, client firm size is defined as the size of the client firm in the marketplace in terms of the number of employees it has (size of the labor force) and its annual revenue (scale of operations). In the study, we found that the number of employees and the amount of revenue have a positive effect on the reference selection for both the telecommunications firm and the financial services firm.

It is therefore in the best interest of the selling firm to strategically select larger client firms to be references; more specifically, firms that have larger labor forces and/or larger scales of operation. Due to their visibility and the availability of information about them, larger firms are often viewed favorably due to inflated perceptions of the firms' activities. Also, information is more valuable when the client firm is trusted or has a good reputation in the marketplace. As such, client firms that are perceived as valuable to the marketplace (e.g., significant size) and whose attributes are visible in the marketplace are more likely to provide an effective reference to prospect firms through their reputation.

Length of Client Relationship: In addition to firm size, the client firm's relationship with the seller firm can also convey information to the prospect firm about the quality of the seller firm. It has been observed that the longer the client relationship, the stronger the bond between the seller firm and the client firm. A closer relationship between the seller firm and the client firm also often indicates to the prospect that the client firm is in some way satisfied with the services and/or product of the seller firm and therefore, reduces the ambiguity of the purchase for the prospect. In this regard, the length of the client relationship is defined in terms of the CLV of the client firm providing the reference and the amount of time that client firm has been a customer of the seller firm. This measure includes the length of the past relationship as well as the expected length of the future relationship.

In the study, we found that CLV had an inverted U-shaped relationship for both the telecommunications firm and the financial services firm. The findings revealed that a firm is more likely to select clients for references who provide more profits to the client firm. This suggests that the influence of a client firm is greater when the firm has been making purchases for a longer period of time and has a greater likelihood of continuing the relationship in the future. It was also observed in the study that tenure has a positive effect on client selection for both the telecommunications and financial services firms. This suggests that the seller firm is more likely to select clients that have had a longer prior relationship as a reference.

As such, the seller firm should strategically select client references according to the length and depth of the buyer–seller relationship. Described as embeddedness, the length and depth of the ties between the client firm and the seller firm has an important impact on the reference selection of a firm. However, as the buyer–seller relationship can become overly embedded and actually negatively impact the relationship, there is a threshold for the embeddedness of the buyer–seller relationship. Beyond a certain point embeddedness may indicate to the prospect that the client firm is unfamiliar with potential alternatives. The prospect will then attribute that the client firm is not capable of making an informed and unbiased reference. As such, the value of the reference from the client firm is increased by the length of the relationship with the seller firm but only to the embeddedness threshold. Therefore, it is suggested that the seller firm select clients with a moderate level of relationship length as references.

Reference Media Format: The medium and the specific format of a reference plays a key role in determining the value of the reference. With each media format the amount of information that can be conveyed changes and the amount of uncertainty from the message content can fluctuate. The most common reference media formats are segmented into the following categories: video, audio, written, case studies/white papers, and "call me" testimonials.

In the case of the telecommunications firm and the financial services firm, it was observed that all of the reference media formats have a positive relationship with the firms. Yet, the value added by each media varied. The richness of the media format, the way that content is delivered, and the quality of the information can all have a significant influence on the value of the reference. We found that references in a video format are significantly more likely to have an impact than audio testimonials. The following was also observed; audio testimonials are more significant than written testimonials, written testimonials are more significant than case studies/white papers, and case studies/white papers are more significant than "call me" references.

As shown, the study confirmed that references presented in richer modes of communication such as video are more likely to add value to a firm. This is attributed to the perception that references in rich media have more valuable information content, convey a greater effort by the client firm to communicate, and potentially provide a more customizable opinion from the client firm. Therefore, a reference that provides information in a richer media format is likely to be more effective in influencing a prospect firm to purchase.

Reference Congruency: The degree to which there are similarities between the client firm and the prospect firm is a key factor in determining the value of a reference. Described as congruency, this degree of similarity can have a significant impact on the value of a reference as trust and reciprocity are believed to be generated when there is congruency between the client firm and the prospect firm. The perceived connection between the client firm and the prospect firm also serves to strengthen the bond between the two parties and further influences adoption. Therefore, it has been observed that prospects may be more inclined to consider references from firms that show some congruency to their firm in key areas. These areas include being from the same industry, purchasing similar products or services, or holding the same role within their firm.

In the study with the telecommunications and financial services firms, a positive relationship was found for the industry congruency (number of prospects in same industry), product congruency (percentage of prospects that valued the reference and purchased the same product/service), and role congruency (the percentage of prospects that valued the reference and held the same role as the person in the client firm) at both firms. This suggests that as the quantity of these variables increases, the BRV of the client firm also increases. As such, increasing the opportunities for congruency can add significant value to a client's references.

Furthermore, the type of congruency can add differing levels of value. Product/service congruency is observed to be the most valuable when compared with industry congruency, industry congruency is the second most valuable when compared with role congruency; and role congruency is the third most valuable in terms of BRV. Thus, if a prospect is interested in a reference, the most influential references will come from clients with product/service congruency followed by industry congruency and role congruency.

The Incremental Benefit of Firm Size: Of all of the drivers of BRV, firm size exerts a greater impact on BRV. When implemented at a telecommunications and a financial services firm, it was shown that larger firms are a more trusted reference; and therefore, have a stronger influence on the effect of the other drivers of BRV. Due to their ability to send a positive signal to the prospect and reduce the uncertainty in the purchase decision, larger firms are believed to incrementally strengthen the other drivers of reference value.

MAXIMIZING BRV

In understanding the drivers of BRV, we can see that references are of paramount importance for B2B firms. As previously discussed in this chapter, BRV focuses on the client firm's ability to influence prospect clients to adopt based on the client firm's characteristics, reputation, and form of communication.

The most effective references often come from referrers that meet the criteria set forth by the drivers of BRV. Therefore, in order to maximize BRV, a seller firm should choose client firms to provide references based on the four key drivers of BRV as well as the CLV of the client firm.

Impact of BRV on CLV

After observing the effect of the drivers of BRV, the relationship that BRV has with CLV at the telecommunications and financial services firms is analyzed. As discussed previously in this chapter, customers with the highest CRV are not the same as customers with the highest CLV. The same observation can be seen in the relationship between BRV and CLV—the clients that have high CLV scores are not the same as those that provide the most valuable references. As such, it is important for the seller firm to manage its client firms based on their CLV and their BRV scores.

In order to establish this relationship between CLV and BRV, the client firms are rank ordered by their CLV scores during a three-year-period and then divided into 10 groups for which the average CLV and BRV for each group is computed. Table 6.9 shows the CLV and BRV for the 10 groups at the telecommunications firm and the financial services firm. For both the telecommunications and the financial services firm, the clients with the highest BRV fall into the third, fourth, and fifth groups on CLV with the fifth group having the highest BRV in both firms.

Unlike the relationship between CLV and CRV, the BRV of client firms in the top two groups (highest CLV) is still relatively high. Also shown in Table 6.8, clients with the highest CLV (Groups 1 and 2) have higher BRV compared to clients with the lowest CLV (Groups 7–10). The contributing factor for this relationship is due to client firm size. Effectually, the bigger the client firm, the higher the BRV of the firm.

However, medium CLV clients (Groups 3, 4, and 5) have the highest BRV due to the length of the client relationship and the congruency effect. As such, a medium-length client relationship leads to higher BRV. In terms of congruency, it was found that many of the prospects being targeted for acquisition had the most in common with the customers in the medium CLV group—therefore, the higher the congruency, the higher the BRV.

Taken a step further, the study revealed that the average BRV scores in the high and medium groups (Groups 1–6 for the telecommunications firm and

Table 6.9	Client Firm Analysis for BRV and CLV			
	Telecommunications (*n* = 9 for All but Tenth Group)		**Financial Services** (*n* = 9 for All but Tenth Group)	
Group	**Average CLV (in thousands)**	**Average BRV (in thousands)**	**Average CLV (in thousands)**	**Average BRV (in thousands)**
1	30.8	34.6	26.2	31.2
2	25.7	40.8	23.6	33.6
3	20.2	49.6	20.5	41.8
4	17.3	55.8	18.1	59.2
5	14.9	61.2	15.7	66.8
6	12.1	30.2	12.8	36.1
7	9.3	6.2	9.6	10.2
8	6.4	3.1	5.5	4.1
9	3.2	1.8	2.9	2.2
10	.8	.2	.4	.18

Source: Printed with permission from V. Kumar, J.A. Petersen, and R.P. Leone, "Defining, Measuring, and Managing Business Reference Value," *Journal of Marketing, 77*(1), (2013): 68–86.

Groups 1–7 for the financial services firm) are higher than the average CLV scores for the clients in those same groups. Based on this finding, it could be more profitable for firms to get their medium to high-value clients (Groups 1–7) to provide references rather than focusing on cross- and/or up-selling to those clients.

Table 6.10 shows the results of segmenting the client firms at the telecommunications and the financial services firms by those that provide high-value references versus those that provide low-value references. As shown, there are significant differences between the high-BRV and low-BRV segments for both of the firms. The following major observations are made:

- The CLV of the high-BRV clients is much higher than that of the low-BRV clients.
- Clients who have more tenure with the firm have higher BRV.
- High-BRV clients are more likely to have provided a video reference than a "call me" reference.
- Larger firms, that is, firms with more employees and higher annual revenue, have higher BRV.

Table 6.10	Segment Description for High- and Low-BRV Clients

	Telecommunications		Financial Services	
Variable	High BRV (*n* = 44)	Low BRV (*n* = 44)	High BRV (*n* = 47)	Low BRV (*n* = 47)
Average CLV (in thousands)	18.4	5.8	18.7	5.2
Average tenure (years)	10.3	4.9	14.7	6.8
Most common media format	Video	"Call me"	Video	"Call me"
Average number of employees	2,710	468	2,158	318
Average annual revenue (in millions of dollars)	59.4	11.2	70.6	18.8

Source: Printed with permission from V. Kumar, J.A. Petersen, and R.P. Leone, "Defining, Measuring, and Managing Business Reference Value," *Journal of Marketing*, *77*(1), (2013): 68–86.

These results add credence to firms selecting clients for references that have higher CLV, longer tenure, more employees, and higher annual revenues. Based on these findings, moving forward, firms may be able to target prospects through the selection of clients for reference in order to increase customer acquisition and profitability.

Impact of BRV on Customer Acquisition

Delving deeper into the use of client references for customer acquisition, the study also shows that client references can be extremely beneficial in adding value to the process of acquiring new customers. Therefore, in addition to traditional marketing and sales force efforts, it is imperative for firms to develop business reference programs and to identify which clients have the potential to add the most value through new customer adoption. In establishing their reference programs and identifying the client firms to provide references, it is important for the seller firm to understand the impact of BRV in terms of its three components; influence, number of references, and CLV.

The influence of client references is vital in encouraging prospect firms to become customers. In the study, we found that references have a profound impact on the purchase decisions of prospect firms for both the telecommunications and the financial services firms. On average, more than 50 percent of the purchase influence resulted from a client firm reference demonstrating the magnitude of the influence that references have on the decision of prospects to adopt. One of the ways that firms can capitalize on this influence is by having a portfolio of client references ready for their sales teams to use during the sales process.

Although it is clear that client references have the ability to influence customer adoption, there is still a need to understand how the number of references impacts the prospect's decision. The question here is: Do prospects place more value on a variety of different references more than only a few references or one key client reference? By investigating the mean number of client references for each converted prospect, we found that usually only a few client references have a major impact on influencing prospects to adopt in the telecommunications and financial services firms. Specifically, converted prospects use on average one to two key client firms as references to influence their decision to adopt. Reference congruency plays a role in this as prospects place more value on client references that match their situation. Within any firm setting, typically only a few client firms will have high congruency; and therefore, only a few references will matter in influencing prospects to become clients. As such, it is important for a seller firm to have a variety of references in its portfolio in order to increase the probability that reference congruency can be achieved.

Once prospects have been converted as a result of influence and congruency, it is important for firms to understand what proportion of value being generated by prospects through their CLV is attributable to BRV. By investigating the CLV for all of the converted prospects, we found that on average the converted prospects that joined during the study time period were profitable customers for the telecommunications and financial services firms. The findings showed that the converted prospects have an average CLV that is slightly lower than the average CLV of the High BRV client firms but much higher than the average CLV of the Low BRV client firms as shown in Table 6.9. This observation confirms that implementing a successful business reference program can help a firm to convert prospects to clients who will be profitable to the seller firm.

LINKING BRV AND CBV

In addition to understanding BRV in the context of CLV and customer acquisition, it can be beneficial for firms to understand the link between BRV and CBV. As mentioned previously in this chapter, BRV is largely impacted by the perception that the prospect firm has of the client firm in the context of the four drivers of BRV. Simultaneously, the perception that the client firm has of the seller firm is at the foundation of BRV. It is the measure of CBV that can spur the client firm to make a reference or testimonial for the seller firm.

Ultimately, the value that the client firm places on the seller firm plays a vital role in the seller firm, securing references that can encourage prospects to do business with them. As shown in Figure 6.13, seller firms can strategically segment client firms based on their BRV and CBV. The segmentation is performed by rank ordering the scores from highest to lowest and then taking the median split of the scores.

A brief description and recommended strategies for managing each of the four segments is described below.

- *Diplomats:* These client firms value the seller firm and are likely to provide favorable references. However, the references provided by these client firms are not as valuable to the seller firm in terms of the reference's ability to persuade prospects to view the seller firm more favorably. If

Figure 6.13   The Relationship between BRV and CBV

	Low CRV	High CRV
High CBV	***Diplomats*** These firms have high regard for the seller firm; however, their references do not provide high value. **Strategy:** Groom references from growth-oriented firms.	***Allies*** These firms highly value the seller firm and can provide value to the seller firm through references. **Strategy:** Target these firms for references.
Low CBV	***Rebels*** These firms do not provide value through references; neither do they think highly of the seller firm. **Strategy:** If CLV is low, minimize investment in these firms.	***Aristocrats*** Although these firms can provide value to the seller firm through references, they do not place high value on the seller firm. **Strategy:** Work on building CBV.

the firm is in a growth industry, references from these firms could be valuable in the future. Therefore, seller firms should groom references from these firms but also ensure that there is a balance with references from firms that have higher BRV. As these firms may tend to be smaller, references from these firms may be easier to secure and as such can help build the client firms' reference/testimonials list.

- *Rebels:* These client firms do not value the brand of the seller firm, nor do they have the potential to provide impactful references for the seller firm. As these firms do not perceive the seller firm well and their perception among prospects is not high, they do not offer much value to the seller firm in terms of their ability to secure future business for the seller firm and should not be approached for references. However, if these firms have high CLV scores then the seller firm can investigate ways to improve the CBV of the firms for future growth.

- *Aristocrats:* Although these client firms can increase the value of the seller firm through references, these firms do not place high value on the brand of the seller firm. As such these firms are not likely to provide favorable references for the seller firm. The seller firm should seek to increase the CBV of these firms by improving the client-firm relationship and potentially encourage future references and testimonials.

- *Allies:* These client firms are very valuable to the seller firm as they have the potential to have the most positive impact on the seller firm's performance. These firms should be targeted by the seller firm to provide references as the references will be favorable due to the high perception that the firm has of the seller firm. In addition, the provided references will increase the perceived value of the seller firm in the eyes of prospects due to their high BRV.

Based on the segments above, it can be seen that it is beneficial for seller firms to seek to understand how they are perceived by their clients as well as the value they can gain from their client references. By moving client firms from the bottom left of the matrix to the top right, seller firms can impact their ability to convert prospects to clients and ultimately increase their bottom line.

FROM REFERRALS TO INFLUENCE

This chapter provides a detailed discussion on the value of referral programs and the customers that they bring, as well as the value of business references in the context of the B2B environment. After introducing a mathematical approach for calculating CRV, its connection with the concepts of CLV and CBV was discussed. We saw how CLV aligns with CRV in identifying the value of customers and enhancing it through optimally designed marketing campaigns. Given the limited applicability of CRV for firms that operate in B2B settings, the concept of BRV was presented, along with a conceptual framework to compute it. The metrics discussed in this chapter enable managers to value customers based on their indirect impact on the firm's profits from both the savings in acquisition costs and the growth of new customers who were referred to the firm by existing customers.

The next chapter discusses the subsequent component of CEV that incorporates the value of the current customer's influence through social media. Known as customer influence value (CIV), this metric will further highlight how customer actions can indirectly impact profits by influencing the behavior of prospective customers.

NOTES AND REFERENCES

1. V. Kumar, J.A. Petersen, and R.P. Leone, "How Valuable Is Word of Mouth?" *Harvard Business Review*, 85(10), (2007): 139–146.
2. Citi Home Loan Referral Rewards, Citibank, https://www.online.citibank.co.in/products-services/loans/mgm/member-get-member.htm?site=PORTAL&creative=NGX&section=INHBN2&agencyCode=XER&campaignCode=&productCode=&eOfferCode=INHBN2 (retrieved on April 1, 2013).
3. 2013 Member-Get Member Programme, HSBC, http://www.hsbc.com.cn/1/2/misc/personal-misc/mgm?tab=1 (retrieved on April 9, 2013).
4. V. Kumar, J.A. Petersen, and R.P. Leone, "Driving Profitability by Encouraging Customer Referrals: Who, When, and How," *Journal of Marketing*, 74(5), (2010): 1–17.
5. Susan, Gunelius, "Panasonic Jump Starts Word of Mouth by Using Top Bloggers," Message posted on January 12, 2009, http://www.corporate-eye.com/blog/2009/01/panasonic-jump-starts-word-of-mouth-by-using-top-bloggers/
6. S. Garfield, "Panasonic Crayon CES 2009," Message posted on January 14, 2009, http://stevegarfield.blogs.com/videoblog/2009/01/panasonic-crayon-ces-2009-153.html (retrieved on April 9, 2013).

7. G. Ryu and L. Feick, "A Penny for Your Thoughts: Referral Reward Programs and Referral Likelihood," *Journal of Marketing*, *71*(1), (2007): 84–94.

8. Microsoft Corporation posted in 2012, "Join Windows U Crew – Be a Windows 8 Campaigner," https://www.microsoft.com/en-in/student/windowsUcrew/ (retrieved on September 9, 2013).

9. P. Schmitt, B. Skiera, and C. Van den Bulte, "Referral Programs and Customer Value," *Journal of Marketing*, *75*(1), (2011): 46–59.

10. Ashworth College, (2012), "Refer a Friend Make $50," http://www.referashworth.com/ (retrieved on February 15, 2013).

11. Schmitt, Skiera and Van den Bulte, "Referral Programs and Customer Value," *Journal of Marketing*, *75*(1), (2011): 46–59.

12. F.F. Reichheld, "The one number you need to grow," *Harvard Business Review*, *81*(12), (2003): 46–54.

13. Kumar, Petersen, and Leone, "How Valuable Is Word of Mouth?"

14. O. Hinz, B. Skiera, C. Barrot, and J.U. Becker, "Seeding Strategies for Viral Marketing: An Empirical Comparison," *Journal of Marketing*, *75*(6), (2011): 55–71.

15. Ibid.

16. Groupon, Inc. (2013), "Refer a Friend and Earn $10 in Groupon Bucks!," http://www.groupon.com/visitor_referral (retrieved on February 15, 2013).

17. Tata Sky, "Chaddi Buddy Gifts Ki Gaddi Tata Sky Refer a Friend," http://www.tatasky.com/friend-get-friend.html (retrieved on September 9, 2013).

18. RefAround.com. (2013), "Bank of America Referral Program: Referees Get $25 to $50, Referrers Get $25!" http://www.refaround.com/bank-of-america (retrieved on February 15, 2013).

19. Marriott International, Inc. (2013), "Marriott Rewards® Refer a Friend," http://www.marriott.com/marriott-rewards/refer-a-friend.mi (retrieved on February 15, 2013).

20. Roku, Inc. (2013), "Refer a Friend." http://www.roku.com/referafriend (retrieved on February 15, 2013).

21. iStockphoto LP. (2013), "Referral Program," http://www.istockphoto.com/participate/referral-program/info/ (retrieved on February 15, 2013).

22. AT&T, (2013), "AT&T Refer-a-Friend," http://referrals.att.com/common/overview.pg (retrieved on February 15, 2013).

23. DIRECTV, LLC. (2013), "DIRECTV Refer a Friend," http://www.directv.com/DT-VAPP/referral/referralProgram.jsp (retrieved on February 15, 2013).

24. Kumar, Petersen, and Leone, "Driving Profitability by Encouraging Customer Referrals."

25. Ibid.

26. V. Kumar, J.A. Petersen, and R.P. Leone, "Defining, Measuring, and Managing Business Reference Value," *Journal of Marketing*, *77*(1), (2013): 68–86.

Chapter 7

Customer Influence Value: Really! Where Did You Hear That?

Find answers for...

- How do customers influence other customers/prospects?
- Can we identify the value of influence each customer has in a customer network? If so, how can we maximize this value?
- How can businesses benefit from actively engaging its influencers in the social media?

INTRODUCTION: SOCIAL MEDIA

Merriam-Webster® defines social media as *forms of electronic communication (as websites for social networking and micro blogging) through which users create online communities to share information, ideas, personal messages, and other content (as videos)*.[1] In addition, social media allows for rich interaction (text, pictures and multimedia) between the users. The key differentiation between earlier online methods of communication/conversation like e-mail or online chat and social media is the "shared view and communication" that it brings into play. Conversations may include a statement or an opinion, a comment, a question or an answer but are not necessarily limited to these categories. When a group of people interact with shared conversation/content by viewing, sharing, commenting, or "liking" the particular thread of conversation/content gathers social momentum among the group of people that are interacting. Every so often, some content that has been shared for general public consumption generates such huge interest that such threads are said to have gone "viral." The definition of social media can be extended to business by marketing your business (product or service) when socializing or networking with clients. Credibility is a must and so are accuracy and professionalism.

With over 80 percent of global consumers across geo-demographic barriers actively influencing preferences and purchase decisions through online social networks and word of mouth (WOM); social media such as blogs, forums, and user networks have increasingly taken a more primary role in the minds of the marketers. In WOM, consumers provide information to other consumers who can become potential customers/marketers of the product/service they gave the information about. Organizations are increasingly investing in social channels to rapidly create or propagate their brand through viral content, social media contests and consumer engagement efforts.[2] Companies such as Geico with its Gecko, and P&G's Old Spice brand are converting the traditional "one way" advertising into a long-term "two-way" dialog[3] and engaging by advertising on channels like YouTube and soliciting comments from customers.

Another example in recent times is of the computer giant, Dell. The company engages the members in the social media platform, monitors 1,500 blogs a day and interacts with most of the people. Dell talks to its customers wherever they want to talk, including Facebook, Second Life, and Twitter. Anyone can suggest ideas for the company, comment on them, and vote for their favorites through IdeaStorm (a website launched by Dell in 2007 to facilitate them to gauge which ideas are most important and most relevant to the public). So far, some 10,000 ideas have been submitted and more than 650,000 people have voted on them.[4]

The top reason why marketers use social media is to generate WOM and communicate brand stories which can enhance sales and profit to reach the aim of maximum return on investment (ROI).

SOCIAL MEDIA LANDSCAPE

Social media is present in different forms including Internet forums, collaborative projects (e.g., Wikipedia), photo sharing (e.g., Picasa, Shutterfly), video sharing (e.g., YouTube), live blogs (e.g., WordPress), micro blogging sites (e.g., Twitter), social bookmarking sites (e.g., Pinterest), and music sharing (e.g., Pandora) to name a few. Many of these services are integrated in the most popularly used sites like Facebook and Twitter, to name a few (Figures 7.1 and 7.2).

Figure 7.1 Social Media Landscape

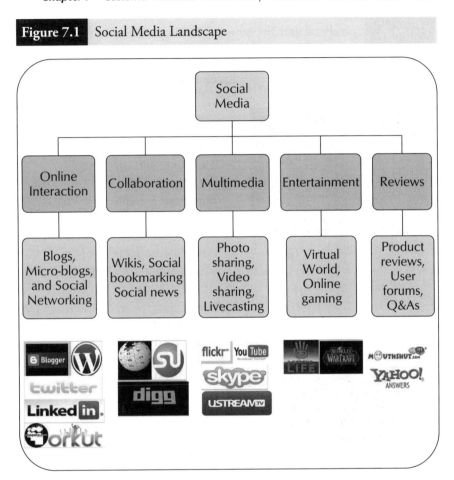

WHY SOCIAL MEDIA CAN BE POWERFUL

Social networks address the three key dimensions that people typically look for while connecting with other people: "who," "when," and "what." These three variables constitute "what" people share with "whom" and "when." Further, questions like how and why they share and from where they share are good for understanding the patterns of sharing and understanding each user's psyche but the power of social media typically lies in the "who," "when," and "what" dimensions. Smartphones, with their ability to capture multimedia

Figure 7.2	Facebook and Twitter—Social Media Giants—A Quick View

Facebook
- One billion monthly active users as of October 2012.
- Approximately 81% of our monthly active users are outside the U.S. and Canada.
- 584 million daily active users on average in September 2012.
- 604 million monthly active users who used Facebook mobile products as of September 30, 2012.

Twitter
- More than 140 million monthly globally active.
- 75% of users are likely to buy the brand that they follow.
- 11 accounts are created every second.
- An average of 340 million tweets posted per day.
- There were 175 million tweets sent every day throughout 2012.

Source: Adapted from www.facebook.com (as of October 2012) and www.twitter.com (as of December 2012).[5]

and connectivity via cellular and/or wireless networks, have become almost ubiquitous among the population that is active on social network.

Today, there are several social networks that serve different purposes. It is extremely difficult to list all categories of social networks available since the landscape is as varied as the individuals are. To list a few, social networks allow one to blog, microblog, connect with people of similar and varied professions, publish audio and video productions, promote products and services, write or record reviews, canvas for votes, conduct polls, and so on.

Businesses have quickly recognized the value of voluntary information shared on these social networks. They are focusing their resources and efforts on using the data and information that they can legally capture from these networks. While there are several uses for this valuable information, businesses have used them in product improvement, new product development, offering enhanced customer service, and targeted marketing to name a few.

Social networking sites are now enabling businesses by gathering statistics on the impact, reach, and progress of a product or service, which in turn, leads to rich analytics on customer behavior, customer preference, and product penetration and branding. Social media thus brings traditional marketing from magazines, billboards, and TV advertisements to a consumer's personal devices like computers, tablets, and mobile phones. Social media has overcome several traditional marketing barriers like limited information, limited reach, one-way messaging, and lack of targeting, to name a few.

While all of the above are key ingredients in making social networks powerful, the most fundamental enabler that fuels social networks is the ease by which WOM information spreads (Figure 7.3). Selection of the right type of social media (right medium) and creating the right message ensures success in social media marketing (SMM).

| Figure 7.3 | Power of Social Media |

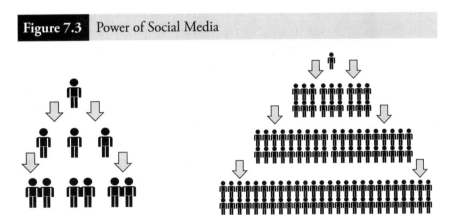

"If you make customers unhappy in the physical world, they might each tell 6 friends. If you make customers unhappy on the Internet, they can each tell 6,000 friends."

Jeff Bezos, CEO at Amazon.com

Source for the quote: www.ebusinessjournals.com/2011/01/25/dave-carroll-versus-united-airlines-when-customer-service-fails/ (retrieved on February 2, 2013).

With the volume of information added and exchanged through the social media portals, companies have started to analyze the data to glean insights on consumer preferences and usage patterns. Since there is a deluge of information that comes through social media channels, selecting the right type of social media platform, designing the right message, and engaging the right user(s) to spread them is critical for the success in SMM. By formalizing the right strategies and harnessing the right tools, businesses can create sustainable WOM marketing; not just the buzz, but meaningful conversations that lead to recommendations.

The question now is, beyond all this popularity and promise, how can marketers know that a social media strategy can be a viable option for generating positive WOM and communicating brand stories, while simultaneously increasing sales, profits, and ROI?

Recent research has shown that by identifying the net influence wielded by a user in a social network and predicting the user's ability to generate the spread of viral information, businesses can determine the "right" individuals to engage in social media conversations to promote WOM. Further, by linking the generated WOM to the actual sales, research shows that social media can be used to generate sales, increase ROI, induce positive WOM, and spread brand knowledge.[6]

As interconnectedness between consumers grows in social channels, consumer-to-consumer communication pertaining to products also increases. This has led to the creation of a new form of WOM marketing that is managed by consumers. Using online messages, these consumer-managed communications involve exchanging product and brand-level messages throughout a network of consumers. Consumers are now communicating with each other on every facet of information regarding the products, which is now more valuable than traditional company driven marketing efforts. Social media has risen quickly to be the first opted platform by consumers to compare products with competitive offerings, read other consumer experiences and also share their own experiences for benefit of the general populace.

SUCCESSES AND FAILURES IN MARKETING THROUGH SOCIAL MEDIA

While it is easy to see how SMM can help businesses, there are several aspects a business has to carefully consider before being able to leverage and realize the true value of "customer influence." There are several instances when SMM has backfired on businesses. A very important point to note about the social media channel is that its strength of "going viral" or "explosive reach" can quickly become an unfavorable characteristic if something backfires on social media. It might even be prudent for businesses to first ensure that their social media campaigns don't backfire before evaluating whether they would be successful. A few instances where social media has backfired on businesses are given below:

- Kenneth Cole—hijacking hashtag #Cairo during Egyptian riots to push their message. Kenneth Cole was finally forced to delete the tweet and issue an apology but the damage was already done (Figure 7.4).
- Domino's Pizza—a couple of employees posted a video on the web that was in bad taste and grossed out all consumers. The CEO then took full responsibility and sent out a very appropriate apology, which helped Domino's redeem itself.
- Kryptonite Evolution vs. ball point pen—a man discovers that he can pick the Kryptonite Evolution 200 U lock—once deemed the "toughest lock in the bike security"—with a Bic ball point pen. Even after this

| **Figure 7.4** | Kenneth Cole Tweet |

@KennethCole
Kenneth Cole

Millions are in uproar in #Cairo. Rumor is they heard our new spring collection is now available online at http://bit.ly/KCairo -KC

4 hours ago via Twitter for BlackBerry®   ☆ Favorite ♻ Retweet ↰ Reply

Source: http://www.huffingtonpost.com/2011/02/03/kenneth-cole-tweet-uses-c_n_818226. html (retrieved on February 2, 2013).

news went viral in blog space as well as *New York Times*, the brand did not respond. The bad publicity had a viral effect with many fake accounts created by users mocking the company with several humorous tweets mimicking the original post.

Yet another form of SMM that we have seen in recent times is the concept of "Social Coupons." For example, Groupon completely flouts the "who-when-what" paradigm but generates transactions by offering deep discounts to whomever that participates in a group buying spree. Are businesses really benefitting by such marketing efforts?

To achieve benefits from social coupons, businesses should design deals carefully, without giving too much away. Businesses considering social coupon campaigns should make an effort to understand how and why coupons work, and how they can affect the economics of the business both in the short and the long term. In a recent article,[7] it has been exemplified how few businesses ended up in losses trying to use social coupons for increasing customer traffic, but in turn, jeopardized their profit margins by extending coupons to existing customers.

The above-mentioned examples are not to deter businesses from using social media but to be careful and smart in their campaigns so that they can maximize the value they can reap from the social media channels. *Timing the content* to meet the expectation of the consumers is another important component for the recipe of a successful social media campaign.

Choosing the right channel and the right people is also key for success in social media campaigns. Yelp, the social networking user review website, provides a prime example of harnessing the power of WOM to benefit customers and the firm.[8] Yelp created the "Elite Program" in order to incentivize the most loyal users who are deemed to have added value to the website through the frequency of their activities, originality, and the positive impact made within Yelp's social community. Among these incentives are exclusive invites to member-only events and other loyalty recognizing perks that strengthen the relationships between Yelp and these influential users, as well as attracting other influential users to become more active in the community.

How does then one know the extent of influence he or she has on another? Can this be quantified and measured?

DEFINING CUSTOMER INFLUENCE EFFECT (CIE) AND CUSTOMER INFLUENCE VALUE (CIV)

We introduce two new metrics called customer influence effect (CIE)[9] and customer influence value (CIV)[10] to help measure and quantify customer influence on others.

- *Customer influence effect (CIE) measures the net spread and influence of a message from a particular individual.*
- *Customer influence value (CIV) calculates the monetary gain or loss realized by a firm that is attributable to a customer (influence), through his/her spread of positive or negative WOM.* Using this metric, it is possible to craft strategies that can weed out or appreciate propagators of negative or positive WOM based on the probable damage or gain that they can cause to an organization in terms of lost or won sales.

By identifying the net influence of a user in a social network and predicting the user's ability to spread viral information, businesses can be selective about whom to engage with in social media conversations for effective WOM. Once businesses associate the generated WOM to the actual sales it would help them create strategies to effectively use social media to widen the brand awareness, influence positive WOM in customers, and spawn sales resulting in an increased ROI.

The next section provides a framework that can be implemented by businesses to create successful social media campaigns based on the above principles.

A SEVEN-STEP FRAMEWORK FOR CREATING SUCCESSFUL SOCIAL MEDIA MARKETING CAMPAIGNS

An effective social media strategy should clearly define the marketing objectives, evaluate the opportunities, and select an appropriate form of social media to communicate. When implemented correctly, social media strategies can drive profit from positive WOM. This can be achieved by a clear "call-to-action" that encourages users to engage in a behavior such as clicking the "Like" button, or sharing (retweeting) the posts. Getting the timing of the social media content right is also crucial to the success (Figure 7.5).

Step 1: Monitor the conversations. Businesses must monitor and capture relevant social media conversational exchanges by customers and analyze them with respect to the context to glean information on customer behavior, customer influence, and brand awareness. They should also make sure that they do not violate any rules and regulations in the process of monitoring, capturing, and analyzing conversations.

Step 2: Identify influential individuals who can spread messages. After monitoring and recognizing the conversations, businesses should identity the "right" individuals who engage in these conversations. This can be achieved by identifying the specific factors that make the individual the right candidate to spread the message (see Figure 7.6).

Step 3: Identify the factors shared by influential individuals. After identifying the "right" individuals (we refer to them as "influencers"), businesses should determine the common factors among them to create "influencer" profiles. Such forms of user profiles allow businesses to identify all the influencers, and design ways to encourage them to talk about the products/services. "Influencers" are seen to exhibit heavy social engagement in three aspects: (*a*) message spread (the number of times a message is forwarded by the receivers), (*b*) influence (the number of times the message is forwarded to their friends), and (*c*) social impact (the number of comments/replies received for each message). Refer to the "Measuring CIV" section that appears later on in this chapter.

Step 4: Locate those potential influencers who have interests relevant to the campaign. Businesses can use the drivers to locate all the influencers throughout the desired social media platforms so that the brand/product/service can be communicated to have the maximum reach. Identifying these drivers calls for a careful analysis of each type and instance of the WOM and how it spreads and can be used to locate all the influencers.

Following the identification of drivers, the Stickiness Index (SI) metric can help businesses locate the individuals who talk the most about the focal product category. *Stickiness Index is a metric[11] that can be defined as an array of the degree to which a user or an instance of WOM is specific to each category of topics.*

Figure 7.5 Seven-step Framework for a Successful Social Media Marketing Campaign

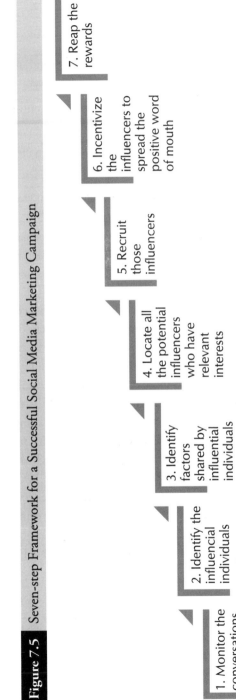

1. Monitor the conversations

2. Identify the influencial individuals

3. Identify factors shared by influential individuals

4. Locate all the potential influencers who have relevant interests

5. Recruit those influencers

6. Incentivize the influencers to spread the positive word of mouth

7. Reap the rewards

Source: Printed with permission and adapted from *V. Kumar* and *Rohan Mirchandani*, "Increasing the ROI of Social Media Marketing," *MIT Sloan Management Review, 54*(1), (2012): 55–61.

Figure 7.6	Drivers of Influencers

Activeness Compatibility	• Number of times the influencer and their network friends "see" and "share" a message.
Host Clout	• Number of user connections and number of users "following" an influencer.
Talkativeness of Receiver	• How often the influencer's message is being retweeted and "hashtagged."
Generosity	• Like-mindedness and similarities shared by the influencer with their network friends.

Source: Printed with permission and adapted from V. Kumar and Rohan Mirchandani, "Increasing the ROI of Social Media Marketing," *MIT Sloan Management Review*, 54(1), (2012): 55–61.

In other words, SI is measured as what percentage of the total conversation an individual has that would be related to the category of interest.

In simple terms, if an influential individual in social media is talking about eat-outs, it is highly probable that the same person is going to be talking (discussing) to his friends about going out for dinner and finding the restaurants near by the location he is in. As we saw earlier, CIE is the measure of the spread of the message and CIV is how much a person can influence his or his friend, and SI is how relevant the conversations are with respect to what is being marketed. Using the information obtained through the CIE and SI metrics, businesses can relate the abstract comments and WOM about the particular product category to specific financial metrics reflecting monetary returns. The financial valuation of such comments can be done through the CIV metric we created. In effect, this step ensures moving beyond simply "listening" to conversations on social media platforms, to actively engaging in the identification of brand ambassador(s).

Step 5: Recruit those influencers with interests relevant to the campaign to talk about the company's product or service. Businesses must enlist the influencers in the social media campaign(s) to spread positive WOM. Recruitment of such influencers is possible by providing users ways to interact online and spread positive WOM that can be tracked and measured (such as survey and online games).

Step 6: Incentivize those influencers to spread positive WOM about the product or service. The next step is to engage the influencers to spread positive WOM and this can be done by incentivizing the influencers. The incentivized diffusion of positive WOM can help businesses retain customers, attract prospects, and further identify potential brand ambassadors. Businesses can choose to offer tangible or intangible, or a combination of both for the incentives.

Step 7: Reap the rewards from increasingly effective social media campaigns. Following the above-prescribed steps will enable businesses to measure effectiveness of their social media campaigns with more accuracy than before. Associating conversations and positive WOM to brand recognition and product sales will result in businesses seeing a quantifiable increase in financial performance, increased customer engagement and stronger brand awareness.

IMPLEMENTATION OF THE SEVEN-STEP FRAMEWORK

This section provides a detailed insight into the seven-step framework for successful SMM, which we implemented at HokeyPokey, a popular ice cream retailer in India (Figure 7.7), with amazing results.

HokeyPokey, a popular "super premium" ice cream retailer has over a dozen outlets based in India. It has 12 locations in Mumbai and seven outside Mumbai spread over multiple cities and is rapidly expanding all over India. They offer "customized mix-in" flavors, which are very popular amongst their strong customer base of youngsters between ages 16 and 25. The concept of customized food services was fairly new in the region, and the retailer felt the need to create a strong brand identity through its passionate customers. Most of HokeyPokey's existing brand advocates fell within the "Millennial" demographic cohort (today's 18- to 29-year olds—members of the so-called Millennial Generation or Gen Y). Given that over 50 million consumers in this segment in India actively spent over three hours on average on various online social networks, we realized the importance of social media marketing to engage its customers and drive a profitable strategy. The main business question then was—"How do we measure the return of investment on social media marketing?"

We decided to implement the seven-step framework for their social media campaign[12] to effectively use HokeyPokey's shoestring budget for marketing and realize a lift in sales and ROI. At the end of the example you will see the

Figure 7.7 HokeyPokey

Source: HokeyPokey website http://www.hokeypokey.in (retrieved on April 5, 2012).

real-world computation of CIE and CIV that enabled HokeyPokey achieve its goals (Figure 7.8).

We came up with innovative ways to market to customers on an individual basis. "Creations on the Wall" and "Share Your Brownies" campaigns were the two pillars of HokeyPokey's success in its outreach to customers. "Creations on the Wall" allowed customers to create their own ice cream flavors and display them on the "Creations Wall" inside the store. We encouraged customers to market their creations with their online peers on social platforms and "share their brownies." This portion of the campaign rewarded customers for marketing their creations and influencing others to try them, or to create their own. These customer creations stayed up on the wall for an extended period of time, allowing other customers to view and choose from these creations. Throughout this period, we monitored the frequency at which certain ice cream creations were selected by other customers. We

Figure 7.8	HokeyPokey's Goals for Social Media Marketing

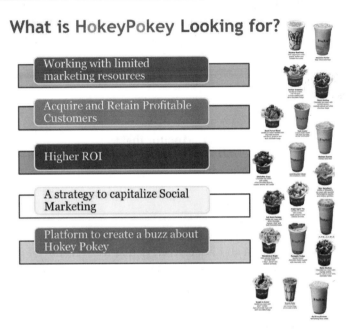

Source: Printed with permission from V. Kumar, Vikram Bhaskaran, Rohan Mirchandani, and Milap Shah (2013), "Creating a Measurable Social Media Marketing Strategy for HokeyPokey: Increasing the Value and ROI of Intangibles & Tangibles," *Marketing Science, 32*(2), (2013): 194–212.

removed the creations that became quite popular from the "Creations on the Wall" and added them to the permanent menu at all HokeyPokey locations. The seven-step implementation was implemented at HokeyPokey over a 30-month period as shown in Figure 7.9.

Figure 7.9	HokeyPokey Social Media Marketing Project Timeline

Project Timeline

Market Research	Software Testing	Pre-Test Phase	Implementation Phase
January 2009	June 2009	December 2009	March 2010	June 2011

Source: Printed with permission from V. Kumar and Rohan Mirchandani, "Increasing the ROI of Social Media Marketing," *MIT Sloan Management Review, 54*(1), (2012): 55–61.

IMPLEMENTATION OF THE SEVEN-STEP PROCESS IN HOKEYPOKEY

First Step—Monitor the conversations (Figure 7.10).

Figure 7.10	First Step

1. Monitor the conversations

Source: Refer to Figure 7.5.

- The first six months were spent in planning, understanding, and analyzing the social media and HokeyPokey's market in Mumbai, India.
- This resulted in monitoring 825,091 conversations involving 1,736 individuals across different social networking channels.

Second Step—Identity the influencers (Figure 7.11).
  HokeyPokey's criteria for the "right" influencers were:

- The individual must belong to a social network that had at least 1,000 users:

  a. To maximize the number of times a single message propagates in the network.

Figure 7.11	Second Step

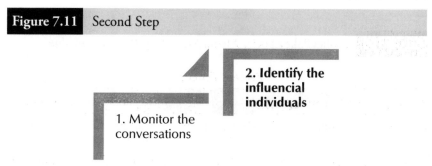

2. Identify the influencial individuals

1. Monitor the conversations

Source: Refer to Figure 7.5.

- The individual must have a minimum of 20 percent connectivity to others in the same geo-location and also belong to the same social network:

  a. To allow for a good spread of the messages.

- The individual must be part of a network that allows easy engagement of users:

  a. This lays the groundwork for the user to be active in the social network.

- The individual must be able to actively engage others within the chosen network:

  a. While the network itself can be an easy platform it also depends on the individual being active in the network.

In addition to the above valuations, it also became necessary to choose social network platforms that would allow for easy data collection. This resulted in Facebook and Twitter being the choice platforms for the implementation.

Third Step—Identify characteristics of key influencers (Figure 7.12).

For this step, we operationalized the drivers of influence by defining preferable characteristics which can also be generalized across the population:

- *Activeness*—number of times that an individual interacts with a message.
- *Clout*—number of people an individual is connected to and being actively followed by.
- *Talkativeness (of the receiver)*—number of times an individual's message gets repeated.

Figure 7.12 Third Step

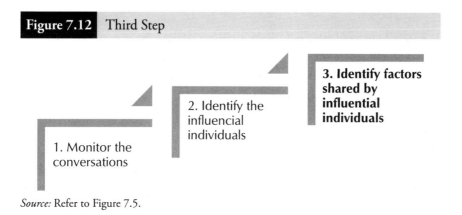

Source: Refer to Figure 7.5.

- *Like-mindedness*—a factor revealed by common interests and similarities between individuals.

These characteristics were identified to help HokeyPokey achieve the following objectives:

- create and spread its brand identity,
- stimulate and encourage a strong brand association among consumers,
- proactively identify brand advocates, and
- reach potential customers through existing customers.

Identification of such characteristics helped in the calculation of CIE.

Fourth Step—Locate potential influencers (Figure 7.13).

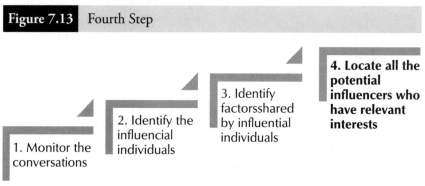

Figure 7.13 Fourth Step

1. Monitor the conversations

2. Identify the influencial individuals

3. Identify factorsshared by influential individuals

4. Locate all the potential influencers who have relevant interests

Source: Refer to Figure 7.5.

- While individuals could have a strong relation by way of shared interests, it was important to group those network individuals who shared interest in ice cream (as measured by the "Stickiness Index" factor).
- This grouping was also important to identify brand ambassadors for HokeyPokey.

Fifth Step—Recruiting influencers (Figure 7.14).

This step consisted of recruiting those individuals that were identified as influencers based on the previous four steps. This group consisted of influencers who were already engaged to participate in HokeyPokey's ice cream promotion campaign.

Figure 7.14 Fifth Step

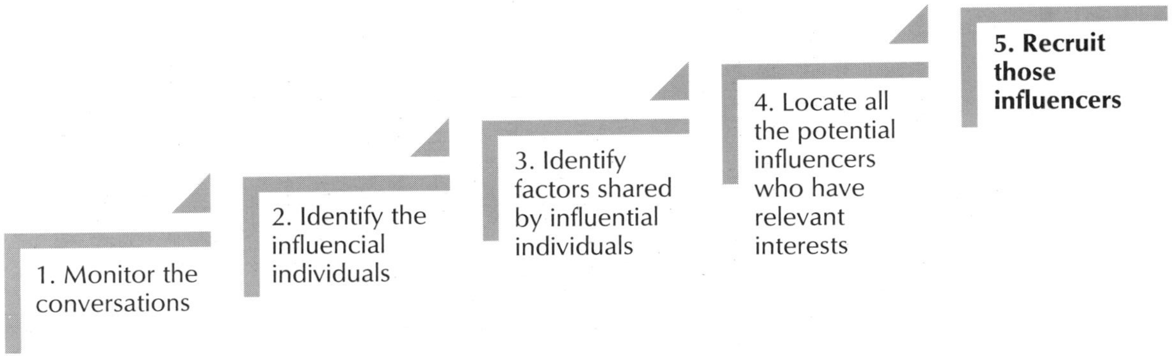

1. Monitor the conversations

2. Identify the influencial individuals

3. Identify factors shared by influential individuals

4. Locate all the potential influencers who have relevant interests

5. Recruit those influencers

Source: Refer to Figure 7.5.

Sixth Step—Incentivize the influencers (Figure 7.15).

This step is a key step while designing social campaigns as the incentive needs to be planned in such a way that it does not tip the balance favorably for the sole reason of existence of an incentive. Hence, we decided to create a unique campaign that combined the intangible and tangible benefits for influencers. The campaign was designed in such a way that influencers who were really motivated and interested could go the extra mile to influence others and the incentive was just a derivative of it rather than the mainstay. This involved developing a two-stage campaign consisting of "Creations on the Wall" and "Share Your Brownies."

Creations on the Wall: The Influencer created custom ice cream combinations that became a part of the menu offered by HokeyPokey. Customers could order these special creations in the same way as they did for those items available on HokeyPokey's standard menu. The influencers were given the freedom to create their own recipes, give their creations the names of their own choice and also identify themselves as the creators. These special creations were given space on a wall in the parlor that was dedicated for the "Creations on the Wall" stage of the campaign.

Share Your Brownies: This formed the second stage of the campaign providing an opportunity for the influencers who had created the special recipes to promote their creations on Twitter. The tangible incentive portion of the campaign was to offer customized T-shirts in exchange for motivated promotional tweets and the intangible incentive was to get a higher standing among the peers when messages were shared on Facebook or Twitter.

The special creations by influencers were shared across all parlors of HokeyPokey for people to order and also to increase the WOM propensity of the campaign. The campaign conversations were tracked four times during its active period: May 2010, September 2010, January 2011, and June 2011. HokeyPokey also provided influencers with "Brownie Points" whenever their creations were purchased or were discussed on the social network, which, in turn, could be redeemed by influencers for prizes and discounts (Figure 7.16).

Several interesting trends surfaced from the tracking of HokeyPokey's campaign. As an example, "Sahara Surprise," which enjoyed just a lukewarm popularity during March and September, 2010, turned out to be the most popular and hotly discussed creation by November 2010 after a few High-CIE customers got influenced. CIE was frequently recalculated to identify influencers promoting their own creations at different points of time to keep

Figure 7.15 Sixth Step

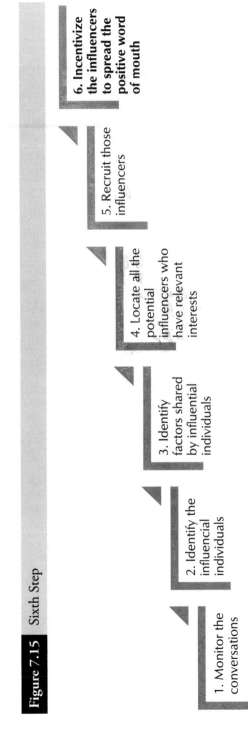

1. Monitor the conversations

2. Identify the influencial individuals

3. Identify factors shared by influential individuals

4. Locate all the potential influencers who have relevant interests

5. Recruit those influencers

6. Incentivize the influencers to spread the positive word of mouth

Source: Refer to Figure 7.5.

Figure 7.16	Happy Family Enjoying HokeyPokey Ice Creams

Source: Printed with permission from V. Kumar and Rohan Mirchandani, "Increasing the ROI of Social Media Marketing," *MIT Sloan Management Review*, 54(1), (2012): 55–61.

interests alive around their creations. The graph in Figure 7.17 shows the distribution of conversations versus the special creations over the course of the campaign. Unfortunately, "Sudden Death" and "Malai Mojito" seem to have suddenly disappeared by May 2010.

Final Step—Reap the rewards (Figure 7.18).

The final step involves converting social media measures like "comments" and "conversations" into quantified financial metrics by computing CIV modeled upon the abstract social media measures.

MEASURING CIV: CALCULATING THE EFFECT AND VALUE OF SOCIAL MEDIA INFLUENCE

When determining the total value of a customer, it is important to include the influence of a customer on the acquisition, retention, and increased share

| **Figure 7.17** | Distribution of Number of Conversations versus Ice Cream Creations |

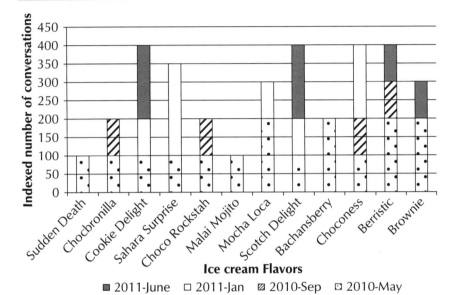

Ice cream Flavors

■ 2011-June □ 2011-Jan ▨ 2010-Sep ▢ 2010-May

Source: Printed with permission from V. Kumar, Vikram Bhaskaran, Rohan Mirchandani, and Milap Shah, "Creating a Measurable Social Media Marketing Strategy for HokeyPokey: Increasing the Value and ROI of Intangibles & Tangibles," *Marketing Science, 32*(2), (2013): 194–212.

of category spending on other customers. Figure 7.19 provides the conceptual approach for measuring CIV.

As illustrated in Figure 7.19, the CIV relies on the "effect" of each customer's influence on other customers. This effect refers to the customer influence effect (CIE). The CIE is determined by taking into consideration three essential components regarding a WOM instance. They are (*a*) whether there is a connection between two users, (*b*) if there is, was the receiver aware of the WOM message being spread? and (*c*) if yes, did the receiver spread the message to other users? In other words, CIE refers to the net spread of an instance of WOM attributable to an individual user in a (social) network. The CIE is also dependent on data pertaining to the user, the type of network in which the communication occurs, the contents of the message, and how much the message appeals to the user for it to spread.

To compute the CIV, the store-level sales were integrated with the corresponding social network, message and influencer social graph through tracking

Figure 7.18   Seventh and Final Step

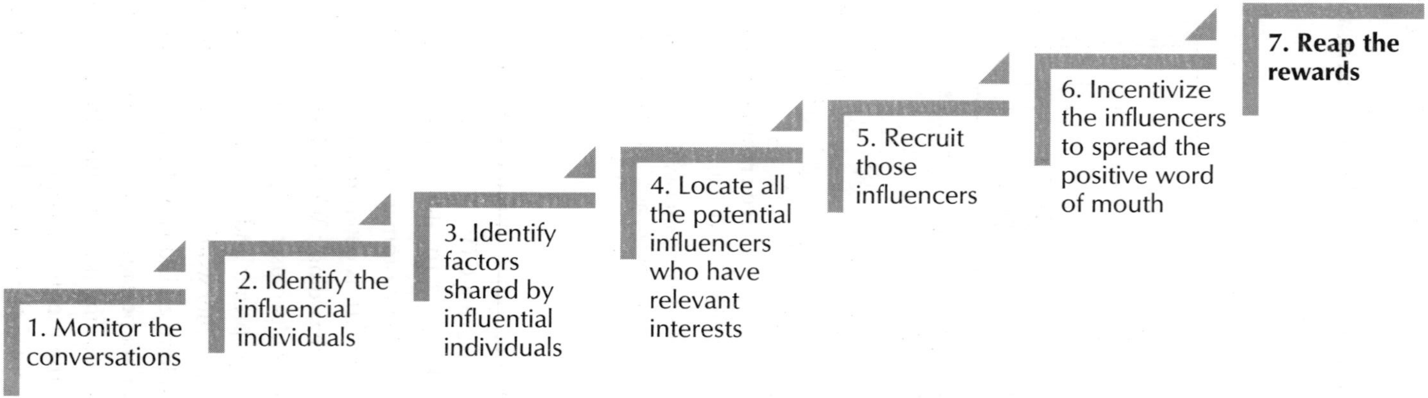

1. Monitor the conversations

2. Identify the influencial individuals

3. Identify factors shared by influential individuals

4. Locate all the potential influencers who have relevant interests

5. Recruit those influencers

6. Incentivize the influencers to spread the positive word of mouth

7. Reap the rewards

Source: Refer to Figure 7.5.

Figure 7.19 Conceptual Approach for Measuring CIV

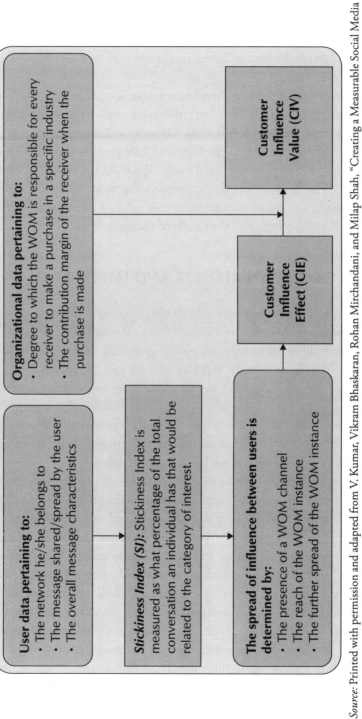

Source: Printed with permission and adapted from V. Kumar, Vikram Bhaskaran, Rohan Mirchandani, and Milap Shah, "Creating a Measurable Social Media Marketing Strategy for HokeyPokey: Increasing the Value and ROI of Intangibles & Tangibles," *Marketing Science, 32*(2), (2013): 194–212.

tags and dynamically generated coupon codes. The monetary value attributed to an individual whose influence resulted in sales for a set of customers is used to compute the CIV.

The impact of this social media campaign was observed at the firm and the customer level. At the firm level, the main impact was in the area of social media accountability. While most firms are still grappling with social media accountability, the use of the CIE and CIV metrics provided HokeyPokey a competitive edge in the social media space. At the customer level, the key impact was observed in calculating the value of an individual's influence in a network, and measuring the monetary value of customer influences of the campaign. The impact of the results of the study is discussed in detail below.

THE CAMPAIGN RESULTS AND IMPLICATIONS

This campaign was effective at both the company and the customer level. At the company level, the main impact was in the area of social media accountability. While most companies are still grappling with social media accountability, the use of the CIE and CIV metrics gave HokeyPokey an important competitive edge. At the customer level, being able to calculate the value of an individual's influence in a network and measure the monetary value of customer influences made it possible for HokeyPokey marketers to greatly enhance the efficacy of their social media campaign. In evaluating the performance of the framework, we benchmarked HokeyPokey's revenue (based on ice cream sales) generated through Facebook and Twitter against the previous 16 months' performance metrics including sales growth rate, ROI, the number of positive and negative conversations, and number of repeat visits. We found that out of the total revenue generated from the "Share Your Brownies" campaign, about 23 percent was attributable to conversations on Twitter and about 80 percent was attributable to Facebook, with a 3 percent to 8 percent overlap between the two social networks. Overall, the campaign was a huge success. HokeyPokey realized increases of 49 percent in brand awareness, 83 percent in ROI and 40 percent in the sales revenue growth rate (see Figure 7.20). The lack of robust methodologies to measure the impact of social media efforts is addressed in this study. It provides tangible metrics and a robust methodology to measure the effectiveness of social media marketing spend and to maximize the ROI of social media campaigns.

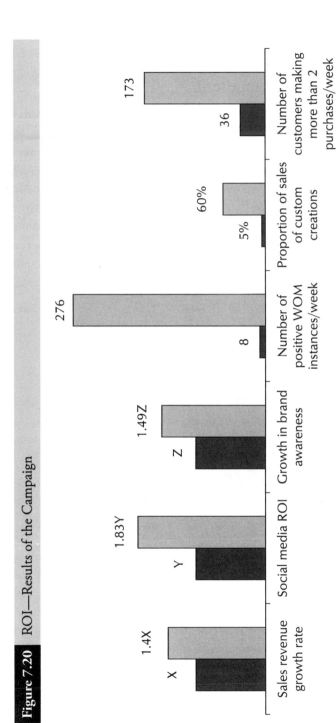

Figure 7.20 ROI—Results of the Campaign

Sales revenue growth rate — 1.4X / X

Social media ROI — 1.83Y / Y

Growth in brand awareness — 1.49Z / Z

Number of positive WOM instances/week — 276 / 8

Proportion of sales of custom creations — 60% / 5%

Number of customers making more than 2 purchases/week — 173 / 36

■ Pre-campaign (January 2009 to February 2010)   ■ Post-campaign (March 2010 to June 2011)

Source: Printed with permission and partially adapted from V. Kumar and Rohan Mirchandani, "Increasing the ROI of Social Media Marketing," *MIT Sloan Management Review, 54*(1), (2012): 55–61.

COMPUTATION OF CIV

How Can This Be Computed?

The CIV is calculated as the monetary gain attributable to each customer's influence by including the following information: (*a*) the degree to which each instance of WOM is responsible for every receiver to make a purchase and (*b*) the contribution margin contributed by the receiver when making the purchase. It is important to note that the above mentioned information is industry specific and therefore, yields a CIV that reflects the characteristics of each industry. The CIV of an individual is calculated by iteratively summing the individual's own CLV, and the proportional CIV of each of his/her influence that is attributable to the individual's influence, as:

$$\text{CIV}_\theta = \text{CLV}_\theta + \sum_{i=0} \kappa_{\theta \to i} \times \text{CIV}_i \qquad \text{(Equation 7.1)}$$

where:
CIV_θ = the CIV of a user θ
CLV = the customer lifetime value
$\kappa_{\theta \to i}$ = the Hubbell's influence of θ on i

For a full example of this calculation, see Exhibit 7.1.

IMPLICATIONS OF CIV FOR SOCIAL MEDIA MARKETERS

The CIE and CIV metrics have enormous applications for firms and marketers using social media tools.[13] The ice cream retailer's (HokeyPokey) study describes the application of these metrics in the case of an offline retailer (localized setting and small business). The same strategy can be extended to online retailers also. Several social media networks like Facebook, Twitter and Google+ to name a few have implemented seamless sign-in so that online retailers can allow their customers to sign-in using social media accounts, which makes tracking conversations easier. However, despite the vast amount of individual and relationship data available through these media, organizations have been unable to directly and efficiently measure the effectiveness of their social media strategy using tangible metrics.

Exhibit 7.1: Calculating the Effect and Value of Social Media Influence

To understand the computation of CIE, let us consider a network of media users discussing a specific ice cream flavor creation. The direction of the arrows indicates the flow of influence of a user over others.

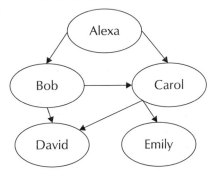

In this network, we compute the CIEs of Alexa, Bob, and Carol as:

CIE of Alexa = Number of relevant conversations posted by Alexa +
     (Influence of Alexa on Bob) × CIE of Bob +
     (Influence of Alexa on Carol) × CIE of Carol

CIE of Bob = Number of relevant conversations posted by Bob +
     (Influence of Bob on Carol) × CIE of Carol +
     (Influence of Bob on David) × CIE of David

CIE of Carol = Number of relevant conversations posted by Carol +
     (Influence of Carol on David) × CIE of David +
     (Influence of Carol on Emily) × CIE of Emily

In this illustration, the CIEs of David and Emily will include only the conversations they spread as they do not influence any other user. We measure the influence of each user on others using Hubbell's influence proposed in the network centrality theory that measures the influence of a user as a function of the influence of the people that she is connected with, plus a factor attributable to her own decision to spread the message. Using Hubbell's influence and the number of conversations the users spread, we computed the CIEs (scaled values) of the users as follows: Alexa: 0.221, Bob: 0.267, Carol: 0.208, David: 0.196, and Emily: 0.140. Conceptually, the CIE represents a share of the influence. Consider the case of C receiving tweets only from A and B. If A and B send 50 tweets each to C, and C does not even respond to B but reciprocates to A and forwards A's tweets to many others, then the

(Exhibit 7.1 Continued)

(Exhibit 7.1 Continued)

relative influence of A on C is close to 1 and the relative influence of B on C is close to zero ... since C has seen the tweet of B but has not responded to that tweet.

To compute the CIV of users in this network, we also consider the value that each individual brings to the firm through their purchase (i.e., future profits known as the customer lifetime value (CLV)). For HokeyPokey, the CLV refers to the profit contributed by a customer through the purchase of the custom ice cream creation subsequent to the spread of the message. We know that the CLVs for the users in this network are: 20 (Alexa), 10 (Bob), 5 (Carol), 20 (David), and 25 (Emily).

The CIV of an individual is calculated by iteratively adding the individual's own CLV, and the proportional CIV of each of his/her influencee's that is attributable to the individual's influence. This is calculated as:

@ CIV of Alexa = (CLV of Bob + 0.5*CLV of Carol) + (CIV of Bob + 0.5*CIV of Carol)

The CIV computation of Alexa can be explained in the following manner. Owing to the influence of Alexa, Bob and Carol purchased the custom created ice cream. These purchases earned them a CLV of 10 and 5, respectively. However, Carol's purchases were also influenced by Bob. Therefore, Alexa's CIV will include only half of Carol's CLV, but all of Bob's CLV. Similarly, Alexa's CIV will also include all of Bob's CIV, but only half of Carol's CIV. Such a way of allocation is for this illustration only. The relative influence of Alexa on Carol over Bob on Carol is determined empirically using historic data. Using a similar analogy; we compute the CIVs of Bob and Carol as:

@ CIV of Bob = (0.5*CLV of Carol + 0.5*CLV of David) + (0.5*CIV of Carol)
    = (0.5*5 + 0.5*20) + (0.5*35)
    = 30

CIV of Carol = (0.5*CLV of David + CLV of Emily)
    = (0.5*20 + 25)
    = 35

Using the three CIV equations and the CLVs, we can compute the CIV of Alexa as 60.

Note: @ It is possible to actually calculate the relative influence of Bob and Carol using past conversational data. For the purpose of computation we assume the relative influence of Alexa and Bob on Carol to be equal.

The lack of robust methodologies to measure the impact of social media efforts is addressed in this study. This chapter (and the book) provides a robust, first of its kind methodology to measure the effectiveness of social media marketing spend and how to maximize the ROI of social media campaigns. Once the customers sign-in, the businesses can directly tie online customer influence to sales. The models can be directly extended to a global setting as well. Following are the key takeaways from this study.

- *Measurement of the value of social media:* Social media has both tangible and intangible values. The HokeyPokey implementation clearly reveals a methodology to simultaneously measure the spread of influence and the impact of social media conversations. It also provides a way to convert abstract social media measures into monetary gains that can be easily understood by businesses.
- *Market sensing:* The HokeyPokey implementation clearly demonstrated the play of CIE which can be seen from Figure 7.19. For the first time, social media marketers have a tool that can be readily implemented as social platforms evolve toward openness. Similar initiatives have been taken up by popular social networks like Facebook by offering "graph search" and market analytics.[14]
- *Accountability in social media marketing:* CIE and CIV measures have armed Chief Marketing Officers (CMOs) with new metrics that can be used to communicate concrete business and monetary gains to the board room compared to former intangible measures like engagements and hits.
- *Generalizable and scalable evaluation framework:* Though the analysis was done for Facebook and Twitter, we have ensured that our models are scalable and can be directly applied across any other online social network. Likewise, the framework can be used for any retailer, any WOM campaign and for promotion of any product/service and in any market which is actively influenced by social media.

ENCOURAGING AND MAXIMIZING CIV

Most of the companies are joining the bandwagon of social media and leveraging the business using all available platforms while on the other hand, most of the consumers are gravitating toward companies that are using social media to dialogue with them about the products and service. Social media has become a two-way road to bridge the gap between the consumers and companies. By choosing the right "influencers" from the pool of consumers and by encouraging those influencers with incentives (monetary and nonmonetary), businesses will be able to maximize the CIV. Some businesses adopt a "broadcast" mechanism by which any customer who has opted to share the business's message will be able to share the message with all the people in his/her network. Some other businesses have adopted a "selective" mechanism by which they go through a selection process of finding those customers who would take their message to their network in an effective manner than opting for a "broadcast" kind of approach. To stimulate and to engage customers for active participation in these new marketing initiatives, businesses are experimenting with novel ways of marketing and are willing to explore ideas that would help them acquire new customers, retain existing customers and, in turn, increase their sales.

One such recent trend has been the *apparently* very successful "social coupons" as offered by firms like Groupon, Scoutmob, and Living Social to name a few. An October 2012 survey by Manta, an online hub for entrepreneurs, showed that 82 percent of 1,087 respondents do not intend to run daily deal promotions this year. Only 3 percent said that these campaigns have garnered them repeat business, while 11 percent said they either lost or made no money on the coupons (Figure 7.21).[15]

In a recent study, the popularity of social coupons was demonstrated and several questions were raised.[16] Are social coupons helping or hurting the small and medium businesses? Are social coupons profitable for the businesses offering them? Can a tool that enables businesses to acquire and retain more customers also nurture profits? Or, is there something fundamentally wrong with the current business model of social coupons and if so, how can they be fixed?

It is important to consider customer acquisition and retention from a customer management viewpoint when it comes to considering social coupon campaigns. When making decisions about allocating resources for marketing efforts, it is common for businesses to target customers who are inexpensive (easier) to acquire and inexpensive (easier) to retain. Such decision-making has been shown to overemphasize the short-term gain of acquiring and retaining low value customers over targeting customers who are going to be most profitable in the long run.[17] In addition, by focusing on either short-term

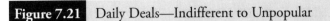

Figure 7.21 Daily Deals—Indifferent to Unpopular

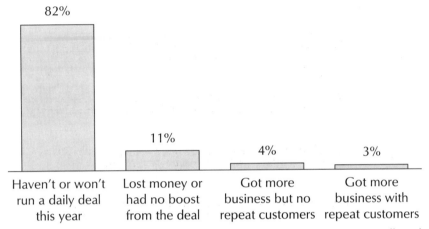

Survey Results of Small Business Owners/Entrepreneurs

Source: Adapted from http://www.businessweek.com/articles/2012-11-12/more-small-retailers-sour-on-daily-deal-sites (retrieved on September 9, 2013).

acquisition or retention, businesses fail to look at the bigger picture of balancing acquisition and retention together.

Since businesses are presented with the option of launching social coupons as an easy and fast way to acquire and retain customers, they are often quick to seize the opportunity and launch a social coupon. And making such easy-way-out decisions makes businesses shortsighted in terms of customer acquisition, retention, and profitability. Therefore, it is important to ascertain the viability of social coupons as a strategy to aid businesses on customer acquisition, customer retention and increased profitability.

The research has shown that social coupons in their current form are not ideally suited to ensure customer acquisition and yield profits for the businesses (see Figure 7.22). The evidence suggests that to prevent social coupons from cannibalizing regular profits, businesses can and should make adjustments to the nature of the deal to influence the profitability of social coupons.

To demonstrate the viability of social coupons and to answer the above questions, the authors of the study investigated three retail businesses. They analyzed the retention rates of the new customers of an ethnic restaurant, a car wash retailer, and a beauty salon. All three businesses had different

Figure 7.22 Social Media Failure

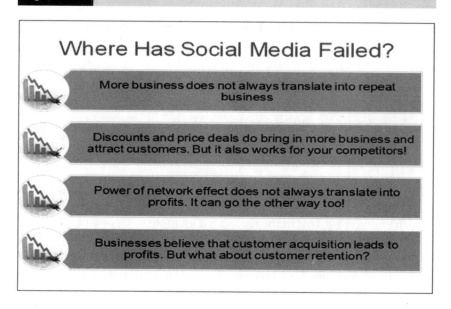

retention rates but quite similar in terms of a decreasing trend in retaining the customers. The results of the study highlight the inadequacy of social coupons in serving the short- and long-term objectives of the businesses. First, the significant losses after the coupon launch created a huge financial burden on the businesses. Second, despite their best marketing efforts, the businesses were not able to retain any new customer who visited them. As a result, their progress of recovering the profit shortfall was greatly reduced or, in the case of the ethnic restaurant, even cut short. Finally, the dismal results of the campaigns discouraged the businesses from considering any further coupon launches until they recovered the shortfall in profits (shown in Figure 7.23).

All the three businesses had a retention rate of 70 percent. However, there were minor variations in the way the businesses retained the new customers. In effect, it was found that:

- The ethnic restaurant will not have any new customers to retain in Month 19 (assuming the coupon was launched in Month 1), and will therefore have to, if at all possible, recover the shortfall in profits by Month 18.

Figure 7.23	Tracing the Dollars

> ➢ *Before the coupon launch*

- Profit contributed by the existing customers of the business
- Regular prices and profit margin rates apply to all customers

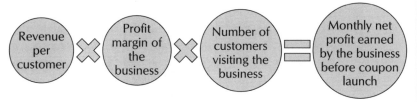

> ➢ *After the coupon launch*

- Profit contributed by the existing *and* new customers of the business
- Prices and profit margins are different for the three sets of customers
- Business will have to give a part of the revenue generated due to coupon sales to the social coupon service provider

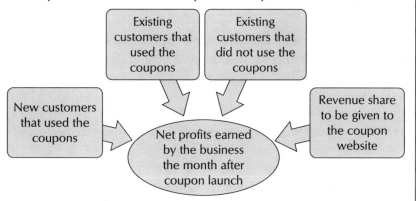

- *Immediate impact on profits*
- All three businesses sustained substantial losses immediately after the coupon launch

- Profits at the end of the month of coupon launch fell between 1 to 3 times that of normal net profits earned before any coupon launches

(Figure 7.23 Continued)

(Figure 7.23 Continued)

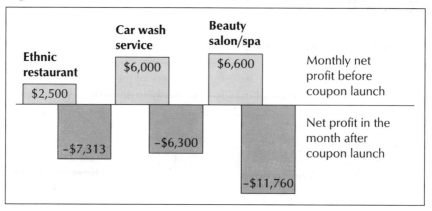

Source: Printed with permission from V. Kumar and Bharath Rajan, "The Perils of Social Coupon Campaigns," *MIT Sloan Management Review,* 53(4), (2012): 13.

- The car wash business will have 140 new customers that availed the coupon visit them every month.
- The beauty salon will have 31 new customers that availed the coupon visit them every month.

Based on the retention rates of the new customers and the business generated by them, we then computed the time each business would take to recover the shortfall in profits incurred during the coupon launch. The results indicated that:

- The restaurant will be able to recover only $1,164 or 12 percent of the shortfall in profits.
- The car wash business will be able to recover the shortfall in profits between Month 15 and Month 16. Consequently, any revenue and profit generated after Month 16 is pure profit for the business and can be directly attributed to the acquisition of new customers.
- The beauty salon will be able to recover the shortfall in profits between Months 98 and 99. Therefore, from Month 99 onward the business can start to see incremental revenue generation from the launch of the social coupon.

These results highlight the inadequacy of social coupons in serving the short and long-term objectives of the businesses. First, the significant losses after the coupon launch created a huge financial burden on the businesses. This was a major setback to the financial health of the businesses. Second, despite their best marketing efforts, the businesses were not able to retain any of the new customers that visited them. As a result, their progress of recovering the profit shortfall was greatly reduced or, in the case of the ethnic restaurant, even cut short. Finally, the dismal results of the campaigns discouraged the businesses from considering any further coupon launches until they recovered the shortfall in profits.

Businesses that launch social coupons not only incur losses in the month following the coupon launch, but also in the following months due to low customer retention. These losses are primarily due to a high number of existing customers receiving the coupons, a high coupon discount rate, and an unsteady flow of new customers visiting the businesses. This cannibalizes regular profits and yields no additional revenue/profits for the businesses. These results call into question the usefulness of social coupons to businesses in their present form.

AVOIDING THE PITFALLS IN SOCIAL COUPON LAUNCHES

The findings indicate that businesses should acquire an understanding of how and why social coupons work, and thereby generate profits. This understanding is critical to evaluate whether social coupons are relevant to their line of business and ultimately helpful for their long-term growth.

Following are some general guidelines that can help businesses in *identifying and avoiding the pitfalls of social coupon launches* and ensure a profitable launch.

Customer acquisition does not always lead to profits. Businesses typically opt for social coupon launches to add new customers to their clientele. The three businesses we studied were no exception. Our analyses have revealed that for every new customer visiting the business due to the coupon launch, the business incurs an additional shortfall in profits. This surprising result is because even though new customers account toward an increase in the customer base, the loss incurred by the business in "acquiring" them (through offering deep discounts and a share in revenue to the coupon service provider) far outweighs the benefits of having them.

However, businesses have the opportunity to mitigate this negative effect. They can up-sell and/or cross-sell other products/services during a customer visit. In fact, despite extra marketing efforts the three businesses we worked with were not able to successfully up-sell/cross-sell that could make the customer visit profitable. However, there may be other businesses that could possibly cross-sell some of their other services to the customer and make the customer's visit a profitable one. For instance, a business providing roofing services can cross-sell its gutter installation and cleaning services. In this regard, the decision to launch a social coupon is likely to be viewed as part of a broader business strategy than as a specific marketing tactic.

Deep discounts could become dearer to businesses. The attraction of social coupons is largely in the deep discounts they provide to consumers. While the low price could be viewed as an incentive for customers to try the product/ service offerings, eventually the new customers will expect to pay the same low price as they continue to transact with the business. As a result, any increase in the price is likely to be viewed by the new customers as a reason to take their business elsewhere. High level of discounts tends to make consumers deal-prone and buy items only through social coupons. The deal-seeking behavior reduces their switching costs and possibly disengages them from the business—all of these have significant negative effects on customer loyalty.

To prevent or reduce the losses from a coupon launch, it is imperative that businesses revisit the existing setup of social coupons and change the discount structure. One way to do this is to launch a coupon that would be valid only on lean business days such as Tuesdays and Wednesdays. This would not only keep the customer acquisition efforts going, but also ensure that the businesses do not incur losses during their busiest time of the week.

Social coupons can cannibalize revenue from existing customers. By launching social coupons, businesses run the risk of inviting their existing customers to pay discounted prices for the same products/services they have been paying full prices for. For instance, a family-owned toy retail chain in Kansas City recently launched a social coupon that attracted nearly 3,000 customers. After the launch of the coupon, the retailer observed that out of the 2,000 coupons that were redeemed, many shoppers bought only the minimum worth of merchandise to redeem the offer, contrary to the store's expectation that shoppers would pick up an extra toy car or doll once they walked into the store. After giving the share of revenue to the online coupon company, the retailer found that it lost money on about 75 percent of its coupon-related sales. Additionally, the retailer observed that roughly 90 percent of the coupons were redeemed by existing store customers.[18] While this is just one example of social coupons at work, it does make a case for revisiting the structure of social coupons.

One way to circumvent the problem of existing customers redeeming the coupons is to target the social coupon only at prospects, and not at existing customers. When existing customers do not receive the social coupon, the subsequent savings in profit shortfall are significant.

What Should the Firm Do to Improve Profits?

To see the effects of avoiding the pitfalls suggested here, a recent study performed a "What-if" scenario with the three businesses on the social coupons they had launched.[19] By changing or influencing the three factors that determined a profitable coupon launch—the number of new customers visiting the business due to the coupon launch, discount rate offered through the coupon on the regular customer fare and, percentage of existing customers that have received and used the coupon—the three businesses were able to make an impact on their bottom line due to the coupon launch (see Table 7.1). The goal of the experiments was to quantify how changing the three variables affects the net profit in the month after the coupon launch.

Specifically, the study was to know the financial impact of a one unit change in the three variables. In other words, businesses expect social coupons to help them in customer acquisition that would ultimately lead to customer retention and profitability. The study also shows the financial impact of adding one more new customer to the business. Does adding more customers lead to more profits for businesses? Let us see what is in store!

With respect to the discount rate of coupons, the study focused on seeing the effect of reducing the discount rate offered on the coupon. While one can expect profitability to increase, it is interesting to know the exact increase in dollars for a one percentage decrease in the discount rate. Regarding existing customers receiving the coupon, it is interesting to know the impact of one percent decrease in the number of existing customers receiving (and therefore using) the coupon on business profitability. The study also experimented with various combinations of the three factors to identify which combination produced the most change in profitability.

Table 7.1	Study Findings		

	It Reduces the Shortfall in Profits for the		
What-if the businesses had...	Ethnic Restaurant by...	Car Wash Services by...	Beauty Salon by...
Increased the # of new customers by 1	−$14	−$17	−$39
Decreased the coupon discount rate by 1 percent	$68	$90	$126
Decreased the % of existing customers receiving the coupon by 1 percent	$187	$225	$495
Increased the number of new customers by 1 and decreased the coupon discount rate by 1 percent	$55	$73	$87
Increased the number of new customers by 1 and decreased the % of existing customers receiving the coupon by 1 percent	$174	$208	$456
Decreased the coupon discount rate by 1 percent and decreased the % of existing customers receiving the coupon by 1 percent	$256	$315	$621
Increased the new customers by 1, decreased the coupon discount rate by 1 percent and decreased the % of existing customers receiving the coupon by 1 percent	$243	$298	$582

Source: Printed with permission from V. Kumar and Bharath Rajan, "Social Coupons as a Marketing Strategy: A Multifaceted Perspective," *Journal of the Academy of Marketing Science,* 40(1), (2012): 120–136.

When changing just one factor, the best results come from decreasing the percentage of existing customers receiving the coupon by 1 percent. When changing multiple factors, the best results come from decreasing the coupon discount rate *and* the percentage of existing customers receiving the coupon by 1 percent. Note that Table 7.1 indicates only the change in financial performance over one month (i.e., between monthly net profit before coupon launch and net profit in the month after the coupon launch).

The results from the "What-if" scenario reveal four key findings. First, contrary to the expectations of the businesses, adding new customers contributed to an increase in the shortfall in profits. Since new customers pay discounted prices and businesses will have to part with a share of revenue contributed by them to the social coupon service provider, the businesses make no money out of having new customers and end up losing money in the process. As indicated in the exhibit "Study Findings," adding one more new customer increased the shortfall of the businesses. When the same result was extended into the future, it was found that this amount only resulted in a bigger shortfall for the businesses. In other words, the businesses were getting into a bigger financial hole as they added more new customers. This finding helped explain the ineffectiveness of the current nature of social coupons to the businesses in generating more business.

Second, the shortfall in profits was reduced the most when the number of existing customers receiving the coupon was reduced by 1 percent. For instance, when the existing customers of the beauty salon that received the coupon was decreased by 1 percent its shortfall in profits decreased by $495.[20] The reason for this substantial decrease is because 30 percent to 40 percent of existing customers of the three businesses had availed the coupon offer. Given the large numbers, even a marginal reduction to this is going to bring in significant reduction in shortfall as the businesses will not have to provide discounted prices and a subsequent share of revenue to the social coupon service provider.

This is also the reason why a decrease in coupon discount rate leads to only a modest reduction in profit shortfall. Since the reduction in discount would apply only to the new customers and one part of the existing customers—a smaller number compared to the remaining existing customers (60 percent to 70 percent for the three businesses) paying full price—the reduction in the shortfall of profit is not as significant as a reduction in existing customers who are receiving the coupon. In other words, between ensuring that fewer existing customers receive the coupon and decreasing the coupon discount rate, the businesses can improve their profitability tremendously than by just adding more new customers. While the previous finding highlighted why the social coupons may not be working for the businesses, this finding helps us illustrate the positive impact of the changes that businesses can make to the existing nature of coupon deals.

Third, it is found that businesses have the option of deciding which factor(s) to alter based on their business setup. If the beauty salon were to choose between changing the coupon discount rate and the percentage of existing customers receiving the coupon, a 1 percent decrease in the percentage of existing customers receiving the coupon would have a similar effect as decreasing the coupon discount rate by 4 percent (all other variables remaining constant). Therefore, based on what is feasible and practical, the businesses can change the factors of the coupon deals to improve profitability.

Finally, when businesses have the flexibility and resources to alter multiple factors simultaneously it is proven that the best results come from decreasing the coupon discount rate and the percentage of existing customers who are receiving the coupon by 1 percent. Given the negative impact of increasing new customers, changing all three factors produced a sub-optimal reduction in profit shortfall.

Redesigning the Social Coupon Strategy

The above findings were based on altering the coupon deals on the three important factors we observed. In light of the poor performance of social coupons, the important question to ask here is—*what else can businesses do to make social coupons profitable?* Extending the outcome presented here, we propose some other considerations that businesses should accommodate in their decision to launch a social coupon campaign.

- *Set clear and reasonable campaign objectives.* To minimize the shortfall in profits, businesses should set reasonable targets and goals while designing and implementing the social coupon campaign. When businesses simulate the analyses described here before their actual implementation, they will know the extent of shortfall in profits they may face. Using this information, they can plan the marketing activities that can help them change the variables, individually or simultaneously.
- *Design personalized and targeted social coupons.* Social coupon websites typically send daily emails that contain the daily featured deals. While the emails serve as advertisements for the deals, they may be considered as spam by people who are not interested in certain products/services. As social coupons continue to evolve into a popular tool for customer acquisition, it is critical to target the appropriate deals at the right audience.

For instance, Groupon has a new program—Groupon Now[21]—that provides deals which customers can buy and redeem immediately. Companies should try to identify and collect the type and amount of customer information (such as demographics, psychographics, past buying behavior, etc.) that is required to issue personalized and targeted coupons. However, the coupons offered through this new program are also likely to be redeemed by existing customers, much like the current setup.

- *Design coupons based on the nature of service offered.* It is important for businesses to review the nature of services offered by them (frequently used services vs. limited use services) while designing the coupons. The businesses we corresponded with and the results presented here are for services that are used frequently. However, the outcome of a social coupon launch is likely to be different for services that are used only once or infrequently (e.g., helicopter tours, parasailing lessons, museum tours, Lasik eye surgeries, etc.). With limited use services, the prospects of retaining new customers are going to be minimal. This constrains the long-term profitability of the businesses. Therefore, this calls for changing the type of offer, identifying the right time to launch the coupon, and determining the validity of the offer. All these would determine the success of the social coupon campaign.
- *Consider alternate promotional campaigns.* If customer acquisition is the goal, businesses should also consider other possible tools such as traditional coupons and referral programs that can yield the same result. Though traditional coupons suffer from low redemption rates and an inability to be shared through social networks, their benefits over social coupons regarding lower discount rates, limited validity, and a higher potential for repeat visits, can turn out to be a more viable option for businesses for acquiring customers. The key takeaway is that businesses should use social coupons only if they can sufficiently demonstrate the success of acquiring new customers and ensure profitability.
- *Location-based targeting using mobile services.* To ensure geographical relevance for promoting social coupons, companies like Groupon and LivingSocial have started offering deals through their mobile applications (location-based targeting). For instance, JetBlue intends to offer its rewards program members, points for checking in at certain airports, and S.C. Johnson will offer promotions and discounts on brands at nearby retail stores.[22] While these initiatives are welcome and refreshing, they still are open to existing and new customers. This is because these location-based services are designed with the social coupon service provider's

customers in mind. The coupons be truly local and truly personalized only when these services are designed and offered with the customers of the businesses in mind.

At the heart of "group discounts" lies the basic requirement that people "need to share information" about the discount so that some of the like-minded people can come together to attain the required minimums for the discount to kick in. More often it was seen that this information sharing again resorted to channels like social networks, e-mail, telephone calls or text messages, which leads to "Word-of-Mouth" marketing.

Based on the above results, it is very easy to see how WOM marketing and SMM go hand-in-hand to deliver mutual benefits to businesses and customers.[23] While the marriage of WOM and Social Media is successful, it needs to be able to offer the following for it to sustain its success in the long run:

1. Ability to adapt to different kinds of businesses.
2. Ability to cater to different sizes of business organizations.
3. Capable of operating in a mode where the identification of the "right influencers" happens automatically in the chosen social media channels once the "right message" is provided.
4. Provide customers with the freedom to share or not share, but still be part of the network without any negative impact on transactions and on the social network.
5. Ability for the network to track WOM messages at message level as well as influencer level.

With all of this we see a strong bond between CIV, CRV, and CLV (inter-relationships) which will be discussed in detail in the section titled "Inter-relationships."

INTERRELATIONSHIPS

CIV, CRV, and CLV

The CIE is inherently aligned with accepted techniques of evaluating customer value, such as the CLV, CIV, and CRV. The monetary value of an individual's influence on a new user may therefore be evaluated in terms of the degree to which the individual influences the new user, and the value that the new user brings to the firm. The monetary evaluation of an instance of WOM or of an individual indulging in an instance of WOM would be invaluable to the marketers and result in improving the bottom line of organizations. This section provides an approach to measure CIV and its relationship with CLV and CRV. It also describes the important distinction between CRV and CIV. While the differences between CIV and CRV may seem subtle, they are in fact, two separate constructs. CRV focuses solely on turning prospects into customers through a formal incentivized referral program, while CIV focuses on both prospects as well as existing customers. Additionally, CRV involves compensation for customers who make referrals, while CIV typically does not. The chapter expands on this important difference that is crucial for managers to know while planning marketing communication campaigns through store-initiated social media conversations in an effort to increase their clout within the social networks.

The Relationship between CLV and CIV

The entire experience a customer has with a business strongly depends on the customer's interaction with that company (e.g., blog postings, WOM, customer-helping behavior, etc.). More extensive transaction volumes and consumption experiences ensure that the customer is experienced with the product and hence knows what he or she is talking about when communicating. Although credibility (purchase history, experience with a product) is an important predecessor to how influential an individual is, it is important to note that credibility can be established without purchase history. Sometimes product "gurus" never actually purchase the same product they are spreading the WOM about. For example, several bloggers "rate" Apple products without purchasing them. Some simply test products without buying them. These "gurus" can be perceived to be highly knowledgeable by their followers and peers, regardless of their purchase history.

In sum, high CLV implies high credibility, making influencers more powerful. As expected, long-term customers might also be able to articulate their ideas making them more influential. This suggests a positive relationship between past purchase behavior (CLV) and the ability to convert prospects (CIV). In addition, high CLV is a factor for a customer developing a binding or positive affinity toward the business. This will make the customer stay with the company for a longer duration which not only strengthens the relationship, but would also pave the way for cross and/or up-selling opportunities. The customers will communicate the positive attitude to other prospective customers and they enhance exerted influence and hence contribute to CIV. However, when a customer is dissatisfied, he or she will shorten the relationship with the business (low CLV).It is also expected that this customer, who has a negative experience, will influence other customers (by spreading negative WOM) and will end up having a negative CIV. So the inference is that CLV and CIV are directly proportional, i.e., when CLV increases, CIV also is high. The reverse is also true.

The Relationship between CIV and CBV

The link between CBV and CLV is established in detail in Chapter 3. What customers think of the brand or how much they value the brand has an impact on the purchase as well as their influence in making others go for the brand. This kind of relationship is well captured in the 2×2 matrix shown in Figure 7.24.

A brief description and recommended strategies for managing each of the four segments are described below.

- *Introverted Fans:* These customers have a high CBV, which means that they value the brand very highly, but they have a low CIV, so they do not influence new customers to buy products/services. They do not influence others as they are not actively engaged in talking about the product/service in the social media. This could be because they do not want others to know what brand they buy or they think they are not going to influence. It is recommended to approach them with marketing campaigns that work on building their CIV, since they value the brand highly.
- *Bystanders:* The customers in this segment do not think highly of the brand, nor do they influence other customers in the decision to buy, which makes them the "bystanders" who have a low CBV and low CIV.

| Figure 7.24 | The Relationship between CIV and CBV |

	Introverted Fans	**Trendsetters**
High CBV	These customers value the brand highly but they do not influence other customers. **Strategy:** Encourage them to be active in social media.	Trendsetters value the brand very high and they also influence other customers. **Strategy:** Nurture them and encourage their social media activities.
Low CBV	**Bystanders** These customers do not value the brand, nor do they influence other customers to buy/use the product or service. **Strategy:** Spend less unless they are high CLV customers.	**Pushers** These Customers influence many others but actually do not value the brand that much. **Strategy:** Impart brand value to them so as to make them Trendsetters.
	Low CIV	High CIV

The recommendation would be to reduce marketing efforts on these customers unless they have a high CLV.

- *Pushers:* These customers have a low CBV, that is, they do not believe in the brand or are not attached to the brand but they have a very high CIV as they are good influencers in the social media. To make the best out of these customers, the strategy is to build brand value in them and once that is achieved and since their CIV is high, they would engage in adding value to the brand and influence others (Trendsetters). High CIV and high CBV will eventually build high CLV customers, who, in turn, will bring more profit to the firm.

- *Trendsetters:* These are the best group of all the customers in this segmentation as they have high CIV and high CBV. Trendsetters believe in the brand they buy and they also love to talk about it to influence others to believe and make a purchase. We would like these trendsetters to grow in large numbers as they are customers as well as marketers.

The Relationship between CRV and CIV

The value of a customer's influence on others, whether incentivized or not, strongly depends on the connectedness of a customer and the number of prospects the customer interacts with. A customer's connectivity depends on how many social networks he is active in and how engaging he is with his friends and how reciprocative his friends are and so on. If a customer is an expert in influencing his network of friends, the CIV is automatically high. Long-term customers are likely to exert more influence. The customer's personality also plays an important role, whereas a customer who is outgoing and an extrovert will have more influence on the people in his or her network than a customer who is an introvert, especially since individuals use specific product-related experiences to initiate a conversation many times. Furthermore, individuals differ with regard to their eagerness to share information with others. Some people generally like to share what they do, why they do what they do, and suggest ideas of improvement but some like to promote only deals and things of their preference. The positive (negative) information shared by these influencers with their peers will enhance (reduce) their own CRVs and CIVs. The peers can then become influencers themselves as they are recognized for the information they give. The cycle continues and becomes a chain as consumers continue to influence their peers by sharing information.

Whether or not one is a market maven, the level of connectedness, and personality traits all have a similar impact on CIV and CRV. Moreover, whether the customer has a positive or a negative attitude toward the firm, also affects his CIV and CRV. Finally, there might be synergies between CRV- and CIV-related activities. It is also expected that a potential customer who has a tendency to do voluntary promotional activity for a product or a firm will be more than happy to do it for some incentive program. Hence, we can easily predict a positive relationship between CRV and CIV. However, it is possible to imagine a situation where incentives might crowd out voluntary activities. Once people get used to being paid for an activity, they are less likely to perform that same activity for free. Also the customers who were won with the help of incentivized influencers may not voluntarily become influencers as they may not be attached to the product by brand awareness or affinity toward the product. This normally brings down their respective CIV as they do not influence their peers.

The positive effects, however, are expected to outweigh the negative effects because even though customers may come to expect rewards for referrals, it is likely that they will still continue to spread (positive) WOM. Even if a customer wants a reward for a formal referral, it is likely he or she will still use product experiences to initiate conversations. So, we see that CIV and CRV also have a positive relationship.

The application of CIV and CIV metrics in social media hold immense importance for firms and marketers. In the digital world, the accountability of social media spending would go a long way in strengthening marketing strategy within a business. The need for businesses to embrace social media and use it as a platform for marketing is inevitable.

As we have already stated, being connected and wanting to share and interact are at the core of any social network and thereby form the basis for CRV and CIV. From the HokeyPokey market trial it was evident that recruiting influencers for an effective message spread is a key step in the SMM. Recruiting influencers is an involved process in itself. If there are several marketing campaigns being run in parallel, categorizing, distributing, and prioritizing campaign messages between influencers can make it more involved. This can be a time constraint since one of SMM's expectations by businesses is its ability for quick launch and spread of messages. One way to effectively recruit influencers is to create a self-regulating SMM network where the principles and mechanism of the network are built in such a way to automatically recruit and govern influencers thereby satisfying the speed to market requirement.

With the above observations, we now proceed to the next section, which builds upon the strength of relationship between WOM and social media and also addresses the above "wants" to make the marriage a long-term success. There should be a mechanism using which, consumers feel encouraged to share messages regarding the businesses with their respective social network friends. These messages, when used by the friends of consumers during transactions, must be traceable to the respective originating consumers. The business can then reward those consumers that chose to share their messages since it helped toward additional business transactions. The businesses can also choose to reward the friends that transacted and encourage them to also share the business's messages.

SOCIAL MEDIA MARKETING (SMM): VERSION 2.0

Effective SMM and measuring its effectiveness through CIE and CIV were presented earlier in this chapter. This section focuses on evolving this to the next step by introducing the concept of "Regulated Social Media Marketing" or in short "Regulated SMM." Regulated SMM deals with the aspect of sharing of a customer's transaction experience in a social network to be perceived in the right spirit without making the customer become a clueless spam agent and become a victim of one's own goodwill in contributing to the society.

Regulated Social Media Marketing

To achieve the stated objective of protecting customer's credibility while encouraging him/her to be an effective WOM agent for a business involves instrumenting the platform for sharing messages to allow the customer to have clear options to share or not share their own form of the message. Such a platform would honor the freedom of expression of individuals and also provide an unbiased and level playing field for businesses and customers alike.

While current social networks can achieve the same objectives stated for Regulated SMM, most social networks have been created for the sole purpose of being a social network and not a marketing specific network. Regulated SMM is to build a marketing specific social network that helps businesses keep their interaction with customers in a separate realm and not intervene with a customer's personal network in social media channels. Messages from the Regulated SMM network would show up in a customer's personal network only upon the customer's own choice and volition and not allow a free ride for businesses or the social network to infringe customer's personal network.

Since it is a customer's personal choice to share or not, they are more likely to be viewed as trusted sources of information than "spam agents" by their friends. Further since any person would not want to ostracize himself/herself from their friends' network, they would be careful in their choices of sharing that automatically bring the governance needed in such a network without having to build additional controls.

Regulated SMM can provide good controls for customers and businesses but businesses should be careful not to reveal customer sensitive and private information. Any violation of these fundamental governing principles can backfire, which is the same risk that businesses take when they accept credit cards for transactions. Creating promotional messages that have the potential to reveal what the customer purchased would not be a good way to implement promotions. Businesses should be cognitive of such situations and rely on fundamentally sound business ethics and sound marketing principles while implementing SMM solutions. Next, we demonstrate a sample framework of how our idea can be implemented.

A SAMPLE FRAMEWORK FOR IMPLEMENTATION

Figure 7.25 shows an activity diagram (Unified Modeling Language [UML]-based diagram[24]) depicting a sample framework that can be used to implement Regulated SMM.

Businesses can choose to implement the above framework in ways that suit their respective business and marketing needs. The diagram also shows the key "touch points" a business has with its customers and customers' friends. It is important to make sure that the implementation stays true to Regulated SMM's objective of providing customers the freedom to choose what they would like to share but also help businesses be able to target their messages to their customers for an effective WOM.

The following are the salient points of the framework:

1. Provide the customer with the choice to share or not share messages from businesses.
2. Allow the customer to have a choice of network where the message can be shared.
3. Messages must be traceable throughout the activity cycle.
4. The timing of the messages is important in making sure that the customer and customer's friends get actively engaged in social conversation.
5. As in any marketing attempt, the message content is of paramount importance.

Table 7.2 shows the benefits of Regulated SMM compared to other online/ SMM means.

Figure 7.25   Activity Diagram

Sample Framework

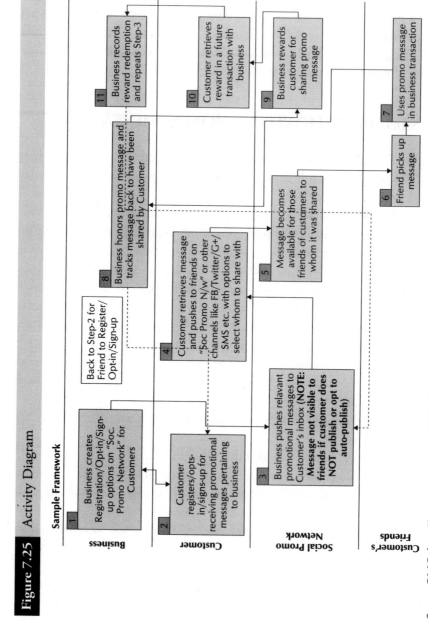

Business	1. Business creates Registration/Opt-in/Sign-up options on "Soc. Promo Network" for Customers — 8. Business honors promo message and tracks message back to have been shared by Customer — 11. Business records reward redemption and repeats Step-3
Customer	2. Customer registers/opts-in/signs-up for receiving promotional messages pertaining to business — 4. Customer retrieves message and pushes to friends on "Soc Promo N/w" or other channels like FB/Twitter/G+/SMS etc. with options to select whom to share with — 10. Customer retrieves reward in a future transaction with business
Social Promo Network	3. Business pushes relevant promotional messages to Customer's inbox (**NOTE:** Message not visible to friends if customer does NOT publish or opt to auto-publish) — 5. Message becomes available for those friends of customers to whom it was shared — 9. Business rewards customer for sharing promo message
Customer's Friends	6. Friend picks up message — 7. Uses promo message in business transaction

Back to Step-2 for Friend to Register/Opt-in/Sign-up

Source: OMG, http://www.omg.org/spec/UML/ (retrieved on February 20, 2013).

Table 7.2	Merits of Regulated Social Marketing—A Comparative Look		
Evaluation Criteria	**Broadcast Social Media Marketing**	**Selective Social Media Marketing**	**Regulated Social Media Marketing**
Ability to Track Message Chain	Low (almost none)	High (can track at customer level)	High (can track at message and customer level)
Ability to Track Customer Acquisition	Low (only on an aggregate basis)	High (ability to track message effectiveness and influencers)	High (ability to track message effectiveness and influencers)
Ability to Track Customer Retention	Low (only on an aggregate basis)	Medium (since repeat purchases are not directly traceable to customers but will have to be traced through messages)	High (ability to track repeat purchases which can be tracked to customers as well as messages)
Cost	Medium (while per message/impression cost might be low, since broadcast is in volume, it might drive up the overall cost)	High (needs selection of media, message and customers)	Medium (no selection of customers but would require some initiation cost to get customer to opt-in/register)
Flexibility in choice of social media	High (Facebook, Twitter, Google+, Groupon, Living Social, etc.)	Medium (customer privacy controls from networks like Facebook may constrain ways of selecting customers or groups of customers to share)	Medium (requires customer intervention to opt-in, which can help overcome customer privacy concerns and controls; allows for cross-network sharing)

(Table 7.2 Continued)

(Table 7.2 Continued)

Evaluation Criteria	Broadcast Social Media Marketing	Selective Social Media Marketing	Regulated Social Media Marketing
Media rich messages	Medium (depends on the channel of broadcast)	Medium (since there is a selection process involved, the richness of message would depend on the channel)	High (same message can be adopted to different formats since cross-channel or cross-network sharing is allowed)
Ability to regulate based on customer activity	Low (almost zero customer level usage tracking)	Medium (ability to track at message level with possibility of extending to customer level with some difficulty)	High (flexible enough to track at both customer level and message level)
Ability for customer to control and maintain his privacy, freedom and profile	Low (mostly pushed by business)	Medium (can choose to share or not and also whom to share with)	High (can choose to share or not, whom to share with, which network to share on and also share on a "trusted but anonymous basis")

Source: OMG, http://www.omg.org/spec/UML/ (retrieved on February 20, 2013).

NOTES AND REFERENCES

1. Merriam-Webster, http://www.merriam-webster.com/dictionary/social%20media (retrieved on February 20, 2013).
2. Nielsen, "State of the Media: The Social Media Report, Q3 2011," http://blog.nielsen.com/nielsenwire/social/ (retrieved on February 20, 2013).
3. Philip Kotler and Gary Armstrong, *Principles of Marketing* (12th ed.) (Upper Saddle River, NJ: Prentice Hall, 2007: p. 481).
4. Ideastorm, http://www.ideastorm.com/ (retrieved on February 20, 2013).
5. Huffingtonpost, "100 Fascinating Social Media Statistics and Figures From 2012," http://www.huffingtonpost.com/brian-honigman/100-fascinating-social-me_b_2185281.html (retrieved on February 20, 2013).

6. V. Kumar, Vikram Bhaskaran, Rohan Mirchandani, and Milap Shah, "Creating a Measurable Social Media Marketing Strategy for HokeyPokey: Increasing the Value and ROI of Intangibles & Tangibles," *Marketing Science, 32*(2), (2013): 194–212.

7. V. Kumar and Bharath Rajan, "The Perils of Social Coupon Campaigns," *MIT Sloan Management Review, 53*(4), (2012): 13.

8. Yelp's, "Yelp Elite Squad," http://www.yelp.com/elite (retrieved on February 20, 2013).

9. V. Kumar and Rohan Mirchandani, "Increasing the ROI of Social Media Marketing," *MIT Sloan Management Review, 54*(1), (2012): 55–61.

10. Ibid.

11. Ibid.

12. Kumar and Rajan, "The Perils of Social Coupon Campaigns."

13. Kumar et al. "Creating a Measurable Social Media Marketing Strategy for HokeyPokey."

14. Facebook, https://www.facebook.com/about/graphsearch (retrieved on February 20, 2013).

15. *Businessweek*, "Small Businesses and Daily Deals: TheAffair is Over," http://www.businessweek.com/printer/articles/84310-small-business-and-daily-deals-the-affair-is-over (retrieved on February 20, 2013).

16. V. Kumar and Bharath Rajan, "Social Coupons as a Marketing Strategy: A Multifaceted Perspective," *Journal of the Academy of Marketing Science, 40*(1), (2012): 120–136.

17. J. Thomas, W. Reinartz, and V. Kumar, "Getting the Most out of all your Customers," *Harvard Business Review, 82* (July–August 2004): 116-123.

18. S. Ovide, "Groupon Merchant: 'There's a Flaw in Their Business'," *The Wall Street Journal Blogs*, January 7, 2011.

19. Kumar and Rajan, "Social Coupons as a Marketing Strategy."

20. Kumar and Rajan, "The Perils of Social Coupon Campaigns."

21. Groupon, http://www.groupon.com/browse/atlanta (retrieved on February 20, 2013).

22. D. Rule, "AT&T Launches Location-Based Coupon Service," March 1, 2011, www.mobiledia.com.

23. V. Kumar and Bala Sundaram, "Winning with Social Media Marketing: An Evolutionary Roadmap," *Marketing Research Journal, 24*(2), (2012): 4.

24. OMG, http://www.omg.org/spec/UML/ (retrieved on February 20, 2013).

Chapter 8

Please Help Us Help You...

Find answers for...

- How can firms measure the value of the feedback provided by customers?
- How can firms encourage customers to provide a feedback?
- How can firms maximize the value derived from customer feedback?

INTRODUCTION: THE VALUE OF CUSTOMER KNOWLEDGE

While brands, logos, taglines, and jingles are common knowledge among customers about businesses, customers are known to possess a lot more knowledge about businesses than just these commonplace items. This suggests that businesses, in turn, have a lot to learn from their customers. Customers can prefer one business over another for certain products and services and it is important for businesses to know the customers' preferences, likes, and dislikes to help improve the business's offerings to attract and retain customers.

Understanding customer preferences is extremely valuable for any business and the knowledge thus gained by the business will serve as a vital ingredient for the success of its products and services. Customer feedback can be either business initiated or customer initiated. Businesses can initiate the customer feedback process through surveys. Typically, such surveys involve incentives for those customers who provide feedback. However, gaining a customer's knowledge about the business can be done in many ways but most notably through his or her involvement in the process. For example, Ben and Jerry's encourage customers to participate in the new product development process by sponsoring a contest where customers can suggest the "best new flavor." "Customer participation" can be defined as the extent to which the customer is involved in the manufacturer's new product development process.

With the ever-growing influence of the Internet, e-Commerce portals, and social networks, it is becoming easier for individuals to search for a certain product or service's merits, demerits, and popularity on the Internet before making the decision to buy the product or service. There is a long list of such helpful sites based on the industry, product, and service that customers can peruse to gain the information they seek. Some examples are google.com, amazon.com, yelp.com, epinions.com, CNET.com, and tripadvisor.com.

In the next sections, we will review three examples of how businesses manage their customers and how they use customers' feedback to improve their respective businesses. Domino's Pizza is the first example that highlights how it turned around its business from strong negative publicity by responding in an appropriate and timely fashion to what customers were saying about its business. The second example is about Zappos, an online shoe retailer, where the focus is entirely on customer satisfaction and how that strong culture within the business has helped it in its success. The third example will focus on Quirky.com, which is a website solely dedicated to collecting customer feedback on new product innovations.

"Show Us Your Pizza"—Domino's Pizza

Customer feedback is of great value to firms, as it allows them to learn what their customers think. This knowledge greatly aids the new product and service development process. When firms truly understand what their customers want and how to deliver their customers' expectations, they have an edge over their competition. Domino's Pizza had a very bad publicity when a couple of its employees posted a prank video on the Internet.[1]

After experiencing a year marked by stagnant sales, negative viral marketing, and customer dissatisfaction, Domino's Pizza embarked on a mission in 2009 to recreate its product, brand, and image based on customer feedback and demand.[2] In stripping the brand and product of all previous concepts, Domino's was highlighting "losing touch" with its customers as the primary reason for its recent struggles. The pizzas were no longer a reflection of customer requirements. In light of this, chief marketing officer Russell Weiner announced that they would be "creating a pizza to reflect what consumers are looking for."

In rebuilding its brand and product concepts, Domino's adopted a new company philosophy that was based on listening and responding to customer feedback. Even after remodeling their product concept and changing the recipe based on customer feedback, Domino's further showed their commitment to listening to customer feedback with the launch of www.showusyourpizza.com. This website allowed Domino's customers to upload pictures of their pizzas to the website (both good, and bad) that the company would then use to improve its products. While Domino's had to go through a bad phase and turn its business around by addressing the gap it had developed with its customers, the next story is about how a company has made "customer satisfaction" as the foremost goal and cornerstone of its business.

"My Expressions"—Tanishq

Tanishq, an Indian jewelry brand launched a promotion called "My Expressions" which acted as a platform for its customers to codesign a new jewelry line "Mia" for working women. The top 10 customer designs were considered for production and the customers were rewarded ₹100,000 each (around $2,200). Tanishq believed that through this promotion they would gain insights to customer's views about Tanishq's jewelry and at the same time find creative and smart designers who were ready to collaborate with Tanishq.[3]

"Culture is Everything"—Zappos

As Tony Hsieh, CEO of Zappos, is fond of putting it: "Culture is everything" and "if you get the culture right, most of the other stuff like great customer service, or building a great long-term brand, or passionate employees and customers will happen naturally on its own." What drives Zappos' culture is an obsession with superior customer service, and there is not a customer or employee that does not know it. Even in these hard economic times, Zappos is meeting internal revenue targets. This is a key challenge for the company in these difficult economic times without drastically reducing prices and diluting the brand for continued growth. Great customer service is what helped Zappos build a loyal customer base. Approximately 50 percent of Zappos.com orders are from existing customers, and an additional 20 percent are from new customers who were referred by existing customers.[4]

"Listening to Customers"—Shoppers Stop

Shoppers Stop, an Indian department chain store, firmly believes in listening to the customers. They believe that by listening to the customers, they will gain more insight into changing customer preferences and they will be in a better position to create products that would satisfy the customer needs. Also, by listening to customer feedback and by proactively addressing customer issues and queries, they feel they will be able build a strong base of loyal customers. The Shoppers Stop management strongly feels that two-way dialogues is the future of customer engagement and wants to capitalize on their customer feedback mechanisms.[5]

"Bringing Ideas to Life"—Quirky.com

One great example of seeking customer input for innovation and new product development is Quirky.com. Since its launch in 2009, Quirky is on a quest to rapidly change the way the world thinks about product development. Quirky engages participants to collaborate in every aspect of product creation—from ideation, design, naming, manufacturing, marketing, right on through to sales. Figure 8.1 outlines "The Quirky Process."

Quirky is a business that is initiated and driven by customer feedback through their Product Evaluation (BETA) program. Thousands of creative people around the world submit their ideas first to be evaluated by Quirky, and then website visitors vote for the ones with the most potential. They bring new consumer products to the market each week, by enabling a fluid conversation between a global community and Quirky's expert product design staff. The world influences the business in real-time, and then they share the revenue directly with the people who help Quirky make successful decisions.

All of the above examples from Domino's Pizza, Zappos, and Quirky emphasize the strong need for businesses to gather customer feedback and apply the knowledge gained for retaining and acquiring customers. Based on these examples, it is clear that there is a huge benefit for other businesses to embark on a journey to better understand their customers and how to value their customers' opinions and knowledge. For understanding the value that a customer brings in for a business in terms of the knowledge about the company's products and services, we need to have the same point of view of the company like the customer.

Figure 8.1 The Quirky Process

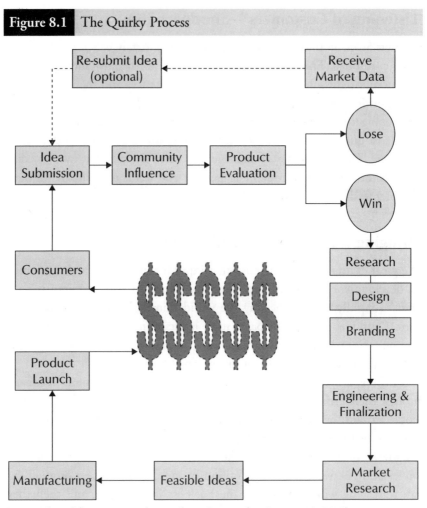

Source: Adapted from www.quirky.com/learn (retrieved on January 03, 2013).

This chapter introduces an approach to measure the value of customer knowledge and lists strategies that can be used to take advantage of the power of customer feedback/suggestion/idea known as customer knowledge value (CKV). As explained in Chapter 2, the monetary value a customer adds to the firm when the company implements a feedback, suggestion or an idea provided by that customer, measures the value of the knowledge gained from customers.[6] Using this knowledge, this chapter showcases how a customer feedback response strategy can be implemented to maximize and encourage CKV. The chapter will also present some examples of how CKV is used in businesses across various industries and then unravel the link between CKV and the other customer engagement metrics (CLV, CIV, and CRV).

DEFINING CUSTOMER KNOWLEDGE VALUE (CKV)

Customer knowledge value (CKV) can be defined as *the monetary value attributed to a customer by a firm due to the profit generated by implementing an idea/suggestion/feedback from that customer.* In some instances, customers can collaborate with the firm to produce new products and services. If more information of this engagement is known and made public, one can then create a separate metric called customer collaborator value (CCV). Here again, customer collaborator value (CCV) can be defined as *the monetary value attributed to a customer by a firm due to the profit generated by the new products/ services arising out of that customer's collaborative efforts with the firm.* In this book, we will focus on the CKV. Customers can add value to the company by helping understand customer preferences and participating in the knowledge development process. This knowledge can be used by the businesses to improve its offerings and innovate based on popular demands from the customers. Customer feedback/suggestions can serve as indicators to businesses about existing products and services and tell them if they are meeting customer expectations. Customer feedback not only identifies areas in need of improvement, but also helps provide suggestions and solutions for future upgrades and modifications. Additionally, such feedback mechanisms also offer new ideas for completely new products and services. This feedback has the potential to not only make the entire offering more attractive to existing and potential customers but also improve process efficiencies (e.g., reduced complaint management).

MEASURING CKV

The process of measuring CKV begins when the customer has ideas for developing a new product or refinements to the existing products. Customers may suggest ideas on their own accord or they could be business initiated. The entire process is summarized in Figure 8.2.

Figure 8.2 Conceptual Approach to Measure CKV

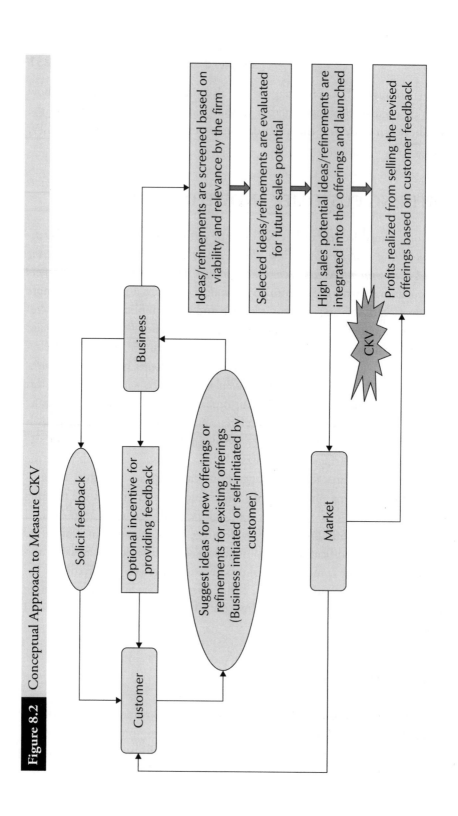

Customer initiated: In this world of social media, it is so easy for a customer to voice his review and feedback to a company about its product/service. It need not be prompted or paid. It could be just a simple "Tell us what you think" on the website that makes the customer share his experience about the product/service which is a rich insight and feedback. In some cases the idea can be from multiple sources (customers).

Business initiated: The business can initiate the idea generation in two ways. The first is to provide incentives upfront for customers to provide feedback. Businesses can reach out to their customers by simply soliciting via email, or by sending a survey or even by human interaction (in phone or in person). To make this process cyclical in nature, organizations typically provide some form of reward to encourage customers to continue to provide suggestions like these. The most common form of reward is monetary or opportunities to win a monetary reward. For instance, Express, a clothing company, launched a contest that entered a customer in a drawing for a $250 gift card for every clothing review he or she submitted.[7] For every picture a customer submitted wearing Express clothing, he or she would be entered five times in the drawing.

The second way of initiating idea generation from customers is a more involved form of reward. Here, the firms provide a share in profits from the sales of the new product. For instance, Brewtopia, a company that specializes in brewing customized beer for its customers, promised its initial members dividends based on how well the beer sold.[8] Perhaps the most involved reward mechanism is the one practiced by the software companies. For instance, Microsoft Corp. is planning to give developers who write software for Windows computers and devices a greater share of revenue sold through the company's upcoming Windows Store.[9] According to this new plan, as long as the software, or app, has made at least $25,000 in revenue, Microsoft plans to give developers an 80 percent cut. Additionally, if a Windows app has not reached the threshold yet, Microsoft will share 70 percent as well. Amongst its competitors, Apple now gives developers 70 percent of the revenue that apps bring in.[10]

To explain the CKV measuring strategy, let us expand on the Microsoft example. As the revenue is $25,000, and if the developers are going to get 80 percent out of it, it would be $20,000. One would think that the CKV is the remaining $5,000, but we have to factor in and deduct the marketing cost and other related expenses (say around $3,000). So, the

CKV attributed to the customer is the remaining $2,000. We have to be mindful that if the idea or development of the software was done by a group of four individuals (customers), the total CKV of $2,000 would be divided among the four customers and CKV of each customer would be $500.

In some instances, certain software companies have also let the customers/users maintain ownership of the patent for the ideas suggested by them that eventually got integrated into the final product. In sum, regardless of the type of reward options, encouraging customers to provide feedback and suggestions for improvement does significantly contribute to the customer–firm engagement levels. The suggestions are then screened on the basis of practical applications and relevance to the company's product offerings. Suggestions that get past this stage are then evaluated for marketability. It is important to remember that *not all great ideas are market-friendly*. Therefore, the organization will evaluate the suggestions on the basis of generating future sales. The suggestions that show promise in generating sales will then be worked upon to be either integrated into the product development process (in the case of new ideas) or updated in the existing product offerings (in the case of product refinements). The profit that the organization realizes from the subsequent sales of these offerings is the knowledge value that can be attributed to the customer, or the CKV. If multiple customers had provided this suggestion, then, the value of the profit is divided among that number of customers and attributed to those individual customers as their CKV (as we explained in the Microsoft example).

Kissan, an Indian ketchup brand, started a new campaign "Welcome to Kissanpur—*where what you grow is what you eat.*" This campaign which was aimed at building brand, focused on customer engagement by getting customers to cocreate the product along with Kissan. The company first distributed tomato seeds glued on to newspapers along with an advertisement explaining the process of growing tomatoes. Customers were then encouraged to post the pictures of their tomato plants in the Kissanpur website and win a chance to get their names printed on the ketchup bottles. This is not exactly an example of cocreation but it certainly was an opportunity for Kissan to gain insights into the knowledge that its individual customers have about the brand (although it is not apparent if Kissan capitalized on this opportunity or not). The insight could help them measure each customer's brand knowledge value.

CKV MEASUREMENT STRATEGY

Since customer feedback gets initiated through multiple channels (to be discussed below) to generate good CKV measures for businesses, the following strategy is suggested as shown in Figure 8.3.

Customer Feedback Channel Identification

In this step, the business will have to analyze the various channels through which customers provide feedback and identify those channels that provide significant and quality feedback that the business can use. There are many ways that a business can keep an ongoing "listening ear" for customer feedback. Some very simple-to-use methods are:

- *On-site Surveys:* On-site surveys may be held by asking customers questions at the point of purchase. One way to do this is by using comments cards on display in stores (example: near checkout lanes or carts) or they can be inserted in the shopping bag along with the purchased goods. For example, "Shortly after Domino's Pizza founder Tom Monaghan opened his first outlet, he asked customers one question every night as they were waiting for orders. He wrote down the answers and learned that delivery was three times more important than issues such as price and service" (Small Business Tax Strategies 1). Although it can be time-consuming, this method does provide immediate feedback.
- *Online Surveys:* Another method of collecting customer feedback is through surveys. Mail surveys can be expensive and usually have a low response rate. This can be solved by providing a stamped survey post-card at the time of purchase saying something along the lines of "Thank

Figure 8.3 CKV Measurement Strategy

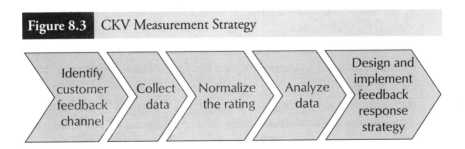

you for using (company name). To help us serve you better, please take a minute to answer the following questions" (Small Business Tax Strategies 1). More information can often be gathered through telephone surveys. Unfortunately, Caller ID has made telemarketing more difficult, so it may be a good idea to ask a customer if you may call them and what time would be most convenient. Online surveys seem to have a higher response rate than mail surveys and they are generally faster, inexpensive, and more convenient to customers. The only downside is that company surveys may get trapped in spam filters or considered illegal soliciting. Some sites such as opinionoutpost.com and surveysavvy.com not only give rewards for taking a survey but they also give rewards for referring new members for taking the survey.

- *Telephone:* The method best preferred by customers when an immediate response is expected (like a complaint or intricate matter). Assigning a toll-free (hotline) number is recommended and it is better to have a human touch to the customer service line rather than expecting the complaint to get resolved by automated machines.

- *Email/Fax:* Fax is now being sent as an email given the advantages of an email communication method. Email saves a lot of human interaction time and is also easier to deal with when sensitive issues are handled (especially when there is a dispute or negative experience). Businesses are using the latest Unique Code Embedded Technology to track email surveys. QuestionPro[11] is one such software in which business can track responses and send reminder emails, etc. The links in the email surveys allow real time responses. Survey respondents can even post their responses to social networks like Facebook, Twitter, or Google+. Once the responses are collected, analysis is done with many features such as real-time summary, trend analysis, etc.

- *Website Feedback Link:* The most important and popular since the boom of Internet is, including a simple feedback button with a box to write the content on your website.

- *Customer User Group:* Companies can invite a certain cross section of interested customers to participate in a special incentive program to share their experience or provide a general feedback of the product/service they launch. As an example, clothing retailer, Express, implemented a customer feedback program, incentivizing customers to participate actively in product design. They launched a contest in which customers who submitted product reviews and pictures would be entered into a drawing that awarded a $250 gift card to the winner. The reviews and pictures allowed Express to see how customers were interacting with their products. Being able to identify trends in how people were combining different articles of clothing to form outfits could be cross-analyzed with demographics, seasons, and other customer characteristics. There are certain companies, such as the online T-shirt printing company Threadless Tees,[12] who take this idea a step further by encouraging fans to create their own clothing. Threadless Tees' model is entirely based on the concept of customer feedback as the customers are in total control of creating a product that is tailored to their individual demand.

- *Focus Groups:* Generally a group of 8–12 customers will meet to discuss a specific topic concerning the business. Focus groups can be difficult to run and may require a hired professional to lead and record the discussion.
- *Follow-Up:* Soon after the sale or service has occurred, calling customers (if the client base is relatively small) or emailing them with a satisfaction-questionnaire asking them to rate if the product/service expectation is met.

If you want to encourage feedback, try and offer customers a choice of feedback mechanisms to use. Also, make each method as easy as possible to use, for example, do not ask a long list of detailed questions and for telephone feedback, consider using a phone number. If the feedback is a specific complaint, do ask for precise contact details and make contact with the person as early as possible to address the problem. And be sure to review regularly, the pattern of comments and feedback you receive so that you can spot trends and identify aspects of your review where you may need to change or improve things.

Collecting customer feedback can help firms in (*a*) evaluating the performance of their existing products and services, (*b*) assessing how well they are able to meet customer expectations, (*c*) identifying areas of improvement in delivering products and services, (*d*) identifying suggestions and solutions for future product upgrades and modifications, (*e*) securing new ideas for new products and services, and (*f*) developing ways to reduce the failure rate of new and existing products. Firms can increase their profits when this valuable customer feedback is effectively implemented in product development and

CRM programs. Therefore, there is a financial value to be gained by utilizing customer insights and feedback. This strategic gain is termed as CKV and is attributed to the customer who provided the idea.

Data Collection

After identifying the channels, the business will have to come up with mechanisms of integrating the channels to collect feedback data. Customer feedback is a resource and it is wasted if not acted upon and used for improvement. By finding out and addressing customer concerns from the feedback, the companies gain a solid understanding of customer needs, wants, and issues. One thing to keep in mind is that various departments within an organization may be collecting customer data, but this data is often not unified. One department may have collected data for a specific purpose and not shared it with the other departments. This is another reason why it is important to set up and manage a customer feedback program. Streamlining and consolidating all feedback data can provide valuable insights into what customers need, want, and value most. For example, in order to understand and satisfy a customer's true needs and wants, LG Telecom in Korea created the voice of customer (VOC) organization. VOC incorporates both the positive and negative feedback by customers and knowledge to improve LG Telecom's service and product offerings.[13] If LG provides incentives for the feedback from its customers and formalizes the process of providing incentives, this would facilitate the tracking of the source of ideas to set the stage for computing CKV. Further, if LG can commercialize the ideas/suggestions/feedback that they get from the customers, then the roadmap for CKV can be implemented.

As a means to collect more data, companies can add a "feedback page" and link it to their company website, which describes the feedback process and the benefits of feedback that can encourage users to share their experience. This page could also have links connected to other popular review sites (like yelp.com) where customers can read about feedback of the specific product/service.

It is not uncommon for unsatisfied customers to go the extra mile to narrate their experience with a product while most satisfied customers do not even jot it down. It is all the more important to create a customer feedback process for happy customers as it can be difficult to manage negative feedback once they appear in the public. Receiving negative feedback is inevitable at some point; however, it is important to remember that consumers want to see feedback and not just positive reviews as it would look like as the company has edited/delete bad reviews. Consumers like to have information even if it is negative as it aids the buying decision. It is better to have a few standalone negative reviews (which have been solved and updated by the person who wrote the complaint) as consumers trust the legitimacy of the business and the feedback more when they see a mix of good and bad reviews.

Does negative feedback help? Let us take the example of the retail giant Wal-Mart and its attempt to handle negative feedback by censuring the negative comments. Needless to say it was just short of a disaster. Wal-Mart started a Fanpage/open forum on Facebook so that an open forum such as Facebook could revive their not so great public image. As expected, in a short time period they acquired a large number of fans for the page, but knowing the number of fans just did not yield any valuable and measurable data for Wal-Mart. As the fans base started growing, their engagement increased, and fearing the negative comments/feedback from the members, Wal-Mart restricted the "comments" option from their wall (page), which negatively impacted the image of the company. This essentially demeaned the whole point of creating a Facebook page. The fan page completely lacked interactivity and became just another place for Wal-Mart to advertise. So lack of planning and abandoning their brand image led the campaign to be unsuccessful.[14]

The key takeaway from this can be summarized as:

- Negative feedback gives a feeling of credibility to the existing positive reviews.
- Negative feedback can help potential customers move toward making a purchase decision as they feel they have zeroed down the product they want, knowing its pros and cons.
- Negative feedback gives businesses a chance to respond and show their superior customer service levels.

Instead of getting alarmed at negative feedback, we can use it to encourage customer engagement, which will become a vital part of marketing. Responding to negative feedback should be highly diplomatic and it is a good practice to have a plan to avoid future customers having to raise the "same issue" for which the negative feedback was given. The more feedback we get from the customers, the better we would be able to serve them to their satisfaction.

Online feedback: reach many, acquire more! When it comes to customers' opinions and the public sharing of those opinions with a huge online audience, there is little businesses can do—except ensure that their service is as good as it can be and to engage with their customers more than ever before. Even though local businesses don't have direct control over what their users write about them, they can influence the conversation and turn a potential threat into a great marketing asset.

Many local search engines, local directories, and local-social sites use customer feedback as a factor for how prominently they show a business in their results. Both the volume of feedback and the sentiment of the feedback received have an effect on how visible a business is and businesses that can successfully encourage their users to share positive reviews will benefit from reaching a wider audience.

Rating Normalization

Different channels may provide ratings from customers in different scales of measurement like "five-star rating scale," "10-point rating scale," "seven-point likert scale," etc. So businesses will have to adopt a standard way to normalize the data collected from the various channels to a "likert scale" of their choice that can be used for further analysis. Graphing the available data using advanced computer systems is another technique. It is easy to visualize a normal distribution, quadratic distribution, etc., by mathematical transformation and then use it to normalize your data.

Data Analysis: Feedback Response Strategy

Once data is accumulated in the repository, the business will need to analyze and classify the feedback data into useful information that can be used in generating CKV.

The feedback information retrieved by the company is business initiated or customer initiated and can further be classified in a classic 2×2 matrix. As shown in Figure 8.4, the type of feedback is represented on the x-axis (positive or negative) and the time to act on the y-axis (immediate or long term). A response for internal and external action is presented within the matrix. In order to analyze the genuineness of the feedback, the matrix can be completed with selected feedback received that is correlated with customer

Figure 8.4	Feedback Response Strategy

	Positive	**Negative**
For long-term action	• Internal Response: Send to R&D and Market Intelligence teams so that takeaway can be implemented in the upcoming product release(s). • External Response: Thank and reward (discount coupons) customers valuing their feedback. e.g.: Coke Freestyle Vending Machine	• Internal Response: Identify the root cause. Research should be done how to incorporate lesson learned from this negative review. • External Response: Provide alternate buying options from the product/service line and satisfy customer in future transactions. e.g.: Iphone 4 having signal problems and rectifying this same in future versions.
For immediate action	• Internal Response: Acknowledge the review and measures to meet and exceed expectation about the product/service. • External Response: Thank and reward (discount coupons) customers valuing their feedback. Encourage the customer knowledge value by increased interaction with these valuable influencers. e.g.: KLM Surprise	• Internal Response: Action should be taken at once to correct the issue and identify the root cause and eliminate reoccurrence of the same issue. • External Response: Damage control and measures to satisfy the affected customer assuring him for continuous support and service. Sending discount coupons and product replacements depending on the situation is recommended. e.g.: Netflix, Verizon

Type of feedback

interactions such as product returns and service calls with complaints during the same timeframe.

Feedback from popular sites (e.g., yelp, amazon, and mouthshut) can be collected and sorted out internally by a business. As we see, the review/feedback reaction can be positive and negative and the action that should be taken from the business side could be immediate or long term. Similarly, the action from the business side can be an internal, circular, or a decision and there will be an external response to the customer by means of a forum, email, or a social media website.

Feedback Response Strategy Design and Implementation

Now let us take some real-life examples of how certain companies have adapted this Feedback Response Strategy in their business and the implications to understand these strategies in detail.

Immediate Action (Positive Feedback): The Royal Dutch Airline, KLM, is going the extra mile with its social media efforts using creativity to create exciting, crowd-pleasing projects.[15] KLM has started an interesting campaign to connect with their customers called "KLM Surprise" at the Amsterdam Schiphol Airport. Designed to track "how happiness spreads," the campaign involves surprising travelers with unique gifts based on their social networking profiles. The way it works is when passengers check in at KLM's Foursquare,[16] a location-based social media site, the KLM Surprise team uses social networks such as LinkedIn, Twitter, and Facebook to find out information about the passenger. Most likely, anyone who uses Foursquare will have a presence on other social networks, providing the team with information about the person and his or her trip. The KLM Surprise team then uses this information to come up with a personalized gift to surprise the passenger. The team follows up by monitoring the conversation generating on social networks by that person and his or her friends. They also take photos of the people they have surprised and post them to the KLM Facebook page. The KLM team has surprised travelers with champagne, notebooks, a watch, and traditional Dutch foods. KLM is keeping tabs on the conversations generated through social media due to this campaign, and plans to evaluate its effectiveness afterwards, but has already said it may be used again in the future. The KLM Surprise campaign is definitely a unique way to get your customers talking positively about their brand, and a classic example of immediate positive action taken by a company using the customer knowledge they acquire.

Long-term Action (Positive Feedback): The idea behind Coca-Cola's freestyle "soft drink" dispensing machine is clearly CKV and is achieved in real time as the data is used for improvising the existing flavors and innovating new flavors.

Coca-Cola's new "Freestyle" Vending Machine[17] was introduced in 2009 as an experiment in Atlanta, Salt Lake City, and Southern California. It has become a revolutionary and interactive machine to customize drinks by mixing and matching different Coca-Cola brands and flavors. The new age touch screen soda fountain uses micro dosing technology that allows the right amount of flavoring for over 100 different drink combinations. Currently, there are over 600 locations around the country using Freestyle including fast-food restaurants, airports, movie theaters, college cafeterias, and theme parks. The machines are interactive and pleasing to the consumers, i.e., instead of levers for different sodas, they have a touchscreen, slick as an iPad, and the system provides daily detailed sales data back to Coke headquarters on flavor popularity, beverage consumption, peak times, popular locations and other data that Coke can use to access the machines to determine customer preferences and act on it.

Starbucks is another classic example of how social media and the Customer feedback mechanism are to be followed. Starbucks has a consumer portal where customers can share ideas or suggestions they have about how to improve the "Starbucks experience."[18] "My Starbucks Idea" takes the concept of crowd sourcing and opens it up to any customer willing to register. This also gives end users the ability to see what other people are suggesting, vote on ideas they agree with and even see the results. Starbucks' "Ideas in Action Blog" acts as a counterpart to the My Starbucks Idea website. This site is written by different Starbucks employees and talks about how they implemented, or are reacting to the suggestions and information from customers.

Immediate Action (Negative Feedback): Below, is a list of examples where the companies have acted upon the feedback given by customers.

Netflix's subscriber base had been on a reliably upward trajectory since it was founded more than a decade ago. The company—widely praised for making it easy to stream films and some TV shows via the Internet—was in the news for the wrong reason recently as the customers were unhappy about a pricing plan, which caused them to lose millions of customers. Finally, the business realized the value of customer feedback and revised the plan to what it was before.[19]

Similarly, Verizon Wireless canceled a planned $2 "convenience fee" for online and phone bill payments after a backlash from consumers.[20]

Long-term Action (Negative Feedback): In 2010, Apple's bestselling smart phone, IPhone Apple, received many complaints from its ever loyal customers about the call "droppings" and signal issues, and Apple released a free software update but it took several weeks to fix the glitch.[21]

IMPACT OF SOCIAL MEDIA IN CKV

All of these methods are an effective means of collecting data from existing customers. What about the noncustomers (i.e., potential customers)? By interviewing potential customers, we get to know about their mindset, why they want this product, and their expectations on the product/service like benefits, willingness to pay, etc. This will also give knowledge on their apprehensions in making the decision to buy a product. By offering trials of a product or service, potential customers may be picked up and useful information can be obtained through optional questioning before and after the trial. Offering an opt-in newsletter can also deliver more information to the customer and promote the future sale of the product being tested.

If a person uses the trial and does not proceed to purchase the product, offer freebies in exchange for a few minutes of his or her time, and talk to them about why he/she chose not to purchase. Continue offering these prizes until feedback starts becoming repetitive. If a product uninstaller is included, incorporate a question asking the reason for uninstallation. Other techniques include providing positive testimonials from existing customers to draw new customers and giving away free products in exchange for feedback.

Gathering data about why the business lost sales can help them create a product, which will be successful in market rather than something that can cause buyer remorse. With an increase in viral commerce and growing web-based communities, products and services are purchased, discussed, and spread at an accelerated rate. Through customers' viral participation with these products and services, companies can analyze and store all of the purchasing habits, comments, and feedback that are readily available. This information is important not only in terms of its cost-effectiveness and availability, but also in terms of the variety and the fairly indiscriminate method of diffusion that it provides. However, due to the volume of information and the vast digital space throughout which it is spread, any manual or case-by-case analysis of this customer feedback is impossible. It is therefore imperative that companies develop automated systems for extracting the knowledge from customer feedback. This process, known as "Opinion Mining" (OM), deals with gathering these customer feedbacks on products and presenting the findings in order to best accomplish certain objectives. Because of the varied findings (customer feedback), the methods and steps in OM keep changing with the objective.

An objective of getting the number of negative and positive reviews of a product, classifying those reviews as negative or positive would be the most crucial step. However, if the goal is to show customer feedback for each aspect of the product, it would be crucial to extract the feature aspects and analyze the overall sentiment for each feature. OM includes feature extraction, sentiment classification, and opinion summarization, with a particular emphasis on the sentiment that the customer is expressing, with various methods based on factors like linguistics and sentiment classification.

Social media has become an increasingly important (and free) method of collecting customer feedback. So many people use it religiously, and sites like Facebook and Twitter may be the most convenient way for them to voice a praise or complaint. Companies that neglect this are missing out on a huge opportunity to manage their customers and product. The companies that are still using call centers to address complaints are falling far behind. Not all customer care centers are open for 24 hours a day, whereas all social media networks are accessible 24 × 7. Customers don't care when your off hours are and they want to deliver their message at a time that is most convenient for them. As part of the exceeding customer service, customer queries and concerns should be responded to as quickly as possible including the feedback/comments which appear in social networking accounts.

ENCOURAGING AND MAXIMIZING CKV

Businesses can help boost the customers' knowledge about the products and services using their interaction toward the customers. Data derived from personal interaction unlike transactional data yields richer content and helps us know what customers do and why. It will also shed light on the reasons for certain decisions customers make. By encouraging customers to write a review or feedback, we get a clear idea of the source of problems they might have, preferences, and needs. Customer feedback provides the best channel to extract ideas for innovations and improvements the customers would like the business to adapt. Having a streamlined process and system to manage and encourage customer knowledge is crucial as this can help us design and launch new products in a timely manner and can aid businesses in keeping the customer loyalty and commitment intact. CKV focuses on capitalizing on information about customer needs to improve satisfaction and increase buying behavior. By encouraging CKV, we can steer the customer from taking the plunge of absorbing high costs and switching to competitors.

The Internet can also be an excellent means to maximize CKV. It aids in establishing contact with customers and it creates value by building a rapport with the customer base (both existing and prospective). We outline the distinct capabilities of the Internet as a platform for customer engagement, including interactivity, enhanced reach, persistence, speed, and flexibility, and suggest that firms can use these capabilities to engage customers in collaborative product innovation through a variety of Internet-based mechanisms. The customer needs to be given the opportunity to easily contact the firm to share his or her ideas or provide feedback. Firms must decide what level of involvement they would like from customers and use suitable social media channels to encourage such interaction with customers to promote this desired level of involvement. Without ease of communication, many valuable insights from the customer base will go untold. Firms should, therefore, take advantage of the Internet when creating initiatives to encourage customer feedback.

In addition to utilizing the Internet, firms should take into account the variety of motivations customers have for providing feedback. For example, some customers may inherently be reward seeking. They are extrinsically motivated and require some kind of compensation from the firm for their ideas and feedback. Firms can offer to buy ideas or can offer these customers a cut of the profits. Firms can also engage customers by sponsoring competitions. Some clothing stores allow aspiring fashion designers to submit their designs and then allow the public to vote on their favorite designs. The winner's design is subsequently manufactured and offered for sale (and the winner is provided monetary compensation). Other customers may be attention seeking and just want fame. Again, contests can provide an excellent means to retrieve their insights and provide them with public recognition. Some other ways to give recognition to the customer could be to name the new product after the customer or post pictures of the customer on the company website. Finally, some customers may only want to offer their direct input to the firm (product reviews) as information providers in contrast to aiding in the new product development process. It is likely that these customers are seeking monetary rewards instead of fame or recognition. As a result, CKV can be maximized when the firm makes communication with customers easy and accessible, provides some form of incentive (monetary or otherwise), and engages the customer in activities through which the customer can offer feedback and collaborate with the firm.

APPLYING CKV IN BUSINESS

An example of creating CKV through the new product ideas contributed by customers is Polyvore.com. This website lets users mix and match images from the web to create and share fashion outfits, interior designs, and other types of collages. The user-generated fashion creations in this website are created by a community of highly engaged stylists and trendsetters. Apart from providing a portal to display fashion creations, the website also lets other users rate the creations and provide comments. Additionally, for users interested in buying any creation listed on the website, the website directs them to other websites that carry the individual items displayed in the creations. All these features have not only enabled the online retailer to recognize and engage the fashion-savvy users, but also facilitated fashion houses and independent fashion designers to interact and gauge customer expectations and preferences. Luxury fashion brands and houses such as Bergdorf Goodman, Rebecca Minkoff, and Prabal Gurung have used Polyvore to engage with customers by offering special promotions including meet-and-greet and branded products. In fact, some of the creations suggested by users of the website have also been showcased in major fashion events across the country. The value accruing from all the customer-suggested creations is most likely realized by the fashion houses and designers by way of increased sales and profits. Additionally, for the website this has resulted in a strong growth in member base to around

6.5 million, who browse luxury products, seek fashion advice from fashion experts, and create collages showcasing their fashion inspiration.

In the airline industry, Delta Air Lines[22] actively seeks ideas from its customers regarding improvements to the airline's travel experience through its online forum called Ideas in Flight, located within their Facebook page. This initiative is part of a partnership between Delta and TED, the nonprofit organization devoted to "Ideas worth Sharing." Within the first few months in operation, this forum has received more than 1,000 ideas. Of the ideas collected so far, Delta has identified that nearly 70 percent of the ideas could become a part of the travel experience. Of that 70 percent, about a third can be tested immediately. The remainder would require much more time as they would be large projects. When Delta sees such ideas to fruition, the profits accruing from these ideas can be directly attributed to the respective customer(s) as their CKV.

Dell is another archetypal example of how CKV is being implemented. Dell IdeaStorm is a website launched by Dell on February 16, 2007 to allow Dell "to gauge which ideas are most important and most relevant to" the consumers. To participate, individuals must join the IdeaStorm community (at no cost) by selecting an anonymous username (you do not have to be a Dell customer to join). After registering, IdeaStorm members can propose ideas as well as comment and vote (promote and demote) on the ideas of others. When the articles are demoted, a "vote half-life" system is used to stop older ideas that are no longer receiving votes from appearing on the popular ideas page. Dell also modifies the half-life vote to prop up ideas that they feel need more exposure. As articles are promoted, their score is increased, allowing Dell to rank which suggestions and requests are considered most important by the website's users. Anyone submitting an idea agrees to give Dell a royalty-free license to use the idea with no restrictions. Dell's feedback response strategy is logged on a page and it demonstrates how they respond to each suggestion and that page is only changed when the status of an idea updates to "implemented" while the information on the ideas being worked on are kept under wraps. An empirical study of Dell's IdeaStorm community reveals that serial ideators (i.e., individuals submitting ideas on at least two separate occasions) are more likely than consumers with only one idea to generate an idea the organization finds valuable enough to implement, but are unlikely to repeat their early success once some of their ideas are implemented.[23]

Before we move on to find out how the components of CEV are inter-related, let us have a close look at the Customer Engagement Management by Hewlett Packard (HP),[24] an information technology leader, which was in the news recently for incorporating social media channels into existing contact center channels to provide organizations with a holistic view of their customers. According to HP, the new HP Social Enterprise Services help organizations quickly implement a social CRM program to improve communications and engagement with customers, while also helping them to better understand those customers. Organizations can rapidly deliver new products and services that are aligned with customer requirements by integrating social media strategy, process, information, analytics, and technology and high-performance contact center teams which establishes a solid competitive advantage. As part of the HP Customer Engagement Management, HP Social Enterprise Services provide two service models: HP Agent Services to engage with customers in social media channels and HP Social Media Analysis to mine the social web for information and insights on customers. Key features include: Listening Service—monitors a client brand or product in social media channels to identify new engagement opportunities); Analysis Service—leverages various analytics to gain insight into client, competitor and industry trends to refine the company's social media strategy; Routing Service—directs engagement opportunities to internal stakeholders, such as customer service, marketing, sales and product development for prompt action; Engagement Service—leverages insights derived from analytics to rapidly respond to customer inquiries and comments in social media channels; and Reporting Service—provides daily snapshots, weekly summaries and monthly reports of insights, analysis and opportunities to measure program success.

When bundled, HP Agent Services and HP Social Media Analysis allow clients to manage customer relationships more effectively by keeping pace with social media and analytical technologies.

INTERRELATIONSHIPS

Linking CKV and CLV

The examples of Polyvore.com, Delta, and many more such companies are classic indicators of firms shifting focus to actively seeking and working with the feedback provided by consumers. Companies are beginning to realize that customers not only provide value through their purchases, but also through their feedback about products/services. This section discusses the importance of realizing the value potential of customer feedback and illustrates the relationship between CLV and CKV.

Normally, customers with low CLVs have little experience with the product and/or they are likely to be unenthusiastic about the firm and, therefore, are likely to provide very little feedback to the firm. In other words, low CLV customers are likely to have a low CKV. Consequently, the higher a customer's CLV, the more are the opportunities for the company to receive input and, therefore, a higher CKV. However, at very high levels of CLV (an indication of a close fit between the company's products and a customer's needs), the customers are likely to be highly satisfied, and thereby have little incentive to communicate with the company. In other words, after a threshold point, high CLV customers are likely to have a low CKV.

While the above relationship between CLV and CKV is likely to be the dominant outcome in most situations, in a small number of cases, it is also possible that a customer with low CLV but one who is highly active through new product idea suggestions may be one of the firm's most valuable assets. This scenario would reflect that the company's offerings are not matched with the customer expectations and identify areas of development. This chapter highlights that the level of connectedness of customers to other prospects and customers can provide firms the capability to better assimilate information from their networks and hence the market when providing feedback, thereby increasing their knowledge value to the firm.

The relationship between CLV and CKV from what we infer is that customers with low CLVs have little experience with the product and/or they are not very enthusiastic about the firm. Hence, their involvement with the company or the product category is probably quite limited. These customers will be, therefore, neither able nor willing to provide new insights into the company on how to manage processes and how to improve its products. However, the higher a customer's CLV, the more positive that customer will perceive the company and its products, and the more are the opportunities for the company to receive input. Very high levels of CLV, however, are indicative of an almost perfect fit between the company's products and a customer's needs. Since these customers are highly satisfied, they would be expected to have little incentive to communicate with the company about how to further improve its products. These customers can, however, offer assistance to less experienced and knowledgeable customers if firms create a communication medium and motivate them to do so.

Linking CKV and CBV

We have seen how CKV is related to CLV. Chapter 4 has a detailed description of how CLV is related to other customer engagement metrics. Since what customers think of the brand and how they value the brand has a major role in making them provide a useful feedback about the product/service to the firm, we have developed a 2×2 matrix combining these two metrics (Figure 8.5). Marketers can implement this to maximize overall customer value and it can be used as a framework to strategically segment customers based on their individual CKV and CBV metrics.

A brief description of the recommended strategies for managing each of the four segments is described below.

| Figure 8.5 | The Relationship between CKV and CBV |

	Low CKV	High CKV
High CBV	**Honeymooners** These customers value the brand highly but do not give valuable feedback to the firm about the product/service. **Strategy:** Encourage them to give feedback.	**Partners** These customers value the brand highly and also help the company by giving feedback. **Strategy:** Nurture their relation as they give reference as well as think highly of the brand.
Low CBV	**Blankslates** These customers do not value the brand, nor do they give feedback about the product or service. **Strategy:** Spend least unless they have high CLV.	**Consultants** These customers do not strongly value the brand but they do give feedback to the company on the product/service. **Strategy:** Promote the brand to these customers.

- *Honeymooners:* These clients have high CBV, which means they value the brand, but their low CKV indicates that they are not sharing their feedback with the firm. The recommended strategy would be to identify potential Partners and understand why they are not providing feedback. One reason could be that they have just started their relationship with the firm and do not have enough input to provide feedback. In this case provide necessary information to the firm and encourage them to give feedback. This could be achieved by sending emails to them with a feedback link, which will prompt them to get back to the business or one can ask them how they liked the product they purchased recently from the company.
- *Blankslates:* These clients have a low CBV and CKV. By this we mean that they neither provide feedback nor think highly of the brand. It is best to minimize marketing efforts on these clients except for the ones with high CLV, as the ones with low CLV, CKV, and CBV are not adding any value to the firm.
- *Consultants:* These clients have a high CKV and low CBV. This means that the client has a good understanding of the firm's products and services but does not think highly about the brand. For a mutually beneficial relationship, customers should value the Brand, know more about it and then share the feedback with the firm. The strategy to make these customers into "partners" is to promote the brand to them. Brand promotion can be done by sending promotional coupons and rewards for repeat buying.
- *Partners:* These customers have high CBV and CKV, which means they provide feedback to the firm and at the same time value the brand. These clients are valuable clients and it is recommended to nurture the relationship with them.

Linking CKV and CIV

It is observed that a customer's CIV will be strongly influenced by his or her online activities and social networking index like the reach of his or her blogging sites, number of active friends in Facebook, Twitter, etc., and also his or her interest in reviewing a product/service. All these activities are excellent channels through which feedback is gained which is translated to customer knowledge and can also act as a medium to influence peers. For example,

Netflix, an online DVD rental retailer, actively seeks feedback from its customers regarding their movie rental experience by observing what its customers are saying to each other. Customers are encouraged to review movies in their website to inform other customers. This information is then used by Netflix to refine the recommender systems that suggest movies to its customers. It is also not uncommon that customers react in extreme situations like when someone is very happy or upset about their purchase. When they are instantaneously happy it comes out as a positive comment or a feedback and if there is some kind of a disappointment either in a product or a service quality, it is expressed as a negative feedback. Although positive and negative evaluations generate valuable feedback for the firm and contribute to the generation of CKV, customers providing this feedback generally are at the extremes in terms of CIV. However, it will be interesting to study whether increased usage of social networking sites such as Facebook has decreased the polarizations of online evaluations. The ease of communication on such mediums may encourage more moderate evaluations.

Linking CKV and CRV

The relationship between customer referral value (CRV) and customer knowledge value (CKV) is very obvious as both depict the connectedness of the customer. The more connected a customer is, the more knowledgeable he or she will be about other customers' usage situations, problems, and solutions related to the firm's products. By soliciting feedback from a well-connected customer, a firm is able to tap into a much broader knowledge base as opposed to soliciting feedback from an unconnected customer.

The same connections to potential customers make it possible for a customer to effectively refer customers to the firm. Also, product experience, knowledge, and involvement enhance both the effectiveness of customer referral behavior and the value of any knowledge transfer between the firm and the customer. The relationship will be strengthened in cases where the firm acquires knowledge from customers through incentivized schemes; as such an action would trigger feedback from customers who are malleable to incentives. For example, Express, a clothing company, motivated customers to submit product reviews by entering them in a drawing for a gift card based on the number of reviews they submitted. It is likely that the company retrieved more knowledge from its customer base by motivating customers to submit reviews (provide knowledge) who normally would not have been inclined to do so.

Linking CKV and BRV

In real life, we see many firms providing references for the firms they do business with. They choose to do it via their website in various formats, audio/video testimonials, case studies, white papers, etc. The firms can also offer other businesses to call or contact them for references. All these add value to the selling firm as they increase the reputation of the firm's products and services and also proof of their consistent service. It also means that the firm that is providing the reference is very knowledgeable about the firm with which they are doing business. To understand this relationship better, we have developed a 2×2 matrix combining these two metrics (Figure 8.6).

A brief description of the recommended strategies for managing each of the four segments is described below.

Figure 8.6 The Relationship between CKV and BRV

	Low CKV	High CKV
High BRV	**Advertisers** These clients provide good references but do not give valuable feedback to the company about the product or service. *Strategy:* Find ways to encourage them to give feedback to the company.	**Collaborators** These clients give good reference and also help the company by giving feedback. *Strategy:* Nurture their relation as they give reference as well as feedback.
Low BRV	**Wallflowers** These are clients who neither refer nor give feedback to the business. *Strategy:* Minimize the marketing effort on these customers except for the ones with high CLV.	**Identifiers** These are clients who give extensive and valuable feedback about the products but do not add value by giving references to the business. *Strategy:* Find ways to make these customers give valuable references.

- *Advertisers:* These business clients have a high BRV, which means that they are referring the firm to other business but their low CKV indicates that they are not sharing their feedback with the firm. The recommended strategy would be to identify potential collaborators and identify why they are not providing feedback. One reason could be that they have just started their relationship with the firm and do not have enough input to provide feedback. In this case provide necessary information to the firm and encourage them to give feedback.
- *Wallflowers:* These business clients have low a BRV and CKV. By this we mean that they neither provide feedback nor provide referrals to the firm. It is best to minimize marketing efforts on these clients except for the ones with high CLV, as the ones with low CLV, CKV, and BRV are not at all valuing adding to the firm.
- *Identifiers:* These business clients have a high CKV and a low BRV. This means that the client has a good understanding of the firm's products and willingly shares feedback but their references are not adding value to the firm. For a mutually beneficial relationship, the firm should provide ideas/ avenues for the clients to give valuable references.
- *Collaborators:* These business clients have high a BRV and CKV, that is, they provide feedback to the firm at the same time refer the firm to other businesses as well. These clients are valuable clients and it is recommended to nurture the relationship with them.

CONCLUSION

As we have already described, customer knowledge value is the value that an individual customer can provide a firm through purchase behavior, opinion mining, and other feedback channels. In both the physical and viral communities, customers leave traces of behavior and opinions (intentionally or unintentionally), which can be analyzed to improve a product and service as well as the various processes and methods that go into bringing it to the customer. Being able to quantify CKV in a consistent fashion would allow companies to maximize the efficiency with which they deal with customer feedback, as well as how they implement it into changing their strategies and products. Being able to analyze, and then quantify the historical value of the feedback from each individual customer would allow companies to locate the customer feedback sources that are most likely to provide insightful feedback. This use could, and should, be broken down into individual product levels, with some customers having greater CKV regarding one product than another.

NOTES AND REFERENCES

1. Youtube (2009), "Domino's Pizza on Today Show," http://www.youtube.com/watch?v=xaNuE3DsJHM (retrieved on February 20, 2013).
2. V. Kumar and Y. Bhagwat, "Listen to the Customer," *Marketing Research—A Magazine of Management and Applications 22*(2), (2010): 14–19.
3. 5 Cocreation Examples, http://www.innovationmanagement.se/2012/02/24/five-co-creation-examples-e-on-coca-cola-mtv-tata-group-and-heineken/ (retrieved on April 4, 2013).
4. Gabbay, Nisan (2006, Sep 17), "Zappos.com Case Study: Why Shoes are Great for E-commerce ... Yes, Really," http://langturn.com/translations/55?locale=pt (retrieved on September 9, 2013).
5. "How Shoppers Stop Is Wooing Customers the Social Way," http://marketingtransformation.informationweek.in/index.php/news/item/26-how-shoppers-stop-is-wooing-customers-the-social-way/26-how-shoppers-stop-is-wooing-customers-the-social-way?limitstart=0 (retrieved on April 1, 2013).
6. Kumar and Bhagwat, "Listen to the Customer."
7. Ibid.
8. Ibid.
9. CNS News, "Microsoft Pledges Windows Developers Generosity," http://cnsnews.com/news/article/microsoft-pledges-windows-developers-generosity-0 (retrieved on February 20, 2013).
10. Apple, https://developer.apple.com/support/ios/iad-network.html (retrieved on February 20, 2013).
11. QuestionPro, http://www.questionpro.com/collectyourdata/ (retrieved on February 20, 2013).
12. Threadless, http://www.threadless.com/ (retrieved on February 20, 2013).
13. Customer Insight Management 'LG' Craze," http://economy.hankooki.com/lpage/industry/200712/e2007122417275847580.htm. (The page is Korean but can be translated into English.) (retrieved on April 8, 2013).
14. Aline, Fatima (December 11, 2011). Let's Learn: Top 5 Social Media Campaigns That Failed Miserably. Message posted on http://blog.askoli.com/social-media-marketing/let%E2%80%99s-learn-top-5-social-media-campaigns-that-failed-miserably/ (retrieved on February 20, 2013).
15. Corina, Mackay (November 12, 2010) Royal Dutch Airline Gives Passengers a Surprise," Message posted on http://thenextweb.com/socialmedia/2010/11/12/royal-dutch-airline-gives-passengers-a-surprise/ (retrieved on February 20, 2013).
16. Foursqaure, https://foursquare.com/p/klm/3450621 (retrieved on February 20, 2013).
17. Cola-Cola, http://www.coca-colafreestyle.com/#!/100-brands/ (retrieved on February 20, 2013).

18. Starbucks, http://mystarbucksidea.force.com/ (retrieved on February 20, 2013).

19. Huffingtonpost (September 15, 2011). Netflix Price Increase Causes Bigger Subscriber Loss Than Expected. http://www.huffingtonpost.com/2011/09/15/netflix-price-increase-subscriber-loss_n_964026.html (retrieved on February 20, 2013).

20. Bloomberg (2011), "Posterior Marketing Response Parameters," http://www.bloomberg.com/news/2011-12-30/verizon-defends-2-convenience-fee-.html (retrieved on February 20, 2013).

21. IBN live (2010), "Apple Apologizes for iPhone 4 Signal Glitch," http://ibnlive.in.com/news/apple-apologises-for-iphone-4-signal-glitch/125891-11.html (retrieved on February 20, 2013).

22. Delta, https://ideasinflight.delta.com/IdeasInFlight/home.action (retrieved on September 9, 2013).

23. B.L. Bayus, "Crowdsourcing New Product Ideas Over Time: An Analysis of the Dell Ideastorm Community," *Management Science*, (2012). http://mansci.journal.informs.org/content/early/2012/11/02/mnsc.1120.1599.abstract (retrieved on February 20, 2013).

24. HP, http://www8.hp.com/us/en/business-services/it-services.html?compURI=1079486#.UQw6Px1fCxc (retrieved on February 20, 2013).

Chapter 9

Managing Customers in a Multi-dimensional World

Find answers for...

- To what extent can the CEV-based framework be implemented in your firm?
- What are the organizational challenges encountered while implementing a CEV-based approach?
- What are the database management issues that are faced while implementing a CEV-based approach?
- What does the future of customer engagement hold?

As we have seen in the previous chapters, firms can undoubtedly benefit from a customer engagement value (CEV)-based framework in terms of attitudinally *and* behaviorally engaging customers so that the profits are maximized. Profitably managing customers is a multi-dimensional task (because CEV is not a single number) for firms as they have many aspects to tend to at once. It is likely that firms will be managing more than one CEV component concurrently; for example, managing the CLV of customers and an active referral system (CRV), as well as a system in place to receive feedback from customers (CKV). When attempting to manage several CEV elements simultaneously, key concerns arise—what is the firm attempting to measure; what can and cannot be measured; and to what extent can the CEV framework be implemented in a firm? Each of these concerns points to how to manage the elements of the CEV framework to the benefit of the firm. However, a company may not know which of the CEV metrics to prioritize for its business, or it may face many organizational and database management challenges in implementing such a framework.

When firms adopt a CEV approach for profitable customer management, it is possible to learn about new and latent customer preferences by observing their purchase and behavioral history. Additionally, when the attitudinal information from the customer is also captured, the firms obtain a differentiating perspective (when compared to competitors) in managing customers profitably. However, collecting, integrating, and utilizing the attitudinal information with customer purchase behavior to drive profits may not be always easy. It requires a concerted effort by the top management to change the organizational-level philosophy of doing business. It may also involve realignment of organizational roles and integration of different functions. Such an upgrade in the organizational philosophy also comes with concerns related to database management. Firms need to collect individual-level data about all of their customers on a large number of variables to compute each of the metrics in order to arrive at the CEV. Although the cost of data collection and storage has decreased over the years, many firms face challenges in identifying the right informational needs, integrating data, and making use of the available information. In Figure 9.1, we see how managers can work their way through the CEV framework. Next, we show how to specifically manage each CEV metric.

The practice of engaging customers continues to evolve, with new dimensions of interaction constantly being added and refined. Even with the evolution of customer engagement, the CEV framework will offer a comprehensive ability to manage the value of a customer in a profitable manner. This chapter explores how and when to focus on managing the CEV metrics, some challenges faced by organizations, issues pertaining to database management, and discussion about the future of engaging customers.

MANAGING THE CEV FRAMEWORK

Chapters 3 through 8 describe in detail how the CEV metrics such as customer brand value (CBV), customer lifetime value (CLV), customer referral value (CRV)/business reference value (BRV), customer influence value (CIV), and customer knowledge value (CKV) are defined, measured, and maximized. Perhaps the most important thing to realize when attempting to understand CEV is that it is not merely an aggregate of the components, but that the metrics are all correlated and constantly interacting. Rather than

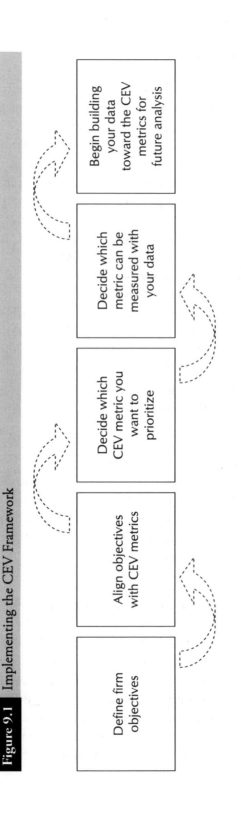

Figure 9.1 Implementing the CEV Framework

Define firm objectives

Align objectives with CEV metrics

Decide which CEV metric you want to prioritize

Decide which metric can be measured with your data

Begin building your data toward the CEV metrics for future analysis picturing the components as separate departments or entities, it is more accurate to think of them as different ropes that are tied together to form a CEV knot. After seeing that each metric has the potential to be maximized (as discussed in their respective chapters), the next step is prioritizing the management of the metrics. Although not impossible, it is very rare that all of the components that make up the CEV framework can be maximized simultaneously; however, some of the metrics can be managed simultaneously. It can be difficult for managers to decide which component their efforts should be focused on. The choice of metric has everything to do with the type of business implementing the framework. The infrastructure, product range/suite, and category, as well as the market/competitive environment are the deciding factors for which metric to prioritize for maximization. Given below is a brief view of when to prioritize the management of each metric.

Customer Brand Value

A strong brand is at the core of any customer–firm relationship. It is nearly impossible to build a long-standing, mutually beneficial relationship for brands that are seen as less than worthy. Brand awareness and perception of the brand or brand image, are the genesis for all potential customer engagement. Before a customer can work his or her way through the CBV framework (and subsequently the CEV framework), the brand has to be seen as viable. A firm has the ability to shape the perception of its brand through various marketing and advertising; Exhibit 9.1 shows an example of this.

The concept of CBV is closely related to the CLV metric because the drivers of CBV promote customer action. As discussed before, linking CBV to CLV can help maximize the lifetime value of customers. To obtain the maximized level of CLV, brand behavior such as brand advocacy and premium price behavior needs to be optimized. This can be done through sending appropriate brand messages to increase a customer's level of brand awareness and favorability of brand image. Such favorable brand knowledge can shape a customer's positive attitude in terms of brand trust and brand affect. Brand purchase intention will be affected and revealed through behavioral brand loyalty (manifested as higher purchase frequency). These efforts can ultimately result in the cultivation of a truly loyal customer who would not only advocate the brand but also be willing to pay a premium price for the quality of the product. Moreover, CBV influences each of the other metrics as

---

Exhibit 9.1: Management in Motion—Building Brand Value

Some brands are ubiquitous, and are known for having a strong perception among their customers, such as the consumer technology brand Apple; conversely, in the CKV chapter we discussed Domino's Pizza and how the brand was in disarray and needed to be repaired and strengthened before it could once again become successful. Old Spice, the consumer-packaged goods brand from Procter & Gamble, is a similar example of a brand that needed to be strengthened before it could be deemed a success again. In the late 2000s and early 2010s, Old Spice sought to update its brand image and reposition the brand from a traditionally older male audience by attracting a younger male age group of 12- to 34-year-olds.[1] This shift in branding was dictated by declining sales and stagnate imaging. Old Spice initiated several changes in order to revamp its brand, including redesigning the deodorant packaging,[2] enlisting celebrity spokespersons' print and television ads for the Swagger scent deodorant,[3] and creating several extensions of the wildly successful television and social media body wash campaign "Smell Like a Man, Man" which was kicked off by a 2010 Super Bowl television commercial before becoming a series of viral videos housed on YouTube.[4] As a result of the campaigns, the sales for the Swagger scent deodorant increased by 400 percent, while the sales for the body wash increased by 107 percent, making Old Spice the number one body wash for men.[5] These examples are important to drive home a single point—as the components of CBV increase (brand knowledge, brand attitude, brand purchase intention, and brand behavior), a customer becomes more valuable to the firm because CBV is the foundation of a customer's relationship to the firm.

---

well. The interactions between a particular metric and CBV can be revisited in detail in each of the respective chapters.

Customer Lifetime Value

Once a strong brand has been established, a firm should focus on building and managing the behavioral aspects of a customer, particularly CLV. Since CLV is directly related to a firm's bottom line, it is the most important CEV metric, and because CLV contributes directly to the profit of the company it should be the first and lead metric to be managed by an organization. In order to calculate CLV proper data is needed, specifically customer level transaction data. Data analytics can then help determine strategies to target high, medium, and low CLV customers. Specific communications—based on understanding the target audience's characteristics—can be developed to drive response and purchase behavior. Sophisticated statistical modeling techniques can aid marketers to not only suggest the optimal resource allocation to each customer/customer segments but also look beyond "who" to target by understanding the "how," "what," and "when" dimensions. Following the adoption of the CLV metric, the portfolio of customer management strategies—known as the Wheel of Fortune Strategies—can be used to maximize the CLV of the customer. The experience (or information) obtained by implementing these strategies is taken into account while making future decisions about customer selection and other strategies, thus guaranteeing a robust process that can be leveraged to maximize profit.

A high CLV is not the only factor determining a customer's maximum profitability. In some instances, increasing any of the metrics—CRV/BRV, CIV, and CKV—which are a customer's indirect contributions to profit but are directly related to profit, should also be the primary focus of a manager. A customer with a medium CLV, which is to say they are not directly generating their maximum potential profit for a firm, could have a high CRV, meaning that they are referring many profit-generating customers to the firm. In this case, the medium CLV/high CRV customer is valuable to the aforementioned organization. This example shows that while a firm may be unable to maximize CLV for a customer, the customer can still be made more valuable to the firm by encouraging incentivized referrals. While a customer's CLV (high, medium, low) is the first line of profit maximization, it is not the end of his or her ability to be profitable.

Customer Referral Value/Business Reference Value

CRV focuses on current customers turning prospective customers (found in the customer's network of friends and relatives) into actual customers for the firm via firm-initiated incentivized referral programs. Current customers are rewarded for the conversion of prospects to actual customers by which the current customers indirectly contribute to the profit of the firm. The referrals are extrinsically motivated and hence customers can be looked at as nonemployee sales people who are compensated for contributing to the firm's profit. A firm can maximize CRV by identifying the right customers who can refer powerful prospects that bring profits for the firm. While CRV is used to calculate the referral values of customers in a B2C setting, BRV is used to calculate the reference value of businesses in the B2B context. As seen in Chapter 5, BRV can be maximized by firms selecting clients based on the four drivers (trusted informant through client firm size, length of client relationship, reference media format, and reference congruency) discussed in the chapter. A client firm with a high BRV value can significantly contribute to the profits of the seller firm.

When referral mechanisms [such as word of mouth (WOM) or testimonials] play a large part in a firm's marketing strategy, it would be prudent to focus on increasing a customer's CRV or a client's BRV, as it would have the greatest impact on the firm's profitability. If a firm has a product/service for which a customer needs more information or for which it is difficult to inspire a trial, referral programs can be very beneficial.[6] An example of the CRV metric being used to convert prospective customers into actual customers can be seen in many apartment communities in the United States. Apartment communities incentivize current tenants (usually done by taking a percentage or dollar amount credited to the current tenant's rent), to act as salespeople to sell the apartment community to prospective tenants.[7] In the B2B context, BRV can be maximized by exploiting the drivers of BRV between the referrer and the client prospect. For example, a construction firm that is responsible for building high-rise condominiums throughout the United States is bidding for a project in South Florida and they want to show that they have come in under-budget on their last three projects in metropolitan areas; the firm can capitalize on increasing BRV by showing references from similar high-rise developments in New York, NY and Los Angeles, CA. These references would be critical in selling their services to the South Florida developers, as they would legitimize the constructions firm's capabilities.

Customer Influence Value

In order for a firm to attempt to capitalize from CIV, its customers should be present on social media platforms. If a firm has a strong social media presence, wants to create a strong social media presence, increase its social media presence, increase brand awareness, or is seeking to sell products via WOM, it would benefit the company if it focuses on maximizing a customer's CIV, as a way to leverage that customer's influencer capabilities. Influencers have the power to legitimize a product among their peer groups and followers. These influencers need not be famous spokespeople; they can be individual taste-makers who have a broad network of people on social media and considerable clout, or social capital. Managing CIV means giving power to the customers engaging them and making them feel important.

By choosing the right influencers from the pool of customers and encouraging those influencers with intangible and tangible benefits, firms can encourage and maximize CIV. To help them acquire new customers, retain existing customers, and, in turn, increase their profits, businesses can employ initiatives that stimulate and engage customers to actively participate in influencer activities such as utilizing social networks and WOM to promote the business. For example, hypothetically speaking, a soft drink company launches a new juice product, then incentivizes the trials of the juice and encourages sharing via social media; the company could then pinpoint the influencers and attempt to maximize the CIV of those influencers. The overarching goal of CIV is to enhance the firms' engagement with the customer through social media. Exhibit 9.2 provides a snapshot of how CIV has been managed by General Motors (GM) via Facebook.

Exhibit 9.2: Management in Motion—CIV

While investing in social media is an important aspect of marketing in this day and age, it is important to know what the goals of a firm's social media presence are, how these goals can be met, and if those goals have indeed been met. Take the recent relationship change between GM and Facebook. In 2012, GM pulled all of its paid advertising from Facebook (valued at $10 million), while maintaining its Facebook pages.

A fundamental difference between Facebook users and businesses leads to GM's pullout:

> The expectation of a business that uses Facebook's ad platform is to be able to not just capture a single user's attention via a click and further action, but to organically expand that click into a series of new clicks by the user's friends and friends of friends.[8]

(Exhibit 9.2 Continued)

(Exhibit 9.2 Continued)

> In other words, the main function of a business is to use advertising to inspire engagement and capitalize off of the resulting CIV. However, Facebook users tend to come to the social media platform to socialize with their chosen group of friends and not to shop.
>
> Kumar and Sundaram[9] suggest four ways in which regulated and targeted advertising in social-media channels has the opportunity to produce a winning situation. The advertising (a) is to be targeted to that population based on context and user interactions, (b) increases the probability of user interaction by offering them incentives, immediately or in the future, based on norms of the business, (c) increases the probability of friends of the user to interact because of shared incentives, and (d) converts the user's interaction and interactions of friends into transactions with the business, thereby gaining customers as well as retaining existing customers.
>
> The lesson here is to understand how users operate in a chosen social media platform, in order to effectively learn how to encourage engagement.

Customer Knowledge Value

Customer knowledge value focuses on capitalizing on information customers provide to improve satisfaction and increase buying behavior. By encouraging customer knowledge value, businesses can steer the customer toward giving the business more feedback, thereby increasing the interactions which will lead to higher profits. In order to maximize and encourage CKV, firms can develop a customer feedback response strategy. Having a streamlined process and system to manage and encourage customer knowledge is crucial as this can help businesses design and launch new products in a timely manner and aid in keeping customers' loyalty and commitment intact. As a result, CKV can be maximized when the firm makes communication with customers easy and accessible, provides some form of incentive (monetary or not), and engages the customer in activities through which the customer can offer feedback and collaborate with the firm. An excellent example of a well developed and functioning feedback system can be seen in Exhibit 9.3.

Exhibit 9.3: Management in Motion—CKV

As we now know, the CKV concept is beneficial for businesses that thrive on ideas generated from customer feedback. More specifically, any business for whom customer feedback is a tool of product/service enhancement, would want to focus on increasing its customer's CKV metric, as it would directly benefit their product suite. CKV is a metric that can enhance business in many different industries by tapping into the wisdom of the customers. Maximizing CKV can be achieved through company provided channels. BMW, a leading luxury vehicle manufacturer, has engineered a great example of fostering feedback on its product offerings via the "BMW Co-creation Lab." The Co-Creation Lab is described as:

> A virtual meeting place for individuals interested in cars and all related topics, who want to share their ideas and opinions on tomorrow's automotive world with one of the leading car manufacturers. It invites people from all over the world to contribute their suggestions for specific topics and to connect with like-minded others. Participants not only evaluate concepts which are developed by the BMW Group but also actively contribute their ideas and suggestions—they become active 'co-creators' of innovative products and services. (BMW Co-Creation Lab 2013)[10]

The Co-Creation Lab online forum allows BMW enthusiasts to become members of the online community and to share traceable ideas about current products offerings, as well as products that are currently under development. BMW sees customer feedback as integral aspect of its future product offerings and thus have made it easy for a customer to give input, allowing that input to participate in the creation of new products. This strategy is not restricted to just the automobile industry, feedback can be a fundamental part of any product or service provider, from software to video games to soft drinks.

A Note on Managing the Framework

As stated before, CLV is fundamental to an organization to value customers. However, of the indirect CEV concepts, it is easiest to maximize CRV because the metric measures an easily quantifiable action, which is to say that because customer references are incentivized, they are painlessly traced to the source of the referral. CIV is a bit more difficult than CRV to maximize because it may be difficult to track, particularly if the firm does not have the software in place to follow the stream of influence on the various social media platforms. Finally, CKV is the most difficult to maximize, especially if the firm does not have a streamlined process to accept, track, and act on the feedback. It is important for managers to understand how their firm functions at its core in order to choose the best CEV metric to maximize.

ORGANIZATIONAL CHALLENGES

There are several organizational challenges that come along with implementing a CEV-based framework. The organization has to become committed to understanding the ever-changing needs and behaviors of its customers. This could be a difficult step for firms who are not willing to step out of the traditional mindset when it comes to understanding their customers and who have traditionally pushed products with very little differentiation or for firms that have improperly segmented their customer base. It is also equally difficult for those who are not willing to listen to the needs or ideas of their customers and who are starting from scratch with gathering customer data, or who have not maximized the use of their customer data.

Loyalty

The traditional school of thought says that loyal customers cost less to serve than disloyal customers, are more willing to pay higher prices for products, and are actively marketing the product to prospective customers. However, managing customer loyalty alone will not deliver the best financial results; firms must also, simultaneously, manage customer profitability.[11] It is maximizing the profitability of a customer that delivers results to the bottom line. When a firm takes customer loyalty and customer profitability into account simultaneously, it becomes clear that different customers will require different loyalty strategies, equipped with differentiated experiences and propositions, as discussed in Chapter 3. It is important for a firm to know who its valued customers are and to stay close to them, and manage the inherent complexity and cost of a differentiated experience effectively. Many companies operate using the traditional thought process; organizations are entrenched in the practice of focusing solely on customer loyalty; because of this, overcoming organizational structure and culture may act as a challenge toward implementing a CEV-based framework.

Customer Feedback

The willingness to listen to customers has become one of the most valued assets of an organization. A plethora of data is available about customers, but not all of it focuses on 1's and 0's; much of the data that is generated by current and potential customers is qualitative. Qualitative data can be found in a number of places including through traditional customer feedback channels (i.e., company/product website, and customer complaints/services) as well as via digital and social media channels. Social media has changed the way many companies are doing business. Because of the proliferation of customers, controlled social media channels, and the rising voice of the customers, it is imperative that firms create an ongoing two-way dialogue using direct (company website) and indirect (company social media) channels. Listening to one's customers allows an organization to have access to customer knowledge, which provides an opportunity for customers to learn about its products from the perspective of the customer. Figure 9.2[12] shows the flow of customer feedback within an organization by illustrating ways in which access to such information provides insights about a product/project and informs other aspects of the company.

Using customer feedback in the B2C context is relatively new in the field. The earlier a firm implements this strategy, the likelier it will have a competitive advantage. It is up to the organization to determine whether or not it wants its customers to act as codevelopers or information sources. Digital and social media are tools that can persuade customers to partake in both roles. Digital spaces such as firm-created virtual communities can cultivate customer-firm codevelopment of new products, while social media platforms can be utilized to garner ideas from customers.[13] Promoting an atmosphere for customer feedback encompasses one of the aspects of the CEV framework—CKV. Benefitting from CKV may present a challenge to firms with very bureaucratic organizational structures. In order to take full advantage of the value of customer knowledge, the internal structure of an organization must have the agility required to respond quickly to the concerns of

Figure 9.2 Customer Feedback Flow within an Organization

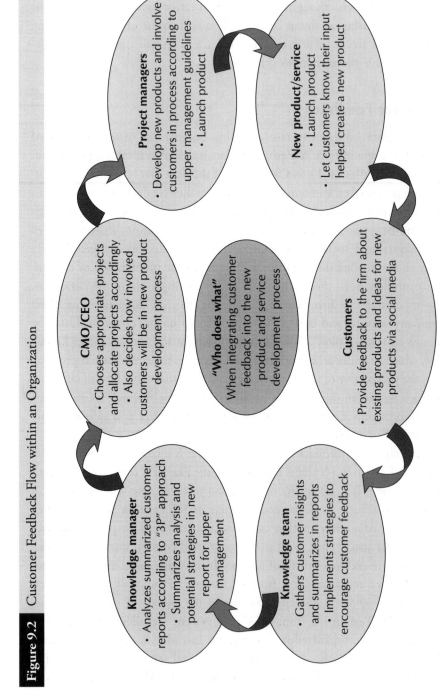

CMO/CEO
- Chooses appropriate projects and allocate projects accordingly
- Also decides how involved customers will be in new product development process

Project managers
- Develop new products and involve customers in process according to upper management guidelines
- Launch product

New product/service
- Launch product
- Let customers know their input helped create a new product

"Who does what"
When integrating customer feedback into the new product and service development process

Customers
- Provide feedback to the firm about existing products and ideas for new products via social media

Knowledge team
- Gathers customer insights and summarizes in reports
- Implements strategies to encourage customer feedback

Knowledge manager
- Analyzes summarized customer reports according to "3P" approach
- Summarizes analysis and potential strategies in new report for upper management

Source: Printed with permission from V. Kumar and Y. Bhagwat, "Listen to the Customer," *Marketing Research—A Magazine of Management and Applications,* 22(2), (2010): 14–19.

customers. Empowering the front lines (or customer-facing personnel) to build trust-based relationships will show customers that not only have their opinions, compliments, critiques, and concerns been heard, but they are also taken into consideration.

Data Availability

The CEV-based framework requires existing data to measure certain key concepts. For a firm to be fully prepared to enjoy the many benefits that come along with implementing a CEV-based framework, it must first be sure that its ability to gather customer data is intact. For example, calculating CRV requires a firm to have access to the actual data reflecting previous customer referrals in order to predict the future number of referrals.[14] The need for access to historical customer data would be a challenge for an organization looking to calculate certain aspects of the CEV framework, if it has not already been storing data related to certain transactions, i.e., customer referral history. In order to meet such challenges the firm should begin storing critical data as soon as possible.

DATABASE MANAGEMENT

The primary challenges facing companies in database management are the continuous growth and increasing complexity of database frameworks, and the difficulty in finding and retaining technical resources that understand the complexities of the databases to effectively manage them. As more companies are switching to a customer-engagement approach that focuses on the overall profitability of a customer, databases have doubled in size resulting in the phenomenon of "Big Data." This exponential growth has had a significant impact on the management of databases in terms. The analytics to support a customer engagement strategy that focuses on calculating customer lifetime value (CLV) requires the employment of databases designed to handle querying of data across various customer interactions with the company. These databases are far more complex than the traditional account/relationship information databases previously used by companies, and offer companies the ability to find out about all of the interactions a customer has had with the company.

Data is one of a company's most valuable assets and serves as an important component in ensuring a firm's success on an operational and competitive level. The proper functioning of a database is the top priority of a firm's IT department and it poses a challenge to firms. Key issues related to database management include (*a*) data integrity, (*b*) data accessibility, (*c*) data security, (*d*) disaster recovery, and (*e*) change management.

Data Integrity

Data integrity is paramount in database management as it ensures that data is of high quality, consistent, and accessible. The trustworthiness of data over time can have a significant impact on a company's operations. Companies now have to retain a greater array of documents and communications for a greater period of time. Maintaining the integrity of data can serve as a challenge to firms and steps must be to taken to ensure that it is not compromised. Threats to data integrity can be minimized by the following means:

- Data Backup—backing up data regularly to be stored in an alternate location.
- Access Controls—controlling access to data through read/write privileges.
- Input Validation—designing user interfaces that prevent the input of invalid data.
- Data Validation—using error detection and correction software when transmitting data.
- Data Encryption—locking data by cipher.

When appropriate measures are not taken, data integrity can be compromised by breaches such as human error during data entry, data transmission errors from one computer to another, software bugs or viruses, hardware malfunctions/crashes, and natural disasters such as fires and floods.

Data Accessibility

Data accessibility is an increasingly important data quality dimension for firms to address. Not only must a greater amount of data be preserved, but it also must be preserved in such a way that it can be easily accessed.[15] For many companies, the fear of losing control over data is outweighed by the ability to readily access data from virtually anywhere. The primary benefit of accessible data is the ability for users to read and update the data needed for the business processes for which they are responsible. Furthermore, a high level of accessibility encourages companies to maintain data that is understandable and well documented. Ultimately, accessibility improves the quality of data by embracing the government of access rights and improving functionality. The increasing adoption of cloud services can also contribute positively to solving many data quality issues through improved accessibility.

Data Security

Data security is a critical task in database management as it ensures that users can only access authorized data. Data theft and loss are real threats that many large companies face on a daily basis. As such, firms must build robust information technology departments and employ database administrators who create, examine, maintain users, determine roles, and profile trails for users as well as security analysts who ensure that data is stored securely, monitor security systems, and repair damage from security breaches.

Through access controls and data encryption, companies can protect their databases from destructive forces and unwanted actions from unauthorized users. In addition, the installation and maintenance of security software and the instruction of computer users on proper security measures can minimize security risks and help ensure that data remains in the hands of those intended to use it.

Disaster Recovery

Disaster recovery involves the steps taken to recover data upon the occurrence of a breach or compromise. Whether due to human error, theft, or natural disasters, these breaches or compromises in security need to be handled quickly in order to get a company back on track. The protection of data is paramount to many firms but sometimes disasters are unavoidable due to uncontrollable circumstances. Like any valuable, data should be covered with an insurance policy to ensure that the investment is not lost or erased by actions outside of the company's control. Instituting disaster recovery control measures highlights processes, policies, and procedures that provide guidelines for the recovery of an organization's technology infrastructure after a disaster. Control measures can be classified into three categories: (*a*) preventative measures that aim to prevent an event from occurring, (*b*) detective measures that focus on detecting unwanted events, and (*c*) corrective measures that aim at restoring the system after the event. Data protection measures such as data backup can also serve as safety nets in the event of a disaster. In addition, cloud computing makes it increasingly more viable for companies to have disaster recovery infrastructures through outsourcing.

Change Management

Change management is a key component for any company's IT management. Database change management is the process of determining which changes need to be made to a database, evaluating the effects of those changes, and then implementing the changes. As a company grows, its needs change which leads to changes in its databases; growing databases can require new hardware, software, and other resources. Changes may also be required due to new business requirements, mergers, legislative changes, and application environment changes.[16]

Change management is often a difficult and time-consuming process for a database administrator but is a necessary evil in maintaining the integrity and accessibility of a company's data. It is important for companies to coordinate schedules and changes with their software-development teams to create unified database applications. Companies that are up-to-date on IT tracking systems are able to effectively manage, change, and prevent unplanned IT issues. Furthermore, companies that systematically manage the lifecycle of IT assets can reduce IT costs.

THE FUTURE OF CUSTOMER ENGAGEMENT

Big Data

As mentioned in the introduction to this chapter, the firm needs to have several data points on the customer. Enter the concept of big data. In May of 2009, Andreas Weigend, former chief scientist at Amazon.com, forecasted that in 2009 more data would be generated than in the entire history of mankind up until 2008.[17] Big data is sourced from many channels—RFID, sensors, geo-location (GPS-enabled devices), audio/visual streaming, and the trillions of bytes transacted through social media—which has become known as the social data revolution. It can also cover many types of data including transactional, marketing, demographics, attitudinal, and firm data (Figure 9.3).

In fact, within these datasets, a single customer profile could have more than two hundred unique points of data. While the understanding and categorizing of big data is a fairly new task for the industry and academia, there are three dominating characteristics of big data that everyone agrees on: high velocity, high volume, and high variety.

- *High Velocity:* Velocity, in this context, refers to the speed at which big data is collected. New information is constantly being formed and collected, whether it comes from the transaction data from a Home Depot purchase

Figure 9.3	Types of Data

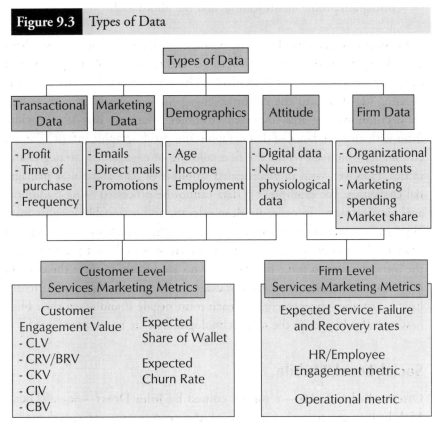

Source: Printed with permission from V. Kumar, V. Chattaraman, C. Neghina, B. Skiera, L. Aksoy, A. Buoye, and J. Henseler, "Data-Driven Services Marketing in a Connected World," *Journal of Service Management* (forthcoming).

or the mountains of user-generated content uploaded to the Internent daily. Information is being formed at a rate that has never been seen before.

- *High Volume:* Big data has been defined as data sets that are too large to be analyzed by traditional software, which means that new analytics software has to be created to manage and query big data in order for firms to gain insights from it. Actual sizes of big data sets can span anywhere from terabytes to exabytes and beyond (for reference, 1 exabyte is equal to 1 billion gigabytes).
- *High Variety:* As big data comes from countless unique sources and has many different dimensions and attributes, it is said to have a high variety. For example, if a user uploads a single photo to the online photo sharing service Instagram, there are several unique pieces of data attached to the action: a date stamp, a time stamp, geolocation, the user's Instagram profile identification, and the photo itself.

Big data is a recent reality in the business world, and as such, many firms are still trying to understand how to get the most out of the plethora of customer information that is available. There are several benefits to incorporating big data into the customer engagement philosophy, such as better decision-making and improved customer solutions. Big data provides firms with an abundance of demographic and psychographic information on customers, which allows for the fine tailoring of engagement strategies and tactics. However, with unprecedented amounts of data come new managerial challenges. For example, big data cannot be processed using traditional analytical software. In order to glean relevant and actionable insights from big data, one needs to be able to query the data, which requires advanced analytics. This could present a problem for firms who do not presently have the infrastructure to mine big data or who are unable to meet the costs of procuring the necessary software. Managers who are seeking to, or currently, have a customer-engagement approach must decide if and when their business can afford to adopt the new technologies that are necessary.

Social/Local/Mobile

Often called SoLoMo—a phrase coined by John Doerr—Social/Local/ Mobile is a concept that speaks of the convergence of social media, location-based services and the proliferation of Internet and GPS-connected mobile devices. Dr Phil Hendrix defines SoLoMo as "situated experiences, enabled by mobile, shared with others. This concept has changed the way that marketers engage with customers."[18] A new world of opportunities is opened up by the confluence of social, local, and mobile data. The depths of available location data allow social media data giants such as Foursquare and Facebook to personalize recommendations, ads, and offers.[19] "Social media is even more useful when linked to location and accessed via mobile devices—with geo-tagging, users can filter social media and access relevant information on a smartphone 'just-in-time' at the point of need, whether in a store, restaurant or other location."[20] The reality of SoLoMo has given marketers the ability to literally pinpoint a customer's physical location and send relevant offers (based on preferences found in social data, i.e., Facebook likes, Twitter follows or mentions, etc.) to an Internet connected mobile device located on the individual.[21] As these technologies continue to become more refined, the CEV metric will be able to accommodate them. For example, CLV, CIV, and CRV can be maximized based on the data garnered from SoLoMo: (*a*) CLV can be encouraged through the delivery of coupons for future purchase to a customer's mobile device, (*b*) depending on the response from a customer's praise or "liking" of a product on a social media platform, an influencer (CIV) can be unveiled, and (*c*) customers can be incentivized to refer a product or service upon publicizing the purchase (CRV).

CONCLUSION

The CEV framework provides an overarching view of the entire customer engagement process, which allows firms to understand the drivers for successful customer engagement. There are many benefits of maximizing the different metrics, depending on the inner workings of a firm. The CEV framework makes different aspects of the process visible to a firm, which then allows the firm to optimally allocate marketing resources to maximize profitability through customer engagement. Not only does the framework clarify various components of the engagement process, it also enables firms to quantify customer engagement.

NOTES AND REFERENCES

1. M. O'Neil, (2012), "How Old Spice Swaggerized their Brand and Men Everywhere," *Social Times,* http://socialtimes.com/how-old-spice-swaggerized-their-brand-and-men-everywhere_b18042 (retrieved on December 10, 2012).
2. Ibid.
3. Ibid.
4. Widen and Kennedy, (2010), Adweek http://www.adweek.com/video/wk-old-spice-case-study-120605 (retrieved on December 10, 2012).
5. Ibid.
6. P. Schmitt, B. Skiera, and C. Van den Bulte, "Why Customer Referrals Can Drive Stunning Profits," *Harvard Business Review, 89*(6), (2011): 30.
7. V. Kumar, L. Aksoy, B. Donkers, R. Venkatesan, T. Wiesel, and S. Tillmanns, "Undervalued or Overvalued Customers: Capturing Total Customer Engagement Value," *Journal of Service Research, 13*(3), (2010): 297–310.
8. V. Kumar and B. Sundaram, (2012), "Lessons Learned from GM's Pullback from Facebook Ads," *Forbes,* http://www.forbes.com/sites/onmarketing/2012/06/18/lessons-learned-from-gms-pullback-from-facebook-ads/ (retrieved on December 11, 2012).
9. Ibid.
10. BMW (2012), "About the BMW Co-creation Lab," *BMW Group,* https://www.bmw-group-cocreationlab.com/about (retrieved on November 10, 2012).
11. W. Reinartz and V. Kumar, "The Mismanagement of Customer Loyalty," *Harvard Business Review, 80*(7), (2002): 86–97.
12. V. Kumar and Y. Bhagwat, "Listen to the Customer," *Marketing Research—A Magazine of Management and Applications, 22*(2), (2010): 14–19.
13. Ibid.
14. V. Kumar, J.A. Petersen, and R.P. Leone, "Driving Profitability by Encouraging Customer Referrals: Who, When, and How," *Journal of Marketing, 74*(5), (2010): 1–17.
15. IT Management. (2006), "Top 5 Issues in Database Management," http://static.itmanagement.com/news/top-5-issues-database-management-053006/ (retrieved on November 12, 2012).
16. IBM (2007), "Introduction to Change Management," http://pic.dhe.ibm.com/infocenter/idm/v2r2/index.jsp?topic=%2Fcom.ibm.datatools.dsa.nav.doc%2Ftopics%2Fchxucoview02.html (retrieved on December 10, 2012).
17. Weigend, A. (2009), "The Social Data Revolutions," *Harvard Business Review,* http://blogs.hbr.org/now-new-next/2009/05/the-social-data-revolution.html (retrieved on December 10, 2012).
18. Hendrix, P. (2012), "How SoLoMo Is Connecting Consumers and Brands to (almost) Everything," *iMedia Agency Summit.*
19. Hendrix, P. and Risley, E. (2011). How SoLoMo Is Empowering Consumers, Transforming Shopping and Disrupting Advertising and Retailing. *GigaOm Pro.* http://www.immr.org/Reports_Whitepapers/reports_1.html (retrieved on November 11, 2012).
20. Ibid.
21. Ibid.

GLOSSARY

Activeness: The number of times that an individual interacts with a message.

Attitudinal Loyalty: The perceptions and attitudes a customer has toward a particular product or service.

Behavioral Loyalty: The observed action that customers have demonstrated toward a particular product or service.

Big Data: Extremely large datasets that require special software in order to be mined.

Brand Advocacy: The customer establishing a relationship (through joining a brand community and encouraging other customers to do so) with other customers who use the brand and/or representing the extent to which a customer is willing to refer the brand to their friends and relatives.

Brand Affect: A customer's positive emotional response toward a brand.

Brand Attitude: The attitude each customer forms about the brand.

Brand Awareness: The extent to which a customer is aware of a brand.

Brand Behavior Intention: Reflects the actual effect of the marketing actions and brand perception on the brand behavior of the customers.

Brand Image: How a firm markets its brand and all other brand-related activities undertaken by the firm which influence the customer's perceptions of a brand.

Brand Knowledge: Customer knowledge of a brand which affects the overall awareness and image toward a brand.

Brand Loyalty: A loyal customer is one who makes repeated purchases of a preferred brand and shows both attitudinal and behavioral loyalty to the brand, and who does not respond to the constant fluctuations in the market.

Brand Price Premium Behavior: A customer's willingness to pay a premium price to buy a preferred brand over other products.

Brand Trust: A customer's willingness to trust the brand to satisfy his/her needs.

Bridges: Individuals with unique connections in a communication network.

Business Reference Value (BRV): The monetary value associated with future profits as a result of the extent of a client's reference influencing the prospects to purchase, discounted to present value.

Clout: The number of people an individual is connected to and being actively followed by.

Customer Brand Value (CBV): The net effect of a customer's brand knowledge, brand attitude, brand purchase intention, and brand behavior formed due to prior brand experience and the marketing of a brand.

Customer Collaborator Value (CCV): The monetary value attributed to a customer by a firm due to the profit generated by the new products/services arising out of that customer's collaborative efforts with the firm.

Customer Engagement (CE): A process followed by the firm to nurture customer relationships in multiple dimensions.

Customer Engagement Value (CEV): The total value (which is multi-dimensional) provided by customers who value the brand such that they engage with the firms: (*a*) through their purchase transactions, (*b*) through their ability to refer other customers to the firm using the firm's referral program, (*c*) through their power to positively influence other customers about the firm's offerings in the social media, and (*d*) by providing a feedback to the firm for product and service ideas.

Customer Influence Effect (CIE): Measures the net spread and influence of a message from a particular individual.

Customer Influence Value (CIV): The monetary value of the profits associated with the purchases generated by a customer's social media influence on other acquired customers and prospects, discounted to present value.

Customer Knowledge Value (CKV): The monetary value attributed to a customer by a firm due to the profit generated by implementing an idea/suggestion/feedback from that customer.

Customer Lifetime Value (CLV): The sum of cumulated future cash flows—discounted using the weighted average cost of capital (WACC)—of a customer over their entire lifetime with the company.

Customer Referral: A type of positive word-of-mouth communication by customers of a firm regarding its products.

Customer Referral Value (CRV): The net present value of the future profits of new customers who purchased products/services due to the referral behavior of the current customer.

Customer Relationship Management (CRM): The strategic process of CRM pertains to selecting customers that a firm can profitably serve, and shaping interactions between a firm and its customers. The goal is to optimize the current and future value of the customers for the company.

Data Accessibility: Data that is preserved in such a way that it can be easily accessed.

Data Integrity: The quality, consistency, accessibility, and trustworthiness of stored data.

Data Security: The degree to which stored data is secured from theft and loss.

Disaster Recovery: Involves the steps taken to recover data upon the occurrence of a breach or compromise.

Frequency: A measure of how often a customer orders from the company in a certain defined period.

Fringes: Individuals with few connections to other individuals in a network.

Hubs: Individuals who have many connections to other individuals.

Length of the Client Relationship: Defined in terms of the customer lifetime value (CLV) of the referencing client and the amount of time the referencing client has been a customer of the seller firm.

Like-mindedness: A factor revealed by common interests and similarities between individuals.

Monetary Value: The amount a customer spends on an average transaction.

Multichannel Shoppers: Customers who have made a purchase in more than one channel in the observed time period.

Net Present Value (NPV): The present value of an investment's future net cash flows minus the initial investment. In other words, it expresses how much value an investment will result in.

Opinion Mining (OM): Deals with gathering customer feedback on products and presenting the findings in order to best accomplish certain objectives.

Past Customer Value (PCV): A metric that measures the value of a customer based on his/her profit contribution in the past, after adjusting for the time value of money.

Purchase Intention: A customer's perception of a brand reflected by his/her intention to purchase.

Recency: A measure of how long it has been since a customer last placed an order with the company.

Recency, Frequency, and Monetary Value (RFM): The technique of using the recency, frequency, and monetary value variables to sort and prioritize customers.

Reference Congruency: The degree to which there are similarities between the referencing client and the potential client.

Reference Media Format: The specific format of a reference and the medium by which it is delivered.

Referral Intention: A customer's stated willingness to recommend.

Referral Program: In the context of a referral programs, a referral is a firm-incentivized recommendation from a current customer (referring customer or referrer) to a prospect (referred customer) about trying the firm's products/services.

Referral Seeding Strategy: A strategy employed by a firm to disseminate information throughout customer networks.

Share of Wallet (SOW): The ratio of the total customer spending with the firm to the total category spending (the firm plus its competitors) for that customer.

Social/Local/Mobile (SoLoMo): A concept that speaks of the convergence of social media, location-based services and the proliferation of Internet- and GPS-connected mobile devices.

Stickiness Index (SI): A metric that can be defined as an array of the degree to which a user or an instance of WOM is specific to each category of topics.

Talkativeness (of the Receiver): The number of times an individual's message gets repeated.

Word-of-Mouth (WOM) Marketing: A way of building active consumer-to-consumer and consumer-to-marketer communications.

Index

acquaintances, 122–125
acquisition and retention of customers, 103, 227
  impact of BRV on, 185–186
  referral programs for, 233
  social coupons for, 233
  strategies for
    need for, 103–104
    pitfalls associated with, 103
    working of, 104
acquisition budgets, 104–105
advertisers, strategies for managing, 275
allies, strategies for managing, 188
Allocating Resources for Profit (ARPRO), 104
American Express, 106
Apple Inc., 18, 27, 39, 59, 101, 235, 253
  "Mobile Me" service, 40
aristocrats, strategies for managing, 188

barnacles (low profitability and long-term customers), 83, 84, 85
Bauer, Eddie, 98
big data, 291, 294–296
blankslates, strategies for managing, 272
brand awareness, 26, 27, 55, 57, 63, 102, 108–109, 114, 130, 199–200, 203, 216, 238, 281, 284
  customer's level of, 115, 118
  and image, 126–127
brand communication, 118
  role in linking brand and customer value, 115
brand equity
  customer-based, 25, 33, 51
  and referral programs, 34

branding
  for building customer base, 101
  linking investments to customer profitability, 101–103
  role of, 46–47, 101
brand management, 123
  customer life cycle, 121
  strategies for, 54, 119–120
brands
  advocacy, 60, 129–130
  affect on customer's emotional response, 58–59
  attitude, 26, 55, 58–59, 102
  behavior intention, 26, 55, 59, 102
  connecting with customers, 48–51
  customer perceptions of, 24–28
  image, 28, 57, 63, 126–127
  knowledge, 26, 55–57, 102, 114, 120
  loyalty, 26–27, 29, 31, 59–60, 102, 117, 120, 128–129, 281
  marketing costs, 61–62
  price premium behavior, 60–61, 63, 102, 129
  purchase intention, 127–128
  recommendations, 61
  strategic implementation of managing, 116–123
  target customer group, 50
brand trust, 26, 55, 58, 62, 115, 130
  affects of, 127
  measurement of, 63
brand value, 27, 118
  aggregate *versus* individual, 54
  in CBV framework, 54–55
    brand attitude, 58–59
    brand behavior, 59–61

brand behavior intentions, 59
brand knowledge, 55–57
predicted behavior outcomes, 61–62
estimated and optimized, 119
linking to customer value, 113
measurement of, 51–54
perception of customers, 54
budgets
acquisition, 104–105
marketing, 82, 104
retention, 104
business reference value (BRV), 23, 35, 107, 171, 283–284
calculation of, 174–177
client firm analysis for, 184
components of, 35, 173
drivers of, 177–178
client firm size, 179–180
in financial firm, 178–182
incremental benefit of firm size, 182
influence of, 179
length of client relationship, 180–181
reference congruency, 181–182
reference media format, 181
in telecommunication firm, 178–182
impact on
customer acquisition, 185–186
customer lifetime value (CLV), 183–185
linking with customer brand value (CBV), 186–188
maximization of, 182–183
measurement of, 172–175
recommended strategies for managing
allies, 188
aristocrats, 188
diplomats, 187–188
rebels, 188
segment description for clients, 185
business-to-business (B2B) industries, 8, 10, 20, 28, 41, 77
purchase decision in, 35
business-to-customer (B2C) industries, 8, 10, 20, 30, 34, 77
butterflies (high profitability and short-term customers), 84
buyer–seller relationship, 180
bystandards, strategies for managing, 236–237

cash flow, 21, 71
Citibank India, 133
Coca-Cola, 57, 263
collaborators, strategies for managing, 275
communication channels, 98
cost-effectiveness of, 87
impact on investment effectiveness, 104, 105
for optimal resource allocation, 87
social media, 22, 24
company's loyalty program, 7
consultants, strategies for managing, 272
consumer packaged goods (CPG), 18, 282
contacts
face-to-face, 105
web-based, 105
cross-buying behavior
consequences of, 92
effect of the drivers of, 90
strategies for, 88–92
cross-selling, strategies for, 92–94
identifying customers, 92
implementation of, 93–94
need for, 92–93
working of, 93
customer attrition, strategies for prevention of, 95–96
need for, 95
prevention of, 95–96
"propensity to quit" model, 95
working of, 95
customer behavior
analysis of, 88
contribution margin, 62
decision-making process, 42
purchase- and non-purchase-related actions, 20, 22
purchase frequency, 62
purchase intention, 59
referral behavior, intentions *versus* actual, 142
toward referral programs, 34
customer–brand relationship, 22, 54
customer brand value (CBV), 15, 23, 24, 25–28, 46, 80, 113, 117, 281–282
definition of, 55
linking of various components of, 114

maximizing of, 63
measurement of, 51–54, 62–63
relationships with
    customer knowledge value (CKV),
      271–272
    customer lifetime value (CLV),
      114–115
    customer referral value (CRV),
      168–170
customer collaborator value (CCV), 251
customer defection, win-back strategy to
    prevent, 71
customer empowerment, 106
customer engagement
    approach to profitability, 13, 14
    CLV for ensuring profitable, 78–109
    different ways for, 6
    firm's approach to, 17–20
    future of
      big data, 294–296
      social/local/mobile (SoLoMo), 296–297
    importance of, 9–15
    initiated by companies, 5–6
    levels of, 7
    management, 269
    marketplace evidence for, 4–7
    metrics, 271
    philosophy of, 2
    product-centric approach to, 12
    profitable, 7–9
    value added by, 10
customer engagement value (CEV), 7, 15,
    24, 25, 46, 278
    benefits to the organizations, 42–43
    database management, 291–294
    five core dimensions of, 22
    framework of conceptualizing, 20–25
    and future of customer engagement,
      294–297
    management of, 279–281
    organizational challenges, 288–291
customer–firm relationship, 77, 106, 139,
    180–181, 254, 281, 291
customer influence effect (CIE), 108, 213
    definition of, 199
customer influence value (CIV), 15, 23, 24,
    35–37, 108, 189, 284–285

computation of, 218
definition of, 199
encouraging and maximizing, 221–227
implications of, for social media
    marketers, 218–221
measurement of, 212–216
    conceptual approach for, 215
relation with customer knowledge value
    (CKV), 272–273
customer knowledge value (CKV), 15, 23,
    38–41, 246–247, 278, 286
    business applications of, 267–269
    comparison with customer referral value
      (CRV), 37–38
    customer engagement under, 24
    data analysis and, 260–262
    definition of, 251
    Domino's Pizza, 247–248
    encouraging and maximizing, 265–267
    impact of social media in, 264–265
    measurement of, 251–254
      business initiated, 253
      customer feedback channel
        identification, 255–258
      customer initiated, 253
      strategies for, 255–264
    Quirky.com, 249–251
    rating normalization and, 260
    recommended strategies for managing
      advertisers, 275
      blankslates, 272
      collaborators, 275
      consultants, 272
      honeymooners, 272
      identifiers, 275
      partners, 272
      wallflowers, 275
    relationships with
      business reference value (BRV), 274–275
      customer brand value (CBV), 271–272
      customer influence value (CIV),
        272–273
      customer lifetime value (CLV), 269–271
      customer referral value (CRV), 273–274
Shoppers Stop, 249
Tanishq, 248
Zappos, 248

customer life cycle, 120
  brand management, 121
customer lifetime value (CLV), 15, 28–31,
  61, 67, 113, 117, 132, 278
  in B2B and B2C settings, 78
  client firm analysis for, 184
  computation of, 74–77, 110
  curve measured at different times, 120
  and customer-centric approach to
    marketing, 31
  definition of, 70–72
  drivers of, 77–78
  for ensuring profitable customer
    engagement, 78–80
    for acquiring profitable customers,
      103–105
    cross-buying behavior, 88–92
    customer selection, 80–82
    interaction orientation, 105–107
    for linking investments in branding to
      customer profitability, 101–103
    loyalty and profitability, 82–87
    for managing multichannel shoppers,
      98–101
    optimal allocation of resources, 87–88
    for pitching the right product to the
      right customer, 92–94
    for preventing customer attrition,
      95–96
    product returns, 96–98
    viral and referral marketing strategies,
      107–109
  future of, 108–110
  impact of BRV on, 183–185
  limitation of, 31
  link with customer knowledge value
    (CKV), 269–271
  looking beyond, 110–111
  measurement of, 72–74
  and profitability of the company,
    282–283
customer loyalty, 12, 14, 30, 67, 78, 82, 85,
  156, 228, 266, 288–289
customer participation, definition of, 247
customer profitability, 1–4, 7–8, 29, 34, 91,
  105, 139, 288
  customer engagement approach to, 13

linking investments in branding to,
  101–103
product-centric approach to, 11
strategies for management of, 82–87
customer purchase behavior, 55, 72, 80, 97,
  279
customer referrals. *See also* referral programs
  process of, 137
  referral behavior, intentions *versus* actual,
    142
  and referral programs, 136–138
  value of. *See* customer referral value
    (CRV)
  "willingness to recommend", 141
customer referral value (CRV), 15, 23,
  31–34, 133, 283–284. *See also* referral
  programs
  calculation of, 34, 147–150
    example for, 150–152
  comparison with customer knowledge
    value (CKV), 37–38
  concept of, 107, 135
  definition of, 147
  implementing of, in business, 158
  limitations of, 34
  monetary value associated with future
    profits, 32
  procedure for maximization of, 152–154
  relation with customer knowledge value
    (CKV), 273–274
  WOM marketing, 136, 140–141, 171
customer relationship management (CRM),
  66, 132
  goal of, 1
customer retention, 14, 36, 92, 223, 227, 229
customers
  advocates, 157
  affluents, 157
  building relationships with, 133
  champions, 157
  main paths for reaching, 120
  misers, 157
  strategic implementation of managing,
    116–123
  types of segments, 83–84
customers acquisition and retention. *See*
  acquisition and retention of customers

customer satisfaction, 9, 12, 14, 40, 62, 71, 106, 115, 136–137, 247–248
customer selection, strategies for, 80–82
customers' future purchases, factors influencing, 19
Customer Spending Score (CSS), 29, 86
customer user group, 256–258
customer value
    measurement of, 66–67
    method for linking brand value to, 113
    profit-based strategy for assessment of, 67
    role of brand communication in linking brand and, 115
    traditional measures of
        backward-looking metrics, 67–68
        past customer value, 70
        receny-frequency-monetary (RFM) value, 68–69
        share of wallet, 69
        tenure/duration, 70
customer value management, 106

data
    accessibility of, 292–293
    analysis, 260–262
    collection of, 258–260, 264
    types of, 295
database management, 279, 291–292
    change management, 294
    data accessibility, 292–293
    data integrity, 292
    data security, 292, 293
    disaster recovery, 293–294
decision-making, 42, 47, 72, 222, 296
Dell, 192, 268
Delta Air Lines, 38–39, 268
diplomats, strategies for managing, 188
distribution channels, 97, 98, 115
Domino's Pizza, 197, 247–248, 255, 282

e-Commerce portals, 247
email/fax, 256

Facebook, 24, 38–39, 42, 58, 192, 194, 207, 210, 216, 221, 259, 262, 265, 268, 272, 273, 297

feedback, customer, 14, 38–39, 41, 289–291
    channel identification, 255–258
    data collection of, 258–260
    Domino's Pizza, 247–248
    flow within an organization, 290
    negative feedback, 259, 263–264, 273
    online feedback, 260
    Opinion Mining (OM), 265
    positive feedback, 262–263
    Quirky.com, 249–251
    ratings from customers, 260
    response strategy for
        data analysis, 260–262
        design and implementation of, 262–264
        immediate-term action, 261, 262, 263–264
        long-term action, 261, 263, 264
    Shoppers Stop, 249
    social media for collection of, 265
    Tanishq, 248
    type of, 261
    Zappos, 248
financial services
    drivers of BRV in, 178–182
    expected gains in CLV, 125
    ROI of the campaign, 125
    segmentation strategies, 124–126
firm profitability, customer contribution to, 20
focus group, 85, 257
follow-up, 17, 257

General Motors (GM), 27–28, 285
geo-tagging, 297
Google, 17–18, 27, 39–40, 60
Google buzz, 39–40

Harley Davidson, 26–27, 57
Hendrix, Phil, 297
Hewlett Packard (HP), 269
HokeyPokey (ice cream retailer in India)
    budget for marketing, 203
    computation of CIE and CIV, 204
    "Share Your Brownies" campaign, 204, 210, 216
    social media marketing (SMM), 203–204
        goals for, 205

project timeline, 205
  seven-step process in, 206–212
  "Stickiness Index" factor, 208
honeymooners, strategies for managing, 272
Houston, Drew, 33
Hyundai, 46–48

IBM, 29–30, 106
  CLV-based management framework, 86
  communication strategies, 87
  Customer Spending Score (CSS), 86
  optimal allocation of resources at, 85–86
identifiers, strategies for managing, 275
interaction orientation
  customer concept for, 106
  and interaction response capacity, 106
  strategies for
    implementation outcome of, 106–107
    need for, 105–106
    working of, 106
Internet, 9, 17, 36, 98, 192, 247, 256, 263,
  266, 297
introverted fans, strategies for managing, 236

LG Telecom, 258
likert scale, 260
loyalty and profitability, strategies for
  management of, 82–87

mail-order catalogs, 98
marketing communications, 4, 8, 61, 88–89,
  96–97, 99, 101, 115, 120, 160, 235
marketing strategies, 22
  for return on investment (ROI), 108
  viral and referral, 107–109
Mercedes-Benz, 22, 48–49
Microsoft Corp., 17–18, 27, 137, 171–172,
  253–254
  Customer Reference Program, 171, 172
multichannel shoppers, strategies for
  management of, 98–101
  implementation outcome of, 99–101
  need for, 98
  working of, 98–99

Nestle, 60
Netflix, 263, 273

net present value (NPV), 23, 29, 67, 72,
  75, 147
Nokia, 52
  change in brand value and net income
    for, 53

online feedback, 260
online surveys, 255–256
on-site surveys, 255
Opinion Mining (OM), 265, 275
organizational challenges, CEV-based
  framework
  customer feedback, 289–291
  data availability, 291
  loyalty, 288–289

Pareto Principle, 66
partners, strategies for managing, 272
Past Customer Value (PCV), 67, 70
Polyvore.com, 267, 269
poor patrons, 123
price discounts, 99, 101
Procter & Gamble (P&G), 18–19, 282
product development, 2, 9, 38–39, 195,
  247, 249, 254, 257, 267, 269
  customer feedback, importance of, 38
  failure rate of, 38
  risk associated with, 12
product improvement initiatives, 19
product knowledge, 39
product ownership, 7
product returns
  drivers of, 97
  impact on customer buying behavior,
    97
  policies for, 98
  strategies for prevention of
    need for, 96
    working of, 96–97
profitability of customers. *See* customer
  profitability
profitable customer management, 3
  CEV approach for, 279
profitable lifetime duration, 61, 77
profit contribution, sources of, 3, 6, 8–9, 70,
  72, 93, 220, 225
profit maximization, 39, 80, 283

purchase behavior of a customer, 28, 32, 71, 102
purchase intention, 26, 55, 59, 63, 102, 114–115, 117, 123, 126, 130, 281–282
pushers, strategies for managing, 237

QuestionPro, 256
Quirky.com, 247, 249–251

ratings from customers, 260
rebels, strategies for managing, 188
Recency-Frequency-Monetary Value (RFM), 67, 68–69
referral marketing campaigns, 108, 171
referral programs
  by Ashworth College, 138
  in B2B setting, 171–172
  benefits of, 138, 172
  and brand awareness, 34
  campaign
    description, 160–162
    preparation, 158–159
    results of, 162–168
    targeting the advocates, 161
    targeting the affluents, 161
    targeting the misers, 162
  concept of, 107
  cost of, 149
  customer referrals and, 34, 136–138
  firm-generated, 8, 23–24, 32
  impact of, 33
  incentive-generated, 31
  influence on customers, 189
  intentions of, 140–147
  linking with CRV and CLV, 154–158
  marketing campaign for, 145
  and relation between CLV and CRV, 156
  by Roku, 154
  seeding strategies, 142–144
    degree centrality and referral rates, 146
    performance of, 144–146
  by Sprint and Scottrade, 134
  strategies to manage customers, 141
  types of incentives, 137
  and value of referred customers, 139–140
  WOM marketing, 136, 140–141, 171
referred customers, value of, 139–140

Regulated Social Media Marketing (RSMM), 240–241
  merits of, 243–244
  salient points of, 241
Rennlist, 36, 60
resource allocation, 96, 283
  strategies for, 87–88
retailers
  profits and the revenues, 126
  segmentation strategies, to manage CLV and CBV, 126
return on investment (ROI), 29, 67, 71, 93, 108, 192, 199, 217

sales campaign, in telecommunications industry, 94
Samsung, 27, 52
  change in brand value and net income for, 53
Schiller, Phillip, 18
Seemingly Unrelated Regression (SUR) methodology, 114
segmentation strategies, to manage CLV and CBV, 122
Share of Wallet (SOW), 9, 36, 67, 69, 84, 100
Shoppers Stop, 249
social coupons
  avoiding the pitfalls in launching of, 227–229
  concept of, 198, 223–227
  customer acquisition and profitability, 227–228
  discounts, affect of, 228
  relationships between
    CIV and CBV, 236–237
    CIV, CRV, and CLV, 234–235
    CLV and CIV, 235–236
    CRV and CIV, 238–239
  revenue from existing customers, impact on, 228–229
  strategies for
    improving profitability, 229–232
    redesigning of, 232–234
social media
  for collection of customer feedback, 264–265

customer influence, value of, 197
definition of, 191
Facebook, 194
forms of, 192
impact on customer knowledge value, 264–265
landscape, 192–193
marketing, 37
network, 36, 42, 189, 195, 247
power of, 193–196
success and failures in marketing through, 196–198, 224
Twitter, 194
user's WOM value in, 108, 234
social media marketing (SMM), 37, 195–196
calculating the effect and value of, 212–216
campaign results and implications, 216
drivers of influencers in, 202
encouraging and maximizing CIV for, 221–227
implications of CIV for, 218–221
measurement of CIV, 212–216
recommended strategies for managing
bystandards, 236–237
introverted fans, 236
pushers, 237
trendsetters, 237
Regulated Social Media Marketing (RSMM), 240–241
return on investment (ROI), 217
seven-step framework for, 199–203
implementation of, 203–205
success and failures in, 196–198
Stickiness Index (SI), 200, 208, 215
strangers, strategies for managing, 83–84, 123

Tanishq, 248
telecommunications industry, 124

customer rankings by CLV and CRV for, 155
drivers of BRV in, 178–182
profit projection for, 167
sales campaign comparison in, 94
segmentation strategies, to manage CLV and CBV, 124
telephone line, for customer service, 256
tenure/duration metric, 70
trendsetters, strategies for managing, 237
true friends, 83, 84
true loyalists, 122–125
Twitter, 24, 42, 58, 109, 192, 194, 207, 210, 216, 218, 256, 262, 265, 272, 297

Unique Code Embedded Technology, 256

value metrics, customer-based, 72, 100, 160, 164
value-oriented referral incentive program, 8
video references, 35, 184
voice of customer (VOC) organization, 258

wallflowers, strategies for managing, 275
Walmart, 59, 259
Web-based sales, 98
Website feedback link, 256
Weigend, Andreas, 294
weighted average cost of capital (WACC), 71
"Wheel of Fortune" strategies, 29, 79, 283
used for maximizing CLV, 81
word-of-mouth (WOM) communication, 4, 9, 22, 31–33, 84, 106, 132
role in firm's marketing efforts, 36
and social media, 192, 199
word-of-mouth (WOM) marketing, 136, 196, 234

Zappos, 247–249

ABOUT THE AUTHOR

Dr V. Kumar (VK) is the Regents' Professor, Lenny Distinguished Chair & Professor of Marketing, Executive Director, Center for Excellence in Brand & Customer Management, and Director, Ph.D. Program in Marketing at the J. Mack Robinson College of Business, Georgia State University. Dr Kumar has been recognized with eight *lifetime achievement awards* in Marketing Strategy, Inter-Organizational Issues, Retailing, Business-to-Business Marketing; and Marketing Research from the AMA and other professional organizations; the *Paul D Converse Award; the Sheth Foundation/Journal of Marketing Long-term Impact Award; The Robert Buzzell Award* from the Marketing Science Institute; and the *Gary L Lilien ISMS-MSI Practice Prize Award.* He has published over 200 articles in many scholarly journals in marketing including the *Harvard Business Review, Sloan Management Review, Journal of Marketing, Journal of Marketing Research, Marketing Science, Management Science,* and *Operations Research.* His books include *Managing Customers for Profit, Customer Relationship Management (CRM), Customer Lifetime Value, Marketing Research, Statistical Methods in CRM,* and *International Marketing Research.* He has won several awards for his research publications in scholarly journals. VK leads the marketing science to marketing practice initiative at the INFORMS Society for Marketing Science (ISMS) and has worked with Global Fortune 1000 firms to maximize their profits. VK spends his "free" time visiting business leaders to identify challenging problems to solve. He plays tennis and basketball to relieve the stress arising out of being in academics. Finally, VK has been recognized as a *Legend in Marketing* where his work is published in a 10-volume encyclopedia with commentaries from scholars worldwide.